SANTANA
WAR CHIEF OF THE
MESCALERO APACHE

To the Memory of
ALMER N. BLAZER

Some seed the birds devour,
And some the season mars,
But here and there will flower
The solitary stars.
— A. E. Housman

SANTANA
WAR CHIEF OF THE
MESCALERO APACHE

Almer N. Blazer

Edited by A. R. Pruit
Foreword by Jerry D. Thompson

Dog Soldier Press
Taos, New Mexico

Dog Soldier Press
PO Box 1782, Ranchos de Taos, New Mexico 87557
PO Box 1842, Worland, Wyoming 82401
www.dogsoldierpress.com

Library of Congress Cataloging-in-Publication Data

Blazer, A. N. (Almer N.), 1865–1949.
    Santana: war chief of the Mescalero Apache / by A. N. Blazer:
edited by A. R. Pruit: foreword by Jerry D. Thompson.
        p.   cm.
    Includes bibliographical references.
    ISBN: 0-940666-69-3 (cloth)
    ISBN: 0-940666-70-7 (pbk.)
    1. Santana, d. 1876. 2. Mescalero Indians—Biography.
3. Mescalero Indians—History. I. Pruit, A. R. II. Title.
E99.M45S353   1995
978.9′004972—dc20
                                             95–33158
                                              CIP

Printed in the United States.
 First printing February 2000
 Second printing September 2000

CONTENTS

FOREWORD

B eneath the towering, snowcapped summit of Sierra Blanca in south-central New Mexico Territory in late 1867 or early 1868, two very different men met for the first time. One was Dr. Joseph Hoy Blazer, a big, blue-eyed, solidly built Iowa Civil War veteran, who never saw an Indian until he was forty years old. The other man was also tall, with a broad, calm face and great dignity of manner. He was Mescalero War Chief Santana. In the years that followed, the two men formed a unique and trusting friendship. In the words of C. L. Sonnichsen, Blazer was "one of the very few white men whom the Mescalero trusted and accepted."[1] Blazer had purchased a sawmill, La Maquina, in the Sacramento Mountains in the heart of the Mescalero country; in time, it became known as Blazer's Mill.

Often preyed on by crooked traders, harassed by land-hungry settlers, starved, lied to, and attacked by the army, Santana and the Mescalero found Blazer to be a striking contrast to other white men they had known. Blazer was to learn much from Santana, who had been a leader of considerable influence among the Mescalero since at least 1830. Long at war with the Mexicans, the Mescalero had watched in 1850 as a new invader penetrated the traditional homeland of the White Mountain Apache. A detachment of blue-coats out of the Rio Grande Valley crossed the Organ Mountains, the arid Tularoso Basin, and rode into the rugged, pine- and fir-crested mountains to the east. With perhaps as many as three hundred warriors, Santana, by sheer intimidation, drove off the invaders. Yet shortly thereafter, Santana, along with the Jicarilla Apache and Comanche, proposed peace to the governor of New Mexico. When peace failed, the chief exerted every effort to keep his band, which never numbered more than a few hundred, as isolated and far away from the white man as possible. Yet again in January 1855 Santana was at the head of the Mescalero band that confronted the army on the Peñasco River and killed Captain Henry Whiting Stanton.

After the death of chiefs Barranquito in 1857 and Manuelito in 1862, Santana continued to rise in the Mescalero hierarchy. During the relentless and genocidal 1862–1863 campaign against the Mescalero by General James H. Carleton, Santana managed, probably by secluding himself and his followers in the rugged canyons of the Sacramento and Guadalupe mountains, to avoid capture and the humiliation of confinement at the Bosque Redondo Reservation.

During the following decade, through clever negotiations and with the mediation of Joseph H. Blazer and other whites who supported the Mescalero, Santana was able to secure a reservation that preserved a substantial remnant of his people's homeland. In the great smallpox epidemic of 1876 that swept the area, Santana, an old man by this time, was seriously afflicted and was taken in and nursed by Joseph H. Blazer at The Mill. Shortly thereafter, the chief returned to his lodge only to die of pneumonia. Joseph H. Blazer died in 1898.

Almer Newton Blazer, son of the doctor, first came to the reservation as a boy of twelve in 1877—a year after Santana's death. The younger Blazer also became a trusted friend of the Mescalero as well as an authority on the White Mountain Apache. Educated at Las Cruces and Santa Fe, he was anxious that Mescalero history be preserved and wrote articles on the Apache and the history of the area.

Over the years, the Blazer family's knowledge and records have proven indispensable for any study of the Mescalero. Any serious scholarship on the subject necessitates the use of these records. J. Evetts Haley, Eve Ball, William A. Keleher, A. M. Gibson, C. L. Sonnichsen, and Robert M. Utley as well as other scholars, have all used the Blazer records and information obtained from the family.

When Almer N. Blazer died in 1949, he left behind a valuable and informative book-length manuscript entitled "Santana: War Chief of the Mescalero." In the manuscript, Blazer repeated much of what he had learned from his father as well as older Mescalero who had known Santana. A. R. Pruit, who grew up with the Blazer family and who has had a lifetime interest in the Mescalero, has at last brought the manuscript to publication. Through meticulous research of historical archives, Pruit verified much of what was in the manuscript and uncovered a considerable amount of data pertinent to the war chief and Mescalero history, even for the years (1855–1872) when Santana was thought by white men to be dead. Much of this information has not previously been seen by scholars.

Because of Pruit's interest in the preservation of Blazer's work, a wealth of Mescalero ethnology and history is now at our fingertips. For his efforts we are grateful. At last, Santana, the great chief of the Mescalero, can take his rightful place in the literature and history of the American Southwest beside Nicolas, Espejo, Josecito, Manuelito, Cadette, Roman, Barranquito, and Gomez, as well as his more famous relatives, Mangas Coloradas, Ponce, Delgadito, Cochise, Geronimo, Juh, Nana, Loca, Chato, and Victorio.

JERRY D. THOMPSON
Gallo Chiquito, New Mexico

Almer N. Blazer as a young man. Courtesy Rio Grande Historical Collections, New Mexico State University Library.

PREFACE

This work was written by Almer N. Blazer during the early 1930s. Upon the author's death in 1949, the manuscript was purchased from the estate by Almer N. Blazer's son, Paul A. Blazer. Although no bill of sale was found among the Blazer papers, a letter from Almer N. Blazer's friend William R. Leigh, the western artist and author, written in 1953 to Paul A. Blazer, stated, "I am glad you have bought the manuscript from the estate and are going to have it published."[1] It was not published at that time but languished for many years among the Blazer papers until we resurrected it and began our present effort to shepherd it into print. When Paul A. Blazer died in 1966, ownership went to his sons, Paul A. Blazer, Jr., and Arthur D. Blazer.

Three generations of the Blazer family have preserved the manuscript, not as a curiosity but as a work of historical value they were certain would be recognized sooner or later. As their uncle and as a self-declared member of the family in which a significant portion of my formative years were spent, I have shared with them their interest in it and have been involved in preparing it for publication.

Almer N. Blazer himself received a good many "pink-slips" from publishers. Although several editors were intrigued by the manuscript, all felt there was insufficient popular interest in Indian subjects at that time. Academic presses had other objections.

The most frequent criticisms dealt with the lack of verification of times and places: "Who were the Blazers?" "Was Santana real?" "There are too few dates." "It is very interesting, but is it actually history?"

To answer these objections has been the present editor's challenge. This entailed researching the available literature to identify the man Santana and finding confirmation of his deeds and the incidents described in the manuscript, as well as writing short biographies of the Blazers. We were careful at all times not to change the meaning of the original manuscript. However, as we researched the military and Indian agent records, some changes in site were necessary (see note 28, Editor's Introduction, page 269, for explanation). We also developed an accurate chronology of events based on historical records.

In order to understand the relevance of the Blazer manuscript to Mescalero history, one must be aware of Almer N. Blazer's unique relationship with the Mescalero Apache. From the time of his arrival at Mescalero in 1877, at age twelve, he was in constant contact with the Indians. He spoke their language (as well as Spanish) fluently, was a friend to them, and was befriended by them. He hunted with them, ate with them, camped with them, and listened to their tales of events past. Both C. L. Sonnichsen and Eve Ball said of him that he knew and understood the Mescalero far better than any other Anglo.

On March 4, 1931, Blazer sent an early draft of his manuscript to western artist William R. Leigh.[2] In an accompanying letter Blazer wrote:

> I am enclosing herewith an original draft and several sketches which I had intended as inserts.
>
> I am also sending some [descriptions of Mescalero legends and customs]. . . . I have compiled them from my recollections of explanations and arguments relative to many subjects, and have heard many of them

with slight variations but believe they are the consensus of the different versions. . . .

I would say too that it is entirely from memory with a mixture of imagination. . . . Most of the incidents I have heard recounted by the participants. . . . Some I have at second and third hand and some details are imaginary.[3]

Blazer has written a history of the Mescalero Apache during a crucial period, 1862 to about 1880, when the entire tribe was threatened with extinction. It is in part a record of the combined efforts of his father, Joseph H. Blazer, and Chief Santana to prevent the annihilation of the Mescalero which many high-level officers of the army recommended and actively sought to accomplish. Almer N. Blazer, basing his story entirely on oral accounts, left encounters between the Apache and the Anglo-Hispanic forces undated and the chronology sometimes awry. In Apache time, the past is not a precise written entity and is, therefore, as Harry Hoijer points out,[4] grammatically vague and sometimes difficult to determine. The pattern of events, however, is clear. Blazer describes Santana's long and difficult negotiations, in which Joseph H. Blazer acted as collaborator and mediator, and the resulting establishment of a reservation on the Mescalero homeland. He also recounts Santana's singular achievement in keeping his people together during this divisive and troubled phase of their history.

Into the fabric of that story Almer N. Blazer has woven another kind of history, an account of the daily lives of the Mescalero people as they were shaped by general beliefs and religion as well as by the external environment. He recorded for posterity the memories and experiences of the Mescalero as they had been told to him, although he was probably unfamiliar with such terms as "oral tradition" or "oral history." He simply put on paper what he had seen and heard. He strove for accuracy in presenting the customs and traditions as he had learned them through his own observation and direct experience and through many conversations with his Mescalero friends. In relating encounters between Anglos and Indians he was objective, although his lack of interest in dates or their verification has resulted in discrepancies in chronology (which I have identified) between his version of events and Anglo historical records.

Where the imagination generally came into play was in devising real life situations to illustrate the traditions and beliefs of tribal life. By using the formal conventions of fiction, Blazer was able to create a living tableau of daily tribal life as it existed before significant contact with European culture, while presenting the Mescalero's experience of the troubled history of that period. The history of power and conquest all too often passes for the history of mankind, and this holds true for the history of Indians of the Southwest. Blazer's version gives the Mescalero a validation which has been long in coming.

The research for this book has been most rewarding. Since the information concerning Santana has never been collected and organized into a cohesive whole, an important segment of the history of the Mescalero tribe has been added. In our view, Blazer's work not only adds to the stature of the Mescalero as a tribe but creates a more realistic, humane picture of the Mescalero as a people than has been commonly envisioned.

It is earnestly hoped that the information herein will confer on Santana the reputation that he surely deserves as an extraordinary man and a great Mescalero chief—one who earned his place beside the other great Apache leaders.

ACKNOWLEDGMENTS

The Blazer family papers still held by Paul A. Blazer, Jr. and Arthur D. Blazer have been of great help in learning details of the family history as well as in gaining a better understanding of the many problems facing the early settlers on that huge, empty, and forbidding frontier.

Paul and Arthur Blazer have been most helpful in jogging my memory with personal details of the many Indian friends we have known. Arthur Blazer, who worked for the Mescalero as manager of their cattle herds and as an overall troubleshooter and friend for thirty-five years, has recounted in detail the customs and attitudes prevailing today among the Indians.

I am especially grateful to Dr. Jerry D. Thompson, Professor of History, Laredo State University, Laredo, Texas, who very carefully read each of the new sections, the Blazer biographies and the introduction, corrected and amended the format, and peppered the whole with many valuable and much appreciated suggestions.

It was my good fortune to correspond with Dr. C. L. Sonnichsen before his death and to continue that correspondence with Mrs. Carol Sonnichsen afterward. Both were most gracious in helping with some missing aspects of the Blazer family history.

Miss Elaine Clark, a linguist who helped the Mescalero develop a written language, has very graciously acted as guide and counsel in the use of and spelling of the Mescalero Apache language.

The archivists have been most accommodating in every instance and deserve a very special thank you for all their help, especially Sarah Owen at the Gilcrease Museum in Tulsa, Oklahoma, and the entire staff at the Southwest Branch, National Archives, Fort Worth, Texas. Linda Blazer and her staff at the Rio Grande Historical Collection in Las Cruces, New Mexico, and Elbers Naiche (Hugar) at the Mescalero Apache Cultural Museum have gone out of their way to help in my research.

Margaret Campbell of Bloomfield, Iowa, also doing research on the early Blazer family, was kind enough to send census reports and Joseph H. Blazer's Civil War record.

Mary Williams, park ranger at the Fort Davis Historical Site, Fort Davis, Texas, and Jane Hoerster, historian for Mason County in Mason, Texas, were most generous with their time in researching specific subjects.

Joan Gold, Diane Kammlah, and Cass Callahan of Fredericksburg, Texas, have all retyped the original manuscript and have been of inestimable value to me throughout the many months I have spent working on the material.

I am much indebted to Dr. Thomas Pruit, English Department, Cistercian Preparatory School, Irving, Texas, for editing the whole manuscript and for his many useful suggestions.

The entire staff of the Pioneer Memorial Library in Fredericksburg, Texas, has been most courteous and helpful. A special thanks is due to Maria Ramos and Candace Noriega for their always cheerful assistance.

Last, but by no means least, I wish to express my gratitude for the help given by my wife. I wrote in longhand. She typed and retyped, corrected, criticized, put up with my work habits, and, in general, ran the tight ship which made this book possible.

A. R. PRUIT

EDITOR'S INTRODUCTION

It is not just coincidence that one of the smallest of the Apache tribes, the Mescalero, was considered by some Anglo-Americans during the era of Santana[1] to be the most destructive and troublesome. Undoubtedly, it was his tutelage and leadership, as well as the bold audacity of his raids, that earned such a reputation for the Mescalero.

That Santana was a real person there can be no doubt. We do not know when he was born or where. We do not know his Indian name. He is a shadowy figure skipping over the pages of time with the intensity and brevity of a whirlwind. His name appears occasionally in dusty archives, usually accompanied by descriptive adjectives such as *fiercest, cruelest,* or *wiliest.*

Almer N. Blazer remembers his father, Dr. Joseph H. Blazer, describing Santana as standing about six-feet in height, broad of shoulder, deep chested, powerfully proportioned. He was also notable for his big feet.

Santana had a poise, assurance, self-reliance, and nobility of manner that marked him unmistakably as a leader. His long experience as a leader of warriors had proved his valor. His way of life was in accord with Apache beliefs and customs of the time. That he occasionally beat his wives, disdained work other than hunting, could be cruel and unrelenting, and accepted the institution of slavery, there is little question. Nevertheless, his skills and ability to make sound decisions under acute stress, coupled with his fairness and generosity in all dealings with his people, made him the person to whom the tribe naturally looked for guidance. Anglos both admired him and dreaded him as a foe.

Other scholars of the Mescalero tribe have pointed out that Cadete and Roman were brothers, both sons of Barranquito, and that Roman and Santana were brothers as well. Though the researchers do not say so, the inference is clear that Santana was also a son of Barranquito.[2] Percy Bigmouth, Mescalero Apache, a friend and contemporary of Almer N. Blazer, thought these men were cousins. Blazer himself believed them all to be sons of Barranquito by different wives.[3]

At the time of Santana's death in 1876, Almer N. Blazer's father judged him to be over sixty years of age. This would indicate his date of birth to be around 1810–1815. In Chapter 18 Blazer describes a raid into Navajo country in which Santana earned his right to be a chief. The fact that neither side used firearms would indicate a date prior to the arrival of the gun trade to Paso del Norte and Santa Fe, with the consequent availability of these weapons to the Indians.

When one begins to understand Santana as Dr. Blazer understood him, and when one adds to that perception the evidence of his deeds recorded in government documents and Indian histories, then, for this writer at least, Santana becomes one of the great Apache chiefs, an equal to Cochise, Victorio, and Mangas Coloradas in wisdom, courage, diplomacy, tactics, and every other quality that makes a man a great leader.

Still in the possession of the Blazer family are two venerable rocking chairs, one a homemade bent-willow rocker of a fashion still made by local artisans, the other an early Lincoln-style rocker with a basket weave made of rush forming the back and seat. The former, Joseph H. Blazer's chair, was later used by Almer N. Blazer and is today fondly called "Grandfather's rocker." The other is still known only as "Santana's rocker."[4] The importance of these two relics becomes more apparent when one realizes that they represent a most unlikely alliance between two men who were polar opposites in terms of culture, beliefs, and their understanding of the purpose of life. Furthermore, over the years, the alliance became stronger and developed into an abiding friendship.

To fully appreciate Almer N. Blazer's portrait of Santana, it is important to understand the conditions and events leading up to the time when Blazer's story begins. Blazer's excellent account of the religion, customs, and daily life of the people needs no further embellishment. Instead, it is necessary to focus on the historical background of the Mescalero's tragic predicament.

In the 1850s, the Mescalero tribe was composed of nine bands, generally consisting of family groups numbering from fifty to one hundred twenty-five men, women, and children. They were hunters and gatherers, like neighboring tribes, but with one great difference—they had horses. With their increased mobility, they could prey upon their sedentary neighbors to the south much more easily and frequently. The Mescalero, however, did not maintain horse herds as the Comanche did. Indeed, it was said of them, only half in jest, that they would just as soon eat their horses as ride them. The great success of their depredations gave them proof of superiority and invincibility, which, to their way of thinking, earned them a natural right to acquisition: "To the victors belong the spoils."

The Mescalero lived in an environment where food and water were always scarce, and life itself was, by necessity, of the hand-to-mouth variety. The harsh terrain and scarcity of food not only limited the number of people per band but also dictated that each band have ample range in which to hunt game and forage for edible plants. In such terrain anyone who survived had to have tremendous physical endurance, the intelligence to outwit and outmaneuver enemies, and the ability to face the formidable realities of existence with a calm acceptance. It is not surprising that Anglo enemies who came from a greener and kinder land were apt to interpret the Apache's actions and attitudes as cruel and indifferent.

Barranquito, the father of Santana and Cadete, was chief of a band and, in the mid-1850s, was functioning as an elder statesman to the entire tribe. In 1854, Lieutenant Colonel Dixon S. Miles learned the following from Chief Barranquito in an interview at Fort Fillmore: "In addition to their two bands [those led by Barranquito and Santos] there were seven others. The most hostile of all was headed by Santana who ranged from the Sacramentos to the Guadalupes [mountain ranges]. . . ."[5] According to Barranquito, except for Santana most of the bands desired peace.

Among the Mescalero there was no tribal chief except in times of acute stress, when one man by consensus of the majority acted as war chief, as Santana did. Santana was both the chief of his band and the war chief of the tribe during the years of trouble.

THE APACHE PROBLEM

When the forces of General Stephen Watts Kearny entered Santa Fe in 1846, when Colonel Alexander Doniphan and others began exploring the topography and routes west through the country, and when the gold rush to California began in 1849, the vast flood of intruding strangers proved profoundly disturbing to the Apache. Aware of the intruders' obvious superiority in numbers, their more effective weaponry, including a constant supply of ammunition, as well as the arrival of seemingly endless numbers of well-trained soldiers, the more astute chiefs realized the tremendous odds against them and their way of life. The wiser chiefs began to search for a solution to a very grave problem: How could they survive? Among these chiefs Santana led the way.

American military authorities repeatedly ordered the Indians to stop fighting and plundering Mexicans and forbade them to depredate any settlers or pillage wagon trains. The military failed to understand that this behavior had for centuries been the only way the Apache knew to maintain their economy in a land of limited resources. An added difficulty was that the democratic structure of the Apache culture—the freedom of each family group to make and follow its own decisions—made peace treaties unenforceable. The bumbling ineffectiveness of United States military policies and procedures posed a further problem. Decisions, treaties, and promises, which had to be made ad hoc in on-the-spot dealings with the Indians, could be rescinded at any time during the weeks, often months, required for written reports to find their way up the chain of command to Washington and the various departments associated with Indian affairs. As a result, neither side was able to keep treaties or even promises, and each side consequently lost faith in the other.

The commonsense query raised by Apache spokesmen was: "What are we to do? We must steal from somebody; and if you will not permit us to rob the Mexicans, we must steal from you or fight you."[6]

In the spring of 1850, Santana and his father Barranquito called for councils with the Comanche and Jicarilla Apache to work out the terms for a treaty with the United States military. The treaty covered a vast territory comprising the eastern half of present-day New Mexico, southern Colorado, all of Texas as far east as Dallas and San Antonio, and south into northern Coahuila and Chihuahua in Mexico. This territory was controlled almost exclusively, as far as the Indians were concerned, by the tribes seeking the treaty. Lack of actual control of this immense area, however, was a major problem for negotiators. One author noted:

> *. . . of all agreements that the Apaches had made with the Spanish au-*
> *thorities many . . . were violated by Indians who had not been party to*
> *them. For Santana and Barranquito to recognize this factor and move*
> *to correct it (if that indeed was their aim) showed perception keener than*
> *that of many who sat on the other side of the bargaining.[7]*

Other authors have referred to this treaty as "the Proposition for Peace."[8] This proposed treaty, which must have required a great deal of verbal exchange, has received very casual treatment in the available records—perhaps another instance of the all-too-common habit Anglo-Americans have of trivializing or ignoring the voices of the Indians.

Testifying to their sincerity was the Indians' offer of an ex-change of captives, whom they considered their most valuable commodity. Although the effort was in vain, the chiefs' initiative appears to have been an honest attempt to find a means to a peace-ful settlement.

Between 1850 and 1865, there was no established Indian pol-icy even within the military establishment. Secretary of War Charles W. Conrad, as well as many of the officers on frontier duty, favored a peace policy—the adoption of some system whereby Indians could be induced to abandon their nomadic way of life, live in villages, and learn how to become self-supporting through agriculture. General Edwin Vose Sumner and Major James H. Car-leton headed a majority who believed that peace could be attained only through a constant show of military force, which included the building of forts throughout the area. Implicit in the use of armed force was the threat of annihilation if punitive force proved unsuccessful.

The civilian Indian agents who shared authority with the mil-itary were largely more hopeful of a peaceful solution. Indian agent James Calhoun, who in 1851 became territorial governor, and Dr. Michael Steck, Indian agent for the Apache, were representative members of this group. The schism between military and civilian attitudes caused many problems and, of course, compounded the bewilderment of the Indians, who knew that only one thing was certain about the white man—he never spoke with "one tongue."

It is understandable that over the next few years Indian raids increased. All depredations east of the Rio Grande were blamed at least in part but usually entirely on the Mescalero.

Santana must have realized the imminent danger of annihilation that threatened the Mescalero. The influx of white people, their superiority in arms and ammunition, and perhaps more than anything else, their new laws and ways of living together made him realize how completely vulnerable his people were. The Anglo-Americans fought among themselves, were cruel, and often spoke with a forked tongue, but he had been told that after fighting they made peace with each other and were no longer enemies. That was not the Apache way.

The new white leader, Stephen Watts Kearny, had come among them with many soldiers, many wagons, and guns and food for all of them, saying:

> We have come with peaceable intentions and kind feelings toward you all. . . . We mean not to murder you or rob you of your property. Your families shall be free from molestation; your women secure from violence. . . . Every man has a right to serve God according to his heart . . . . We esteem the most peaceable man, the best man. I advise you to attend to your domestic pursuits, cultivate industry, be peaceable and obedient to the laws.[9]

It was true that they did not fight with the Pueblos or the Mexicans except when they broke the white man's laws, but it would take a very long time for the Mescalero to understand these laws. What was to be done in the meantime?

SANTANA'S DEATH REPORTED

By 1854, there were many Anglos, civilian and military, who believed that reservations of some kind were a better solution to the Indian problem than extermination. The idea of reservations led to a plethora of ideas about where and how big such reservations should be, what Indians should be placed on what reservations, how and under whose authority they should be regulated and administered, and so forth.

The territorial governor, David Merriwether, worked out a number of elaborate schemes for such reservations, with various forms of government assistance provided until the Indians learned how to be self-supporting. But, like all such schemes of the day, they came to naught. However, it must have been the growing number of such suggestions upon which Santana pinned the one faint hope left to him for the survival of his people.[10]

At the same time, there was more and more talk from the military depicting the Mescalero, led by that most cunning and capable chief Santana, as the worst of the Apache. The intention, so the rumor went, was to conquer and subdue the Mescalero. To Santana, this surely meant that he and his band and probably the whole tribe were to be exterminated. This rumor came to have the face of truth for Santana. The only possible escape, he thought, was to appear to "throw away" or abandon a portion of his tribe[11] by reporting his own death and then disappearing. His band would live by the only means they knew—hunting, gathering, and depredation—but they would be as elusive as the fox, and no one would find them. Santana would give time a chance. He did not intend, of course, to lose contact with the remainder of the tribe.

In October 1853, Brigadier General John Garland, military commander of the Department of New Mexico, wrote to the adjutant general of the army, in Washington, D.C., that he "had an account to settle with the Mescalero Apaches of the White Mountains for their attacks upon California emigrants during the past summer."[12] A number of punitive raids into the White, Sacramento, and Guadalupe mountains were made throughout 1854.[13] The frequency of these expeditions undoubtedly confirmed Santana's suspicions and hardened his resolve. He had a plan.

Early in December 1854, a band of Apache raided "the grazing camp of Messrs. Beck and Giddings [Gittings, according to Captain Richard S. Ewell] on the Pecos, near Anton Chico, and ran off the entire herd of some 2,500 sheep in the direction of the White Mountains. Captain Richard S. Ewell led a combined force of 180 men—dragoons and infantry—in search of the depredators."[14]

In Captain Ewell's final report on the success of this raid, he described the ambush of Captain Henry Whiting Stanton:

> About 3 p.m. on 18th Jan'y, I came to the first of their abandoned camps where my command was halted for the night and Captain Stanton was directed to take his company with some additional men to examine a small open valley to the right where were some abandoned lodges about 500 yds distant, and endeavor to find the direction taken by the Indians when they left.
>
> This officer after reaching the point designated charged after some Indians he saw in front and in following up the steep hillsides in the ardor of the chase, became separated from some of his men, badly mounted which were unable to join when he sounded the rally. After rallying about a dozen of his men, he proceeded up the valley until he became satisfied that the Indians had not retreated in that direction and he started back leading his horses. About ¾ of a mile from camp, the valley narrowed, with trees and here he was ambushed and fired into, the first fire killing one of his men. He ordered his party to take to trees but the Indians being in too great force he mounted and directed his party to retreat remaining in rear himself, firing his Sharps Carbine, when he received a shot in the head and was instantly killed.[15]

In a report to the War Department dated February 28, 1855, General Garland expressed his "feelings of more than ordinary

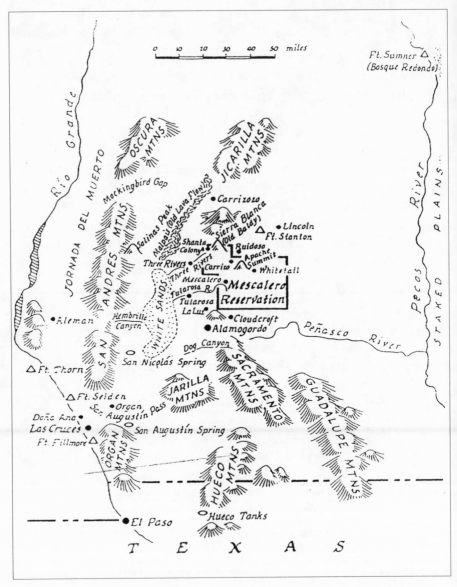

Map of the areas in which the Mescalero were active. From C. L. Sonnichsen, The Mescalero Apaches (Norman: University of Oklahoma Press), page 254. Reprinted by permission.

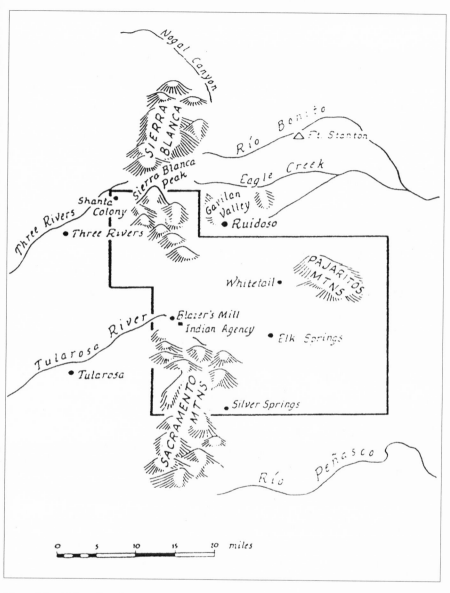

Map of final Mescalero Reservation area showing the location of Blazer's Mill. From C. L. Sonnichsen, The Mescalero Apaches, page 78. Reprinted by permission of the University of Oklahoma Press.

satisfaction" with the result of Captain Ewell's expedition in pursuit of the Mescalero Apache, adding:

> The Apaches lost in the fight fifteen men and I am gratified to say that I have positive information that their great war chief "Santa Anna" [emphasis added] and one of his sons were killed.[16]

Since Captain Ewell's full report did not identify any of the dead Indians, General Garland's "positive information" was in all likelihood obtained from the Indians.

On March 6 Dr. Michael Steck, the Apache agent, wrote:

> I was visited today by a delegation of Mescalero Apaches, who stated that a "Junta" of the tribe was held a few days ago. They say that their roads are open to the Americans, that the source of all their difficulties with us, Santana, is dead and they want peace, etc.[17]

That the original raid was a planned tactic intended to gain for Santana and his band a respite from the neverending search-and-destroy missions of the American military there can be little doubt. The strategy worked; Santana was presumed dead and quickly forgotten. By the early 1870s, when Santana began to reappear in the reports of the various agents, he was not remembered as the "infamous chief" of the Captain Stanton incident. What he did or where he was between 1855 and 1870 is not known.

RESERVATIONS VERSUS ANNIHILATION

Late in 1855, the year Captain Stanton was killed, a military post was established at Fort Stanton. From that time on, with the exception of their years in the concentration camp at the Bosque Redondo Reservation, it was to this post that the Apache returned when they were worn out by their pursuers, when they were starving and ready to sue for rations and peace.

In the years before the Civil War, nothing changed regarding the Indian question. The army forces continued their search-and-destroy missions, while the Indian agents, notably Dr. Michael Steck, continued to press for reservations and the pursuit of peace. The Indians, however, were losing ground. Most of them seemed to realize this but were unable to do anything about it. On October 29, 1855, Lieutenant Colonel Dixon Miles at Fort Fillmore wrote:

> Barranquito made a very pertinent remark to me yesterday, which is so thoughtful and just that I will transcribe it. It was in answer to my question: "That he must hunt up recently stolen mules and deliver them to the owner, if he did not he sanctioned the breaking of the treaty which meant war, and if he and his band wanted war, to say so, I was ready." Answer: "Since I formed and signed the treaty, I have had my horses stolen by the Mexicans, bridles and saddles taken off my horses by Mexicans, also blankets and other things—some of them before my face and in disregard of my remonstrance. I have complained to you and to the Alcalde of these outrages but you have not made these Mexicans give up my horses, bridles or saddles. They have also with impunity outraged my women and beat my men and children. The U. S. Government has given me or my people no redress. Have you not broken the treaty? But I want peace not war. I have borne all these wrongs patiently and now that someone, you don't know who, has stolen a few mules you charge my people to say I must and shall return them. Where am I to look for them? Where am I to get them? I have none. I am 'afoot' for all my horses and mules have been stolen. But I want peace. To obey your orders I'll hunt up the mountains and through the valleys, and if I can find them I will bring them to you. If I can't find them and you make war I will bow in submission to whatever you direct. I will not nor shall my band fight."[18]

On August 13, 1856, Major Jefferson Van Horne reported that "Cadete, son of Barranquito came in today [to Fort Stanton] to announce the death of his father at the Sierra Blanca and that he would succeed him as chief of the band."[19] He also noted that some horses and the mules in question had been stolen by Mexicans from Manzana and then taken by Shawano's band. Shawano's band harbored about the San Andres Mountains east of the Rio Grande, and as there was no friendship between that band and his, he could not get the mules back without fighting them. Shawano is almost certainly the full name of the renegade half-brother of Cadete, Roman, and Santana, whom Almer N. Blazer describes as Cha,[20] and who figures importantly in Santana's story.

By 1858 the plight of the Mescalero was becoming acute. Cadete's band was reported to be camped on the Rio Bonito in destitute condition, half-naked, with no gunpowder, and with game too scarce to kill with bows and arrows. Consequently, they were entirely dependent on rations from the post, which were insufficient and of poor quality.[21]

The dissident Mescalero bands led by Agua Nuevas and Shawano (Cha) continued their depredations. The Mexicans around Mesilla, organized as the Mesilla Guard, were attacking and wantonly killing other Mescalero who, like Barranquito's band, were trying to live in peace. Dr. Michael Steck was advising them to wait and abide by the decision of the United States courts or there would be war.[22]

While the Mescalero chiefs visited General Garland in Santa Fe to ask for help, the citizens of Doña Ana County were petitioning the same General Garland for protection. Some of the Indians (probably most, since they were destitute) kept depredating, and the settlers remained fearful, angry, and demanding. The military began preparations to finally subdue the Mescalero by force.

GENERAL CARLETON AND THE BOSQUE REDONDO

The beginning of the Civil War on April 12, 1861 changed everything overnight, except the plight of the Mescalero. Fort Breckenridge and Fort Buchanan were immediately abandoned. Fort

McLane and Fort Stanton would be evacuated within the year. The Western Apache watched the forts in their area burn and went on a pillage and plunder rampage. Soon Confederates under Lieutenant Colonel John Robert Baylor marched west from San Antonio to occupy Fort Davis and Fort Bliss. By July 1861 Baylor had pushed north to occupy Mesilla and forced the surrender of the Seventh United States Infantry at St. Augustine Pass in the Organ Mountains. Baylor, an Apache-hater, began skirmishes with the Mescalero, causing them to abandon their ripening crops and return to their old ways. In one infamous order directed to the commander of Rebel forces at the Pinos Altos Mines, Baylor wrote:

> I learn . . . that the Indians have been into your post for the purpose of making a treaty. The Congress of the Confederate States has passed a law declaring extermination to all hostile Indians. You will, therefore, use all means to persuade the Apaches . . . to come in for the purpose of making peace, and when you get them together kill all the grown Indians and take all the children prisoners and sell them to defray the expenses of killing the Indians.[23]

Mercifully, when this directive reached Jefferson Davis he countermanded the order and removed Baylor from office.[24]

Then in June 1862, following the evacuation of New Mexico Territory by the Confederates, the famous California Column, made up of California adventurers, including some of the "forty-niners," arrived on the scene. The leader of the column was the newly commissioned Brigadier General James H. Carleton. With the defeat of the Confederates in New Mexico, General Carleton on September 18, 1862, took command of the Department of New Mexico and turned his attention to the Mescalero.[25] Within a week he issued his infamous order:

> All Indian men . . . are to be killed whenever and wherever you find them. The women and children will not be harmed, but you will take them

prisoners, and feed them at Fort Stanton [which he immediately reoccupied] until you receive other instructions about them.[26]

The upshot of this was the development of a pincers move-ment in early September 1862 under the commands of Colonel Joseph West, commanding the District of Arizona, and Colonel Christopher "Kit" Carson. Two separate expeditions under Colonel West entered Mescalero country. The maneuver was very effec-tive. The Mescalero, completely routed, fled to Fort Stanton and were sent under guard to the Bosque Redondo located on the Pecos River near Fort Sumner.[27] The Bosque Redondo (Round Forest) was not a forest at all but consisted of clumps of cottonwood trees growing along the river. The rest of the Bosque Redondo was a forty-mile square area where the water was what the natives called "gyp" (bitter gypsum) in taste, wood was very scarce, and the win-ters were harsh. The mountain-loving Apache were forced to live on an uninviting plain a long way from home.[28]

General Carleton wrote General Lorenzo Thomas in Wash-ington in September 1863 that all the Mescalero were in the Bosque Redondo "with the exception of a few who had either run off into Mexico or joined the Gila Apaches."[29] But Mescalero depreda-tions continued.

There is absolutely no evidence in any of the reports relating to the Apache that Santana was among those at the Bosque Redondo.

Dr. Michael Steck, meanwhile, continued to oppose General Carleton's ideas. He and many settlers began to support the idea of putting each tribe on its own reservation in its own homeland. Santana, no doubt, was listening.

During this time the Bosque Redondo turned into what can only be called a concentration camp. General Carleton, thinking the sub-jugation of the Mescalero was almost completed, turned his attention to the Navajo, a much larger tribe with approximately 12,000 members. He began by capturing them and then, by forced marches, removing them to the Bosque Redondo with their thousands of sheep and other livestock.

At the Bosque Redondo there was not enough grazing for all the animals and not enough water to irrigate all the land necessary for the crops which might support them. The Navajo, natural enemies of the Mescalero, outnumbered them by fifteen to one.[30] Cutworms killed all the crops. Some of the meat they were fed was from diseased cattle, the flour was frequently adulterated with plaster of paris. All in all, it became a hellhole. Still, in August 1864, General Carleton, the radical optimist, was able to write to John P. Usher, secretary of the interior: "The Indians on the Reservation are the happiest people I have ever seen."[31]

In February 1865 General Carleton reported that more than 9,000 Indians were held in custody at the Redondo Bosque.[32] On November 3, 1865, there were only nine Mescalero left there. The rest had stolen away and scattered themselves to prevent recapture, most ending up in their old haunts. Any other life, or even death, was better than staying at the Bosque Redondo.

With the return of the Mescalero to their old homelands, it must have seemed to them, as well as to those settlers whose lives and livelihoods were involved, that nothing had changed. However, changes were in fact occurring, although they were not readily apparent to the embattled Mescalero.

At this time the always inefficient coalition between the military and the civilian territorial Indian administration showed definite signs of breaking down. Dr. Michael Steck and General Carleton disagreed more often and publicly. The "Indian Rings," which profited from the theft and sale of land allotments meant for the Indians, were becoming more insolent and more unscrupulous. Even Washington was aware that the situation was becoming intolerable.

That Santana, though officially in hiding, was still in control of tribal affairs during this period is evidenced by the singularly remarkable fact, almost unbelievable in those troubled times, that La Maquina was not once molested by the Mescalero. Despite the bitter enmity between the Anglos and the Mescalero, neither Nesmith, Dixon and Ryan during their ownership, nor J. H. Blazer during his, suffered any loss at the hands of the Mescalero. Even a sequestered Santana kept his promises. He was truly a man who talked with one tongue.

THE PEACE POLICY

The prohibitive cost of subsisting the Indians over an eighteen-month period ($1,114,981.00 from March 1864 to October 1865),[33] coupled with the disorder already present in the Department of Indian Affairs, precipitated a long overdue decision by the central government to wipe the slate clean and start over. Dr. Michael Steck was the first casualty. He was relieved of his superintendency in April 1865.[34] General Carleton was relieved of his command on September 19, 1866.[35] A short time later, December 31, 1866, a written agreement between the War Department and the Department of the Interior was signed in which the War Department happily transferred the entire Indian problem to the Department of the Interior. The actual transfer was not made, however, until November 1, 1867.

The "mills" of bureaucracy "grind slowly" but not "exceeding fine." [sic] Committee hearings were begun in 1865. In an effort to develop a more humane policy of peace with the Indians, the churches were asked to enter discussions. A Board of Indian Administration was organized within the Department of the Interior with Vincent Colyer, a Quaker, appointed to be the secretary.[36]

By the time Colyer made his first trip to the Southwest in 1871, the decision had already been made to place the Indians on reservations, on lands of their choice when possible. Therefore, Colyer's visit was intended to establish sites satisfactory to all concerned. He did not visit the Mescalero but, remarking that the "Mescaleros had been at peace for a long time," he authorized that a reservation be established for them in their old homeland.[37]

Perhaps not by coincidence, Santana first officially reappears in 1872, shortly after Colyer's authorization for a reservation had been made. That first official appearance, occasioned by the murder of his brother Cadete, was almost as dramatic as his first, more clandestine appearance at Blazer's Mill around 1869.[38]

Santana had apparently become concerned when Cadete did not return from a court appearance in Tularosa when expected. He set out to search for him, crossed the blood-marked trail, and followed it up the canyon to the place where he found Cadete's remains. He buried him there somewhere near the trail, then returned to his camp to report the killing. This incident is described in reports by A. J. Curtis, Indian agent at Fort Stanton.[39]

From the time of Cadete's murder in 1872, Santana appears fairly regularly in the official reports.

L. Edwin Dudley, superintendent of Indian affairs in New Mexico Territory, after visiting the Mescalero Apache Agency at Fort Stanton on February 18, 1873, wrote:

> I counseled with as many of the chiefs as could be collected together including Roman, the successor of Cadete, Paulgonia [probably Santana's medicine man Gorgonio], Santana, Francisco, Pablo, and Jose Pino relative to a reservation and without exception they desire to have set apart for them the east side of the White and Sacramento Mountains.[40]

This rather casual mention of Santana leads one to believe that either he was there to observe and evaluate without making himself known, or that Dudley, a newcomer, simply had not heard of him.

The peace Santana had tried to attain for twenty-three years was now a real possibility. For Santana—an old and tired Santana—the deprivations, the self-imposed isolation, the work, the planning, and the hardships of the last fifteen years at last came to fruition with the establishment of the reservation. It was his greatest triumph. Like Moses, he had brought his people out of the wilderness and back to the promised land. Unlike Moses, he would join them there for the few years left to him. His work was done. True triumph does not require the sound and the fury of the multitude. It is found in the quiet places of the heart.

SANTANA

Three Indians stood in the shadow of a lone pine tree on the mountaintop, where scrub oak brush also partly concealed them. Their gaze was fixed with deep concern on two horsemen, who had stopped a quarter of a mile below them on a fire-denuded ridge where it abutted the steeper slope on which the watchers had maintained their vigil since daybreak.

The Indians had been watching the horsemen's movements for several hours as the riders followed the trail of a single horse. It was now nearly midday, and the snowfall of the night before had begun to ball badly on the shod hoofs of their mounts as the bright sun began to melt the covering, here exposed to its direct rays.

Along the ridge the horsemen had been following the grade, which had not been steep; but ahead the mountainside rose abruptly and shaded the ground so that the frozen snow, driven by a light breeze, had obliterated the trail tacking up the slope before them, making it difficult to follow. There was no trace of the route taken by the horse they had been following.

"They can ride no farther," asserted the larger of the Indians, "and they cannot see the tracks from there on and might turn back."

A short consultation between the horsemen appeared to ensue, and they turned back, retracing their steps down the ridge, and disappeared as they descended into the valley.

These horsemen were scouts sent out from a detachment of cavalry that had arrived at Tularosa the evening before—intent on punishing the Indians for their depredations.[1] Their object was to locate the Indians' rendezvous and guide the troops in an attack. Had they persisted in their efforts for another hour, they would have reached the summit of the mountain, from where, with the aid of their field glasses, they would have seen the wisps of smoke rising from the little fires, and probably other evidences of the presence of the Indians' camp.

Had the scouts been killed, which would have been likely had the Indians' camp been found, the resulting search for them would have certainly resulted in discovery of the camp by the cavalry. The escape of the scouts would have been equally disastrous for the Indians and the history of the Mescalero very different from what it is.

The military campaign of 1867 was probably the first time in their history the Mescalero had been concerned over the encroachment of immigrants into the territory they had roamed almost unrestrainedly for centuries.[2] The Spaniards and the Mexicans, it is true, had resisted their raids, but with little loss to the Indians, and occasionally these immigrants had attacked them. However, on the whole the Mescalero had benefited from, rather than been injured by, the intruders: the booty from their successful raids more than offset the losses in their repulses.

But now, since the conclusion of the Civil War, the United States troops had kept them on the move so that their supply of food for the winter was insufficient. If the campaign was continued through the winter, hunting on the plains, where the soldiers were more effective, would be curtailed, and the snows in the mountains would drive the game to the lower levels, leaving the Indians in a state of famine.

The Indians were not concerned for their immediate safety, for they had usually been able to avoid the troops, but the soldiers were now less than a score of miles away. A single Indian scout, one of a considerable number who had gone to hunt on the plains, had reached the camp the night before to report the arrival of the troops at Tularosa, and to help them formulate plans. The hunters had decided to divert the troops from the vicinity of the camp of the Mescalero. The Indian scout had not followed a beaten trail but had ridden east into the mountains, then had doubled back by a devious route to the southwest and located the point he had crossed the summit of this mountain by its lone pine. There his trail could be watched for many miles.

Santana and his two brothers backtracked the messenger to this point to determine if he was being followed, for if so, it would be necessary to move camp or a pitched battle would ensue—something the old chief was determined to avoid if possible.

The day had been clear, and the bright sun had melted the snow from the southern exposure of the hills while the three brothers had remained on the mountaintop. The watchers remained at their post until late in the afternoon before they saw the smoke signal rise from Golondrina Peak, some thirty miles to the north, which told them that the ruse the hunters had proposed to use was succeeding. The soldiers were following the trail prepared for them, expecting to be guided thereby to the main camp of the Mescalero, which in fact they were leaving behind as fast as their well-fed horses could carry them.

The area occupied by the Indians' camp covered some sixty square miles and contained nearly two thousand Mescalero.[3] On every side high summits of the range, rising to altitudes of about eight thousand feet, surrounded the encampment, except to the northeast, where the several canyons draining the watershed converged to form Nogal Canyon. This canyon formed an opening to the northwest and emptied its flood waters into Tularoso Canyon and the Rio Tularoso flowing westward.

Scores of springs provided an abundant and well-distributed

water supply for the Indian camp. Deep canyons between the hills and ridges ranged down to as low as five thousand feet in altitude, where piñon and cedar were the predominating timber, with junipers scattered in groves and clumps. The higher reaches were heavily timbered with magnificent pines and firs, and the heads of these canyons contained dense groves of quaking aspen now brilliant with the frosted leaves turned to quivering gold. Here and there ash, maple, and wild cherry lent their variegated autumn hues to the color scheme embedded in the many shades of green shown by a dozen species of conifers.

The snow still lay untarnished in large patches where shaded, for the air was chill at these elevations, the difference in temperature between bright sunshine and shade within a distance of a few feet being often thirty degrees.

Somber shadows, cast by the mountains to the west, were climbing rapidly up the main range to the east of the bowl-like depression occupied by the Indians, before the watchers left their post to begin their three-mile tramp toward the meager comforts of the camp. The setting sun still bathed the mountaintops in its last rays while the Indians cleared the western brow of the mesa, and hundreds of sparklike points of light gleamed through the dusk of the trees below, where the small, solitary fires of each family unit were being fed with dry twigs.

The habitation of the Indians had been selected with the idea of escape rather than defense, should they be attacked. Most fires could be seen from other fires and were easily within hailing distance of each other. Thus word could be quickly passed to every part of the camp, over the miles of distance, and any important communication could be delivered throughout the area in a few minutes. There were no guards, for the Indians depended on their dogs to give notice of the approach of strangers, and no one approached a fire without first calling out and receiving an answer.

The fires and the sun had dried the ground within the brush

walls of the wickiups, and with loose hides placed to windward comparative comfort had been restored since the snow of the preceding night. Stormproof shelter for the people was very limited as there had been no buffalo hunt to provide hides for new tipis. The canvas tents, issued by the government while on the reservation, had long since been reduced to rags and abandoned, and many tipis had been left standing while their occupants fled for their lives when surprised by sudden attacks. A few tipis still remained, however, which were given over to the sick or injured, or for the housing of infants.

While not communists in the strict sense, common interests of the Indians led to communistic practices as a matter of self-preservation. There were a few whose superior intelligence made their lot easier than that of others, but the Indians' mode of life prevented the accumulation of property to any considerable extent, except for women and horses. But there was nothing comparable to the poverty of white civilization. Food and shelter were equally necessary to all and equally available since nature's storehouse was their only resource. In the abstract, personal property was sacred to the owner, and in excess of immediate needs, was stored for future use, in which case it was protected by the most stringent laws and customs. The accumulation of such stores was of no great advantage to the individual, however, for in case of scarcity, all were entitled to a portion for the relief of the common distress, though not in the owner's absence.

Nature provided bountifully or sparingly according to the seasons and in restricted areas where such supplies were indigenous. All were equally enabled to acquire and store so that the energy required was the only thing that might have a barter value. This, too, was discounted by the fact that many special tasks were performed by experts, and light tedious tasks were performed by aged or convalescent persons or children in exchange for more strenuous efforts during the seasons of accumulation.

Luxuries were usually prepared by the individual desiring them, not for the public, but occasionally in sufficient quantity to distribute as a treat to special friends and relatives. And certain articles were prepared by secret formulas for barter.

Essential food was eaten by all wherever found, in proportion to the supply available. This was a natural cause of their nomadic habits, for when the food supply was low in the locality of an established camp they moved to a place where their wants could be more easily supplied. Seasonal moves were the rule, for their range included high, well-watered, and shady districts as well as low plains and foothills where winter storms seldom bothered for long.

Conditions at the time were not normal with the Mescalero, however, and the brush walls of the wickiups had been reenforced, so occupants could protect themselves from the cutting wind of the coming night. And about each little fire in the deepening gloom a carefree, happy group assembled. The old, the sick, and otherwise indisposed crouched in silence where some friendly nook provided a measure of comfort; their stoic natures enabled them to bear their suffering without complaint, for custom denied them that.

This had been the first snow, and now the cold weather must be expected with increasing severity. Most of the game would leave the high mountains for the lower hills and the plains, which would make their existence more difficult. But generations of hardship enabled them to contemplate the future without apparent concern.

Frost flakes glittered in the air as Santana approached the wickiup that U'ah, his old wife, had prepared for his comfort. He called and was answered by Ntsaaze, his only son. Santana had eaten nothing since leaving camp long before daybreak, when he and his brothers had begun their tramp and all-day vigil in the snow. A slice of venison from a frozen ham had been his only ration that day.

Katsuue, his daughter, brought him a roasted bone to scrape for his supper, which, with the marrow secured by crushing it, was more than many of his followers had, for the meat they had expected the hunters to have brought in had not been forthcoming on account of the intervention of the troops.

A small buffalo hide tipi was the only stormproof shelter he owned, and this was now given over to his three wives. U'ah, the wife of his youth, was caring for the twin sisters he had taken to wife in middle life. Each of these later had borne him a son, but both of these children had died in infancy. Now Anna had given birth to a girl during the week, and Etta was disabled with a broken leg caused by the fall of a horse.

Santana's son and daughter who ministered to his comfort were the last survivors of a large family of children born to him and U'ah during many years of their early lives. Ntsaaze was grown to men's estate and was, like his father, a noticeably large man as compared to the Mescalero generally. Katsuue was about fifteen years of age and a comely maid.

"Bima [mother] is with the others," she told her father. "She said for me to call her if you wanted her, but she thought they could sleep and would not come if not needed."

Beside the son and daughter, the group about Santana's fire included an aged sister of the chief, a *yadeche* (priestess) who was charged with the spiritual welfare of Katsuue during her adolescence.

The women kept to their side of the fire crouched beneath the trailing smoke, and wrapped in their robes soon fell asleep on their pallets of fragrant branches and grass.

A number of the head men gathered later in the night to discuss the situation and decide what was best to do. The hunters on the plains had proposed to try the plan, of making a false trail for the troops to follow, which, if successful, would be indicated by the signal for which the three brothers had waited on the mountaintop.

By an unfortunate chain of circumstances, some of Santana's people had been engaged in the massacre of some Mexican immigrants at Carrizo Springs, and this punitive expedition of the troops was believed to be in reprisal of that occurrence. The Indians had thought that if they were to be harassed by the soldiers on account of the trouble at Carrizo Springs it would have occurred long ago, for several months had passed since it had happened.[4] Now the troops were within twenty miles of the camp and might be followed by reenforcements. The food situation was also discussed. The present rendezvous had been established by Santana for the purpose of a capitulation. However, an additional objective was several months hunting in the nearby mountains since sustenance of the Indians had depleted the game to the extent that it was now difficult to supply their needs, and the approaching winter would soon increase their difficulties.

The question was, should hunters go onto the plains where the vigilance of the troops and the settlers would make the discovery of the camp more likely? The location of the Indians' camp had been chosen near the only organized settlement in the Mescalero country, as best suited to their purpose. It was too far from the town to be in danger of discovery by anyone engaged in the ordinary affairs of life. Centrally located in the rough mountainous country into which the Indians might flee for safety if discovered, it was off the usual routes of travel, above the summer heat and below the heavy winter snows, well timbered with abundant water, and so near the settlement as to be unsuspected. They decided to avoid the plains and resort to the few remaining horses when necessary.

A serious split in the tribe had occurred when Santana had decided to sue for peace due to a difference of opinion over resisting invasion of the settlers. Santana had observed a fundamental difference in the character of the recent arrivals and insisted that they were a different kind of people from the Indians and not subject to the divine laws in which the Mescalero believed. He was supported in this by a majority of his followers, but of course they had no conception of what would happen. He, however, realized that his people could not contend successfully with the increasing numbers of settlers.

Contrary to the conventional idea of some right of possession claimed by the Indians to the land, the Mescalero had no conception of ownership. They believed that Eyata (something above the sky) had made the world, and it was his. They were fatalists and believed that all good things, including the world, were provided by the Deity for the use of all his creatures in a predetermined manner, and that all bad came from a malignant influence (Chete Neh) permitted to contend with their good thoughts. They believed that all Eyata's creation was good, and, since the strong in all nature exploit the weak, this was right and justified.

Consequently, their belief was that it was right to take what they wanted, if they could. In this there was no discrimination between humans, beasts, or other creatures of nature and violence in the taking was incidental, with the contention between the natural right to take and the malignant thought as exemplified in resistance.

Valor was their cardinal virtue. If a man showed fear under any conditions, he was considered a pariah. Timidity was a trait permissible only to women without incurring the contempt and ridicule of a man's associates. They almost never fought in the open or in mass, although they were loyal comrades. They depended on surprise, ambuscade, sniping and individual enterprise. An enemy seldom had more than a glimpse of one in action. They did not go into a fight in traditional war bonnets and finery. They used paint for camouflage and identification, not for adornment, and they stripped to their breechclouts and moccasins when going into battle.

The warriors did not often scalp or otherwise mutilate their victims. Such mutilations were usually committed by fury-crazed females, in retaliation for the death or injury of their man. There was no shouting of orders, and the disconcerting yells indicated that an individual was safely concealed, rather than signaling the beginning of a charge.

For many years Santana had been the undisputed leader of the Mescalero. Santana's word was law, subject only to the traditional law of Eyata, equivalent to a constitution, and the supplemental tribal laws as interpreted by the council of head men assembled as a court. He was strongly supported by his own valor and ability, and the head men of the various subdivisions of the tribe submitted to his leadership in all matters of importance because of his superior qualifications.

There were four half brothers in Santana's immediate family. Beside these three—Santana, Roman and Cadete—there was another, Cha, who was several years younger than his brothers. All the half brothers had lived harmoniously under the old regime. Cha had been well treated but resented discipline by his older brothers. When the older brothers refused to continue the general warfare on the invaders on account of Santana's beliefs, Cha had gathered a band of desperate characters and left the tribe.[5]

Because Cha was his brother and because he had removed a large number of a disturbing element from among his people, Santana permitted the secession with the stipulation that Cha and his followers should not allow any depredations in the Tularoso country—specifically the eastern portion of the plains and the Sacramento Mountains—where Santana proposed to assemble the Mescalero with the object of capitulation. And on their failure to observe this condition rested Santana's threat to exterminate the renegades.[6]

The Mescalero were not ruled by hereditary chiefs but by persons of unusual qualifications and personal ability who assumed the leadership and commanded sufficient respect and loyalty to maintain the position. This was accomplished by force to a greater or lesser extent and often resulted in bloody encounters among the tribesmen. The result was the survival of the fittest as demonstrated by the contenders' ability to cope with emergencies.

There were eight principal subdivisions of the tribe, each consisting largely of closely related families but all of the same general stock.[7] Each band was independent of the others in the ordinary affairs of life, and in a general way was controlled by its own head man, who in turn held his followers by personal ability. These head men voluntarily submitted to their acknowledged leader, who in matters concerning the tribe as a whole was looked up to and obeyed—not infallibly, however, for there were always jealousies. Thus, the tribe as a whole was ruled by Santana as their chief from about 1830 until his death in 1876.

The American troops that occupied the country during the Mexican War had subdued the Mescalero and some of the other tribes, in a measure, placing them on a reservation at Bosque Redondo on the Pecos. Fort Sumner was later created for their surveillance.[8] The Civil War, however, practically ended this control, and, although nominally still on the reservation, the Mescalero, at this time lived where they pleased. Cha's insurgents numbered nearly a hundred men. They had abandoned their wives and children to be cared for by relatives with the main tribe. Having established a rendezvous in the Jarilla Mountains, they depended on the proceeds of depredations—attacks on settlements and on travelers along the roads—for a living.

The Jarillas were an isolated group of hills where the Indians knew of hidden water, and were surrounded by miles of desert country wherein no permanent water was known to exist. Here Cha's insurgents defied their pursuers with the help of the desert when menaced by the troops or by organized bands of settlers intent on punishing the outlaws. It was an inhospitable location, bleak and rocky, where the scant, scrubby timber and brush provided little shade or fuel. In summer the sun beat mercilessly on the granite hills, and in autumn the cold winds reached great velocity. They had driven in numbers of stolen horses that had tramped out the grass near the water so that the blowing sand made their existence there more trying; consequently, they remained in this location only when compelled to do so by their pursuers.

Individuals from Cha's band had, clandestinely, visited some of the scattered fugitives from the main tribe in the Sacramentos and taken back a part of their own families and some stolen women with them. They had also been joined by some renegades from other tribes, making a mixed and vulnerable community, had they not been protected by their location. The increasing discomfort had at length driven them to take their dependents into the San Andres range, where, although more exposed to attack, they were more comfortable. Thus, they had accumulated a considerable number of dependents they could not protect—for the fighting men must retreat to their rendezvous when pursued—and their scattered women could be visited only occasionally.

Many of the stolen women were only too glad to be rescued, and all were in constant fear of being discovered, which would be death or capture for them. Thus, through the women Santana had found means of reaching some twenty of Cha's fighting men who had repented of their desertion. They were all tired of the life they were living. Upon Santana's proposal that they rejoin the tribe at their camp in the Sacramentos and his assurance that they would be received back into their former status, they were glad of the opportunity to desert Cha.

It was during their movement across the plains that the trouble at Carrizo Springs had developed. The mutilated bodies of the victims had been found and the massacre reported at Tularosa, where a party had been organized to investigate. After giving the victims burial, the Indians' trail had been followed for a distance but lost without overtaking the murderers. Unusually large tracks about the scene resulted in the belief that Santana had been present when the atrocity had occurred. The military had been notified, but until now, several months later, there had been no attempt made to punish the perpetrators.

The mountaintop from which the watchers had followed the movements of the scouts had been denuded of timber by some long

past forest fire and was now covered by a thick growth of scrub oak
with an occasional surviving pine. This was the highest of the isolated elevations about the rendezvous and was maintained as a
constant lookout, occupied throughout the daylight hours by one
or more sentinels. Their duty was to watch for alarming appearances
and signal to the camp, or to any individual or party beyond the
surrounding hills in case of necessity. The main traveled road

*Santana's twin wives were forced by Santana to have their picture
taken in 1870. This is the first picture to be taken of Mescalero
Indians. Courtesy Rio Grande Historical Collections, New Mexico
State University Library.*

through the mountains and the country as far as the eye could see in all directions, except to the south, was in sight, and it was on the summit dividing Tularoso Canyon from the Indians' location.

This lookout was located about ten miles from the town of Tularosa, situated at the edge of the plains at the mouth of the canyon to the west. A few miles to the east, near the mouth of the north fork, another settlement known as The Mill[9] was located. And these were the only settlements closer than Mesilla Valley, a hundred miles to the west.

In years gone by, Santana had arranged a peace agreement with each of these settlements. But Cha had attacked parties of the Tularosa people on the road, and the affair at Carrizo Springs, where Santana's own tracks had been found, had shaken their confidence in his promise of immunity from attack by Mescalero. Consequently, his emissaries had not been well received at Tularosa.

At The Mill Santana had also failed, for he found that none of his old acquaintances was there; and he had not approached the newcomers but had set his spies to watch their movements, to learn their habits and, if possible, their dispositions.

He had counted on an assistant from one or the other of these settlements to intervene for him in contacting the military authorities and arranging his capitulation without delay, which would have avoided this shortage of food for his people and allowed them to be safely on the reservation long ago. Now, there was no hope of assistance from the Tularosa people, and he was not yet satisfied that his advances would be well received at The Mill, although he had made plans to try. In the meantime every precaution must be taken to avoid discovery of the location of his people. For, although their intentions were good, until Santana's desire for peace had been made known to the military there could be no discrimination, and any Indians found within many miles would be treated as hostiles. However, he believed that once amicable contact was made, a treaty could be arranged on favorable terms.

TULAROSA

Tularosa was originally settled and fortified by a few hardy Mexican pioneers in 1862, and being isolated and a community of little importance, had escaped attention during the Civil War. Although never invaded by hostile Indians, a relatively large number of its residents had lost their lives to marauding bands while on the roads performing the various duties requiring their presence beyond the protection of the settlement. A number of attacks had also been repulsed by the people.

The fertility of the lands and a bountiful supply of water for irrigation, however, was attractive and gradually induced additions to the inhabitants until by 1867 Tularosa had become a village of some three or four hundred souls.

The buildings were of adobe with heavy walls capable of resisting rifle fire, and many were surrounded by adobe walls enclosing gardens, orchards, and vineyards that provided additional discouragement to an attacking force.

At the close of the war several military organizations had been disbanded at points that left government equipment available, and the Mexican *carretas* (wagons), which had been their only vehicles of transportation prior to that time, were now largely superseded by the iron-axled government wagons.

A number of these wagons were employed in freighting lumber from The Mill to various destinations throughout the country, whereby the oxen used in plowing were kept busy while the crops were being tended in the old way by hand. Most of the employees at The Mill were also members of families living at Tularosa, and the settlements were more or less interdependent.

A recent addition to the inhabitants of the town was an American who had established himself as a merchant and built a large residence, store, and other buildings near the center of the settlement surrounded by a large adobe corral. He had the appointment as forage agent at this location and handled the surplus crops of the area. The people of this community were in general poorly provided with arms, however, and although they had sufficient number to protect themselves, they could render no assistance to their neighbors.[1]

When the troops sent to punish the Indians for the massacre at Carrizo Springs arrived at Tularosa, they were accommodated by the forage agent; but on account of the lateness of their arrival nothing was done until the following morning.

The soldiers' tents had been pitched within the high walls of the corral, where they and their stock were shielded from the wind. Here the stock had abundant hay and grain, and in some measure the soldiers were entertained at a native dance where wine and brandy of local manufacture contributed to their enjoyment.

The next day the dozen or so scouts accompanying the expedition were sent out to look for Indian signs while the officers remained in comfort, provided with a warm room by the forage agent. Scouring the country in every direction, the scouts, riding in pairs searched for signs of their quarry and found the Indian hunters' night camp. Early in the morning they reported that the Indians' trails, which led off in every direction, were being followed with the expectation that they would converge and lead to the main camp of the Mescalero.

All but two of the scouts had reported by midnight. The Indians' trails all led away to the north, heading toward the Mal

The first hotel built in Tularosa, 1887. Courtesy Rio Grande Historical Collections, New Mexico State University Library.

Pais (lava beds), where the scouts believed they converge. The last two scouts did not arrive until near noon of the next day and reported that the trail they had followed was that of a single horse, which led them toward White Mountain in an apparently direct course for some fifteen miles, until darkness and the snow compelled them to wait for daylight. The light snowfall had been followed by a bitter cold night with little wind, which had left the depressions of the horse's tracks still visible to the trained eyes of the scouts. These they had followed when daylight came and found they turned back to the southwest and across the summit. This they believed indicated that they had followed someone who had been initially intent on going into the White Mountain country but had been discouraged by the storm and had turned back toward the more comfortable climate of the foothills and was not headed for the Indians' camp—supposed to be somewhere to the northeast in the White Mountain country.

This last report was that of the two scouts the Indians had watched from the mountaintop, and indicated Santana's wisdom in the selection of this location for his camp.

The military campaign had been organized with the object of avenging the atrocities committed at Carrizo Springs several months before. The undertaking had been delayed by the continuous hostility of the Indians in Mesilla Valley, where all available troops had been attempting to drive the Indians back to the Jarillas.

The captain in command had already decided to lead his men northward, where, at a distance of some thirty miles, it was believed the Indians whose sign had been discovered were heading for a rendezvous and would leave a defined trail to their destination at the main Mescalero camp.

This last report had been awaited with some anxiety, for it was possible that these men had met with some misfortune that would require the assistance of some part of the troops; but all preparations for travel had been made and no change of plans was made, so that within the hour the troops and their packtrain were on their way.

There were more than two hundred veterans in this expedition, but Santana was supposed to have a thousand warriors. The danger of engaging this great a number of warriors unawares made every precaution necessary, while every hour of delay meant more time for the Indians to prepare for an encounter or an escape.[2]

It was assumed that the Indians' diverging trails indicated that the proximity of the troops was known and were a ruse to divert them from their goal. That their movements would be noted was a foregone conclusion.

The scouts, well in advance, were deployed at considerable intervals to give timely warning of a concentration of Indians anywhere ahead, thus reducing the danger of a sudden con-frontation.

Before reaching the Mal Pais, however, the trails were seen bearing to the east of the route they were following, joining from time to time, and finally leading to Carrizo Springs, where night found the expedition.

No fires were allowed, for the troops had learned by experience that sentries outlined against the firelight made an easy mark for the Indians' arrows as they crept invisibly through the grass. And a guard of twenty men relieved every two hours was detailed to keep watch over the stock, for they had learned that the Indians' cunning was more to be feared than their numbers. Large detachments of soldiers had been left afoot by half a dozen Indians stampeding their herd in the face of rifle fire, while a few others diverted the attention of the camp by a feint attack from another direction. Consequently, every animal was hobbled.

The fresh signs found at Carrizo Springs indicated a concen-tration of a hundred or more Indians who had made a short stop for water and grazing their horses. Water splashed about the spring still lay unabsorbed upon the ground, indicating that they had not left more than an hour or so before the arrival of the troops. It was believed to be a war party, for all the tracks had been made by men and showed sign of the fringes of Mescalero warriors' moc-casins, while no women's tracks were found.

From the spring, the trail left by the Indians in the deep grass was plain as a wagon road leading northeast toward the foothills. In that direction was open country, undulating plains; but now, obscured by the deepening twilight, no horsemen were visible.

To the west, at a little distance, loomed the ancient lava beds rising from the level plain, an impassable barrier. Beyond this, the distant peaks of the Oscuro Mountains outlined an undulating horizon still sharply distinct against the sunset sky. And, crescent-like, to the north, east, and south, the Jarilla, Capitan, and White mountains, still illuminated by the fading light, were emphasized by Carrizo, Capitan, Nogal, and Baldy peaks, rising majestically above the contour of their summits.

An early start brought the troops to the foothills by noon, where, on rolling, gravelly ridges intersected by deep ravines, the trail was much less distinct but could be easily followed. The terrain here made slower progress advisable, for deep gorges must be paralleled as well as steep hillsides, clothed in dense growths of cedar and piñon. And the visibility was reduced since the trail meandered among the hills, where the scouts' lateral reconnoiters were obstructed by impassable barriers. Consequently, the day's march was less than twenty miles, with the Indians' trail becoming less pronounced as if by a reduction in the number of horses.

After two more days with similar conditions the only tracks visible were those of a half-dozen horses crossing a barren flat, which were then lost on a rocky ridge. The trail was not found again, although a day was spent in cutting sign for miles around.

The strenuous march had told on the soldiers' horses. Not an Indian had been seen. The troops were in "bad water" country with rations getting low and no supply point within a hundred miles. There was nothing to do but abandon the campaign and go home.

THE MILL

The Mill was the reoccupied site of a very old settlement. It had been established, originally, during the first occupation of the Rio Grande Valley by the Spaniards. Here the efforts of the padres had in some measure secured the amity of the Indians and made possible the manufacture of lumber from the local pine for use in the construction of their settlements, particularly the churches. An abundant supply of pine timber grew immediately adjacent, and selected trees produced perfect material for the adornment of their shrines.

The Rio Tularoso is a permanent stream rising in the south fork of the Tularoso Canyon only a few miles from its junction with the north fork to form the main canyon of the Tularoso. This juncture is about a mile above The Mill. The north fork provided the main travel route from the west across the mountains to Lincoln, Roswell, and beyond. In the early days the north fork of the Rio Tularoso arose less than a mile from its junction with the south fork. The large spring from which it arose has not been running for many years. The volume of water carried by the Rio Tularoso, coupled with the relatively steep downgrade of the canyon where the mill itself was located, allowed the use of power machinery in the sawmill, which replaced the crude whipsaw that had to be operated by man power.

The machinery had been improved from time to time, and a

considerable settlement had grown up during the Mexican administration. During the Mexican War the settlement was garrisoned and an attempt was made to defend it against the American troops. This resulted in the defeat of the Mexicans and the destruction of the settlement during the winter of 1846–1847.

During the early 1850s the lumber industry was resumed here under the protection of the United States troops to provide lumber for the construction of the forts being established in the newly acquired territory, although it was a private enterprise. Returns from the selected lumber required by the military made it possible to provide for the necessities of the settlers at reasonable prices, and the business prospered for a time in spite of the constant menace of Indians—until the settlement was finally destroyed in 1855 by the Comanche.

Several years before the forts were abandoned in 1862, probably about 1857 or 1858, a man known as Skilicon,[1] along with a number of kindred spirits, made some arrangement with Santana whereby they would not be molested by the Mescalero, and again lumber was manufactured at what was already known for hundreds of miles in every direction as The Mill. Some land was also cultivated at The Mill, and both lumber and agricultural products were sold at Fort Fillmore during the late 1850s.

On January 18, 1855, Captain Henry Whiting Stanton was killed in a battle with the Mescalero on the Peñasco River near present-day Mayhill. The Indians were soundly defeated. From that day the total subjugation of the Mescalero became inevitable; it was only a matter of time. The Mescalero no longer were able to protect The Mill, and it was again destroyed by the Comanche in 1859. By 1862 the defeat of the Mescalero was completed. They were rounded up at Fort Stanton and transported to the Bosque Redondo near Fort Sumner.[2]

In 1861, Whitlock[3] acquired such rights as remained of the Skilicon enterprise and reestablished the settlement by employing

Blazer's Mill, 1879. Blazer Family Collection.

a mill crew and a number of extra men required for their added protection. These extras, when not guarding the loggers, were occupied in agricultural pursuits on lands adjacent to The Mill.

By late 1865 all the Mescalero escaped from the Bosque Redondo and scattered in small bands over the Sacramento, White and Guadalupe mountains, and even as far south as Mexico. Cadete and his band took refuge with the Comanche.[4]

In the meantime, the proprietorship of business at the mill changed several times, although the occupation of the property had been continuous and undisturbed. In 1868 Dr. Joseph H. Blazer acquired an interest in the property and by 1869 was in charge of operations.[5]

One day Jim Walters, the cook, was alone in the kitchen, and four men were stacking lumber in the mill yard while acting as guards for the property, with their guns at hand. All the other men were out with the loggers, who made such trips once or twice a week as the supply of logs required. The kitchen was in a log cabin a little distance from the mill and above it on the mesa. There was no window in the kitchen, and the door, facing south, stood open. The sun streaming in provided plenty of light while Jim prepared the noonday meal, but when a shadow obscured it he turned, instantly alert, for his companions would not have approached in silence and an enemy was the only alternative in his mind.

His reaction was spontaneous; he picked up the rifle and presented it at full cock in the same movement. But a sobbing wail from the apparition in the doorway gave him pause before he pulled the trigger. The figure standing in the sunlight was not distinct against the glare, and he did not recognize the visitor.

As Jim stepped forward the apparition drew back so that the light reflected upon the visitor, revealing a wizened, wrinkled, red-brown face with piercing black eyes and a mat of tousled gray hair, a body stooped with age and wearing a calico garment of some kind about the torso, a skirt nearly touching the ground in front but

Dr. J. H. Blazer, circa 1864. Courtesy Rio Grande Historical Collections, New Mexico State University Library.

disclosing the dirty brown calves at the back as the visitor turned as if to retreat. One scrawny hand grasped a long crooked staff while the other carried a rag of some filthy looking cloth.

"*Valgame Dios*" ("God bless me") came from the old Indian woman as she began to move away.

"*Que quieres?*" ("What do you want?") demanded Jim angrily, as he stepped into the doorway.

The old woman stopped and, turning her head, replied, "*Qualquier cosa*" ("Anything"); then she continued speaking in Spanish, "I am cold and starving but would rather live than die."

"Wait then," said Jim, and going back to the fire brought out a smoking hot biscuit from the Dutch oven on the coals.

This she devoured ravenously, and he also brought her a chunk of boiled beef, which satisfied her hunger to some extent and released her tongue.

In reply to Jim's questions, she told him that her people had abandoned her to starve and that she and some other old Indians had lived during the summer on little animals that they could catch and wild fruits and vegetables to be found in the mountains. But now that it had snowed they had eaten hardly anything for several days; and there were two old men besides some other women in her party that were all older than she and some were sick.

She finally asked who was boss and was told that he was a big man with white hair and beard. Then she wanted to talk with him and was told that he was out with the men getting logs and would not be back until late but that she might wait for him. This she declined to do and after begging more bread and meat said she would come again the next day and left.

Jim had been in the country for a number of years and had heard of the favorable arrangement formerly enjoyed by the settlement here when Santana's Indians had acted as protectors to the industry, and the loss of protection resulting from their captivity. Now there was apprehension and suspense caused by the frequent reports reaching The Mill of depredations committed elsewhere by the Mescalero. Jim believed this old Indian to be a Mescalero and a spy. As to the object of her visit he was doubtful; that her sole errand was to beg food was not likely, for there were half a dozen hams of venison hanging in the shade behind the kitchen that she could just as easily have stolen as make such a visit. Any scruples about stealing would have no weight, and risk of being shot would, of course, be understood.

He watched her tottering gait as she climbed the trail behind the cabins. She did not rest nor falter while in sight, and he believed her decrepitude to be largely a sham. He looked for tracks around the other cabins and found none.

When the men from the mill yard came for dinner, he asked if they had seen any strangers, and as they had not he decided to say nothing about his visitor until he could tell Dr. Blazer and let him decide what should be done. There was no opportunity to talk with the doctor alone until after supper, and when he heard the tale he remarked that he was glad that she had been well treated and that he would like to talk to her if she returned. They then talked of the arrangement in former years whereby the Mescalero had befriended the settlement at The Mill, but Jim knew nothing of the means employed in making the arrangement, or of the terms or method of payment.

The doctor had been in the country only a few months and had had no dealings with any Indians; in fact, he had never seen an Indian except in hostile attitude on a few occasions when his mule train had been threatened with attack. The doctor believed, as Jim did, that the sole object of the visit could not have been the little food the woman might be able to beg and hoped that the incident might lead to some friendly relation with the Indians. At any rate they knew of nothing to be done for additional protection if the Mescalero were near in force; and if the old woman's story was to be accepted her friendship was cheap at the price of a little food.

Blazer's sawmill and behind, the new grist mill, 1882 or 1883. Blazer Family Collection.

The doctor sent for an old Mexican, Cavino, who had served him faithfully as wagon boss before he had acquired his interest here.[6] Cavino also believed that the friendly attitude that had been assumed was in their best interests, and that it was well that the men knew nothing of the possible proximity of the Indians. He pointed out that they were as alert as possible, and would be more apt to see an Indian if expecting to, while no doubt if the Indians were in the vicinity in force The Mill would be under constant observation and any unusual action would be noted and might be misconstrued to the detriment of a friendly approach. It was decided that the three should keep the matter to themselves. Cavino was in charge of the extra men and, being old, gave most of his time to directing the others so that he might watch for Indians without appearing to do so; at the same time the doctor and Jim, on the higher ground around the cabins, also were on the alert.

Thus, nothing was done to arouse suspicion, but the doctor saw to it that the daily cleaning and inspection of the arms was not slighted. And the extra men were put to work husking corn in a shed near the mill so that all the workers would be close together.

The level floor of the canyon where the farming was done was a quarter of a mile in width and extended for nearly a half-mile above and an equal distance below the mill, which was located at the foot of the mesa on the north side of the canyon. The cabins were above on the higher ground. High mountains shortened the horizon to the north and south to a mile or so, while down the canyon to the west of the San Andres range, seventy miles away beyond the plains, could be seen through a gap in the hills. To the east and south the mountainsides were pineclad, and the southern exposure of the hillsides to the north were thickly covered with piñon and cedar.

Since early morning the doctor strode conspicuously before the cabins and about the clearing on the mesa in anticipation of the arrival of the expected visitor. The mill was running, and a shout or even a gunshot on the mesa could not have been heard there above the noise of the machinery. However, a rope was extended from the doctor's quarters to the mill roof, where it was attached to a hammer so arranged that, when the rope was pulled, it would strike a discarded saw to serve as an alarm signal that could be heard throughout the fields.

Noon came and went while the doctor pondered the situation. He knew that Santana was the chief through whom the protection of The Mill had been arranged in former years, but his name was throughout the country a synonym for atrocious cruelty. His tracks, recognized by their unusual size, had been found around the massacre at Carrizo Springs within the past few months. By common report he was the leader of the Mescalero. Unscrupulous, cunning, and resourceful, his control of the tribe was absolute. His fighting men were estimated at near five hundred warriors, poorly armed to be sure, while The Mill was provided with the best to be had in guns and abundant ammunition.

The cabins at The Mill had been sited and constructed with the object of defense. The cabins all faced south and the undergrowth was kept cleared away for a hundred yards around them to prevent the concealment of an approaching enemy. They were made of heavy logs chinked with blocks and clay without and within, and had no cut windows. Portholes could be improvised at a moment's notice by removing sections of the chinking from between the logs. The doors were of heavy planks and the roofs of dirt which could not be set on fire.

The location of the settlement, however, was more than a hundred miles from any source of relief, and a considerable number of hostiles could starve out the defenders long before succor could reasonably be hoped to reach them.

The enterprise in which the doctor was engaged could not be carried on if opposed by even a few hostiles, for while his men were in the woods, where the logs had to be obtained, snipers could destroy them without hope of any effectual defense. His conclusion was that conciliation was the only possible means of continuing the business. It was now profitable and represented the investment of not only all his own resources but those of his partners as well.

Jim had seated himself near the kitchen door with his lighted pipe when his visitor of the day before spoke from but a step away. Neither he nor the doctor had seen or heard her approach; but both were alert, and a moment later the doctor joined them.

The doctor did not speak Spanish well but managed ordinary conversation and understood most that was said. Jim knew more Spanish and after a few words of salutation the old woman said she had brought her companions and asked for food. The food was brought, and at a call from the visitor two other women and a man appeared from behind the house. They were older and more decrepit than the original visitor and after gorging themselves with bread and meat and a pot of coffee, they all seated themselves upon the ground and talked freely.

The substance of their revelation was that there were a considerable number of Mescalero in the Sacramento Mountains, but they insisted that they were all good people who wanted to be friends. When asked about the recent fighting, they denied vehemently that any of these Indians had anything to do with that and insisted that they personally had been by themselves all summer but knew that the others had not been away.

When inquiry was made for Santana, they did not reply at once but conversed among themselves for a time, appearing to have a diversity of opinion about something. However, finally they admitted that he might be in the Sacramentos somewhere, although they didn't know where he was.

The doctor told them that he wanted to talk to Santana himself and make friends with the Mescalero. This caused another argument among the visitors. Further talk brought about an arrangement whereby the doctor was to furnish them food for a few days while they tried to find Santana and deliver his message. They were given a sack of bread, a couple of hams of venison, coffee and sugar, a few dried peaches, and the promise of more if they succeeded in bringing the chief to The Mill for a friendly talk.

They left by the trail the old woman had followed the day before, which was in plain sight from the cabins for a quarter of a mile as they climbed up the mountainside toward the north. After reaching the cedar brakes, where they could no longer be seen from the cabins, they ceased their pose of decrepitude and threw away their staffs. They watched for a time through the screen of cedars to discover what, if any, action would be taken at The Mill.

There was no commotion or unusual activity; all the men continued in their usual occupations, smoke rising from the kitchen chimney indicated a renewal of the fire there for the preparation of the evening meal. The doctor had resumed his pacing back and forth before the cabins, head down with his hands clasped behind his back, a characteristic pose by which the Indians soon learned to describe him as in a meditative mood.

Assured by this resumption of usual activity at The Mill, the emissaries left the trail and trotted down the mountainside in a southeasterly direction, reaching the canyon a half-mile above The Mill, where, screened by a dense willow thicket, they crossed the stream and hurried into the mouth of a broad, open gulch. Here in a clump of trees they were awaited by a dozen warriors with horses for all, and they rode off up the canyon and over the summit to the extended main camp of the Indians.

The old woman who had first visited Jim at the kitchen continued on to Santana's habitation, where the chief awaited her. Her experience of the day before had already been reported, and her meeting with the doctor was recounted in full detail while Santana listened without remark. Every posture and gesture of the doctor was described in illustration of his remarks as interpreted by Jim; and the woman noted that she had first found and counted the men to be sure that none was absent who might have gone to report the presence of Indians in the vicinity.

She was then questioned and described the doctor minutely, "He is as tall as you," she declared, "and as heavy, and he looks old, for his hair and beard are white. But he is not old, for his eyes are not old and his face is not old where there is not beard, and he moves quick and easy like a young man. He talks slow, but he thinks fast; and the other man thinks he is very wise, for he says nothing but what the *shizhi* (white one) says. His legs and his arms are long, and his body is short, so that when he sits down he looks short and when he stands up he looks tall."

"But does he talk straight?" asked Santana.

"Yes, I think he talks with one tongue," she replied. "His eyes are blue, and he looks quick and he says what his eyes look. I saw him talk to all the men when they went to work this morning, but he is not afraid and did not tell the men that I had been there. The men were not afraid because he was not afraid, and they know he is the boss for they do not talk when he does not tell them to talk. I think he has very strong medicine."

Santana's conviction that his people must submit to the on-coming tide of white invasion had, in some measure, weakened his rule. He had been compelled to resort to persuasion to a greater extent than ever before and proceed with discretion in order to retain his leadership. His success in bringing the tribe together had had a good moral effect, however; and the fact that Cha had to worry constantly about evading his pursuers—who had formerly been but an occasional trouble—was proving Santana's attitude justified. Consequently, he was gaining more support.

The settlement at The Mill had appealed to him as a suit-able place to look for assistance because of his previous connec-tions there. His secret observations had revealed that none of his acquaintances was now there, and he had been making a study of the newcomers with the object of securing their assistance.

The defection of his brother Cha and his insurgents had been unfortunate in that they had continued their depredations much as had been the custom of the whole tribe during the years gone by. They had used a white flag, on occasion, to gain advantage of their victims, thereby causing such means of contacting their opponents to be disregarded.

The former actions of the tribe under the direction of Santana himself had been the cause of his bad repute, so the late atrocities had naturally been laid to him. A large reward had been posted for his capture dead or alive, leaving little hope that the Indians could contact the military without some intermediary.[7] The Mill was at his mercy, but his desire for peace was sincere, and its destruction would only be as a last resort in the protection of his people.

The troops the hunters had decoyed away from the proximity of the Mescalero camp might with equal facility have been led into an ambuscade and annihilated, for he had several times their number of warriors available and every advantage of perfect knowledge of the country. But his intelligence foresaw something of the future, although vaguely, and at this time his only object was peace.

Santana had had The Mill watched by his spies all summer without their presence having been detected and knew every phase of the activities there, even what freighters came for lumber and when they might be expected to arrive. Thus, he knew from the small amount of lumber on hand that none were expected before the end of winter. Ox teams from Tularosa had been loaded out the week before, and the lumber lay drying in the town, where it would be allowed to season for a month or more before being hauled to its destination. A knowledge of the personality and attitude of the people at the settlement was all he lacked, and the report of the old woman seemed favorable to the accomplishment of his objective. And if his attempt failed there would be nothing lost as there was no way these people could escape him if they proved obdurate.

First house built by J. H. Blazer. The cupola served as the lookout and vantage point of defense. Courtesy Rio Grande Historical Collections, New Mexico State University Library.

THE ARMISTICE

Several days had passed without event, and the doctor was engaged in the double cabin, which served him as a combination office and living quarters, when the decrepit Indian woman who had first called on Jim appeared at the door.

"Santana's wife is here," she said.

The doctor stepped outside and invited a woman standing at a little distance to come in. This she declined to do but approached and stood just outside. From the kitchen Jim saw the visitors and joined them. The older woman moved away and disappeared as the other woman approached.

The newcomer, a woman past middle age but in no way looking old, spoke fluently in Spanish. Her hair hung loose and reached well down toward her waist and, although showing a little grey, was abundant, black, glossy, and smoothly combed. She was dressed in a neat, yellow buckskin suit, modestly trimmed with fringes on the waist and skirt, and high-topped moccasins. A single strand of large beads encircled her throat, and beaded ornaments adorned the tabs upon her breast. The usual "fire bag," owlcase, and other ornamental containers and a knife were pendent from the silver-trimmed leather belt she wore.

She said her name was U'ah, that she was Santana's wife, and that Santana wanted to have a friendly talk with the people at The Mill.

"Where is he?" asked the doctor.

"Over there," she replied, waving her hand indefinably toward the mountain to the east, "and will come if you will be friends." And on being assured that all the people at The Mill wanted to be friends with everyone, and that the doctor would talk with Santana whenever he cared to come, she drew a red cloth from beneath her blouse and waved it above her head.

Both the doctor and Jim had assumed that they were dealing with these women, emissaries of Santana, to arrange for a meeting with the chief at some future time. They did not realize the ability of the Indians for concealment and stealthy approach, in spite of the fact that they had been surprised on two former occasions by their visits. The doctor's arms had been left in the inner room of the cabin, and Jim's gun leaned against the wall inside the kitchen door, all a fate-laden moment beyond their reach.

At U'ah's signal a dozen warriors appeared at the edge of the thicket on the hillside, two a few steps in advance of the others. All carried lances in their hands and shields on their left arms, and bow and arrow quivers projected above the right shoulder of each. But they were not painted.

The two men mistook this sudden appearance as a hostile demonstration and for the moment were surprised into inaction. Then Jim started for the kitchen to get his gun. The doctor pulled the signal rope to sound the alarm for the men at the mill, but there was no response. The rope had been disconnected from the hammer and tied to the roof of the building. The doctor then turned to enter his cabin, where he had left his arms, but the woman still stood before the door calmly observing the agitation of her hosts. A hostage, thought the doctor, and pushed her through the door, which he shut and fastened. However, his arms also were in the cabin.

Finally, the doctor looked toward the Indians on the hillside. The two in advance had thrown down their arms and stood, a hundred yards away, hands up and palms forward, the peace sign. He returned the sign, and they advanced. Jim had watched the doctor from the kitchen door, and when he saw his hands go up he raised his own and joined him as the two Indians moved toward them and the others seated themselves as though to await developments.

All this had occurred in a very few minutes. One of the two Indians advancing was a large man some fifty years of age, tall, broad of shoulder with narrow hips, well muscled, and who moved in graceful strides. His face was full and unwrinkled with his queues of hair falling from behind his ears and resting on his breast. His tawny shirt, close-fitted to his form and reaching to his waist, nearly matched the color of his skin, and buckskin fringes decorated his shoulders, swinging free halfway to his elbows.

Beside him came a different type of man, apparently older by twenty years and in comparison small. Slim and active in his movements, his shorter steps made his progress seem a trot. His complexion was darker than his companion's, and his buckskin suit was plain, close-fitted to wirelike muscles.

Meanwhile, the woman in the cabin was pounding frantically on the door with her fists and calling at the top of her voice.

"What do you want?" demanded the doctor as the two Indians approached.

"A friend we want, one that will help the Mescalero to be friendly," replied the larger Indian, who proved to be Santana.

The older Indian interrupted, "I would talk to the woman," he said, and at a nod from the doctor moved up and held a short conversation through the door. "She is afraid of the bearskin on the floor," he said, "let her out, and I will go in and stay as long as you want me to."[1]

The doctor had been giving little attention to what was being said, although Jim was interpreting faithfully. He was thinking of the futility of a hostage under the circumstances, of his responsibility and his helplessness. But the offer somehow reached his consciousness. He stepped to the door and threw it open.

The woman staggered out and sank trembling to the ground, and the Indian moved inside the room but the door was not shut. "You need not take her place," said the doctor as he turned to Santana, who had assumed a statuesque pose with his arms folded on his breast and was studying the doctor's face intently, without giving the least attention to the condition of his wife.

The smaller Indian, who proved to be Gorgonio, the principal medicine man of the tribe, had gone to the side of the prostrate woman who had fainted and was ministering to her, while Santana awaited the doctor's reply.

The usual calmness of the doctor's nerves had been sorely tried by the suspense of the past few days and now at a critical moment failed him. His responsibility, his helplessness and isolation were all forgotten in an overwhelming wave of anger at the proud, arrogant, heartless attitude of the man. "How can you ask for a friend here when the Mescalero are killing our people all the time?" he demanded.

His quick temper had betrayed him. His intention had been to use all the diplomacy at his command. Now, he assumed, the Indian would be affronted, but he was able to control the trepidation he felt and by force of will stared Santana in the face.

The old chief, however, took no offense, but seemed to be impressed by the doctor's temerity and replied, "Some Mescalero are bad and do bad things, but all my people are good people and want to be friends. Some of my people are very foolish, and the bad ones got some of them to run away from the reservation. And now my good people want to go back to the reservation and be friends. And the bad ones are not with us.

"They are along the big river [Rio Grande] and are doing bad things that make the soldiers mad, and must run from the soldiers all the time. But my people want to be separate and not run, nor fight the soldiers or the people."

The doctor observed Santana's attitude with relation to the

indictment he had unintentionally pronounced with a feeling of great relief and decided to change his plans to the extent of talking back with some show of independence.

"The people killed at Carrizo Springs were not on the Rio Grande," he asserted, "and others were killed on the Rio Grande about the same time. They say the Mescalero did the killing at both places and that your tracks were found at Carrizo Springs where the people were killed."

Santana persisted in his conciliatory mood, pleased rather than offended at this challenge of the sincerity of his assertions.

"That is what your people know," he replied. "Some of my people did kill those Mexicans at Carrizo Springs, and my tracks were there, but I was not there when they were killed. But if I had been there when they were killed, I would have helped to kill them. And if you had been there you also would have helped to kill those people, for you do not think first before you do things when you are mad. I will tell you what I know about that, and you can say who did the bad thing."

The doctor, still perturbed, felt weak and shaky while the Indian stood confidently before him, and in an effort to regain his composure seated himself on a stump nearby. He had been dividing his attention between Santana and the Indians seated on the hillside above the edge of the mesa where the path from The Mill appeared. He had looked several times, first in one direction and then in the other, wondering what would happen if some of his men appeared and saw the Indians. They had not been warned of the presence of the visitors and would have loaded guns in their hands. Could an outbreak of hostilities be prevented?

But Santana was not uneasy, and seating himself on the ground nearby, said, "My men will do nothing unless I tell them to, and your men will not come until the middle of the day, for I had the rope fixed in the night but they do not know it."

The doctor realized that to attempt to warn them by means

other than the signal would be frustrated and likely to precipitate a clash, so he did nothing.

"What about the people who were killed at Carrizo Springs?" he asked without comment on the chief's remarks.

Santana began: "Some of every kind of people are bad, and some are good. But most of every kind of people are just common people, not very bad and not very good, and some of every kind of people are very good and some are very wise. And some of every kind of people are foolish; and some are very bad and do bad things when they think no one will know who did it. And when bad people and good people are together and the bad people do bad things to other people, the other people cannot know which are bad, and the other people are made with all the bad people and the good people, too, because they are all together, and some have done the bad thing to them.

"Maybe some of those Mexicans that the Mescalero killed at Carrizo Springs were good people—I do not know—but some of them were very bad; and if any were good they were killed because they were with those that were bad. My people who killed those people are common people and good people. They had been foolish and gone with Cha, but that was because the Mescalero are a proud people and have always been a free people; and when they were on the reservation they could not go anywhere until the agent gave them a paper.

"The agent is a good man, but he does not know what the Mescalero must have. He does not know that things must be gotten when it is the right time, and he would not give them a paper when it was the right time. So they could not hunt when the meat was good, and they could not get things that grow in the mountains that the Indians eat when it was the right time, and the weeds we use for medicine when it was the right time.

"Some of my people went for medicine when they were sick, and when they came back the agent said they were fools, for the white doctor would give them better medicine, and he put them in the guardhouse. But when some were sick they went for medicine and did not come back, because some that took the white doctor's medicine died. And some who went to bury their people that died did not come back because the agent said, 'Bury your dead like white folks do' and would not give them a paper.

"Then Cha had a bad heart and told the bad Mescalero that I was 'like an old woman'—afraid to fight—so they went with Cha to fight the soldiers and the people. Then some of the good people who had gone to the mountains went with Cha, too, and they killed people on the roads and in the settlements, and the soldiers could not catch Cha's people. So some of the common people who were foolish, said 'Cha is very wise,' and they went with him. And they took some Mescalero women when their men were not there and did other bad things. And I told them to keep away from the Sacramento Mountains, where my people lived, or I would have the Mescalero kill all their people.

"But the stolen women and the good men did not want to be with Cha's people and came back to the Sacramentos with me when I went to them in the San Andres Mountains. And we came back in little bands to make no big trail. And one good man had two wives and a big girl, and they came near Carrizo Springs. There he killed an antelope early in the morning, which was with some oxen that were lost. The Indians sometimes use gentle stock to cover their approach within arrow range of antelope. Then when he went to get his other wife and their things, he left one wife and the girl to fix the meat. When he came there again, the woman was killed and the girl was taken away for he could see where she had been dragged through the grass. And he followed to see if he could find the girl; and she was screaming in the camp where the wagons were by the water."

At this point a shout from the path at the brow of the mesa recalled them to the present time. The men were coming from the mill for their noonday meal. Those first catching sight of the Indians shouted to their companions, and the Indians on the hillside started a rush toward their chief. An excitement ensued that required the action of both the doctor and Santana to prevent an outbreak of hostilities. But the leaders were between their respective forces. Thus, the doctor's men held their fire to avoid endangering him; likewise, Santana's uplifted hand stopped his warriors until the peaceful nature of their mission could be explained.

Explanations, however, left suspicions, and the doctor's men kept to themselves. Food was prepared for all, and Santana and Gorgonio dined with the doctor. By the time the old chief was ready to continue his narrative, all had agreed to leave their arms in the cabins, and at Santana's command the Indians left theirs at a distance; then without more ado the two groups arranged themselves to listen.

"There were eight men and two women," continued Santana, "and the girl was tied to the wheel of a wagon. The man was alone, and there were too many of the Mexicans for him to take her away, so he went away and made a signal for help. When enough Mescalero came they went and fought the Mexicans and killed all the men and one woman. The other woman ran away, and a Mescalero man caught her and was going to have her for his woman. But when his two wives came, they did not want him to have her and killed her.

"The girl was tied to four ox yokes on the ground, not by the wagons, and all her clothes were taken off and the Mexicans had done whatever they wanted to, but she was not dead. Then many Mescalero came there, and when the girl's grandmother came and the girl told her which Mexican had been the worst to her and had killed her mother, the grandmother cut that Mexican with a knife. And some other women cut the other Mexicans, because one Mescalero was killed and some were shot and not killed. And the girl died.

The Blazer "big house" was at one time the office and quarters for the Mescalero Agency and Agen F. C. Godfroy. Courtesy Rio Grande Historical Collections, New Mexico State University Library

"Then I came there, and I made the women quit cutting the Mexicans. Then I told them to go all together and make a trail toward the Capitan Mountains— to leave the others a few at a time and go into the White Mountains and then to the Mescalero camp in the Sacramentos. That is the reason my people killed those Mexicans at Carrizo Springs and not because they are bad people."

Santana's version of the massacre fitted in very well with what had been found by those who had gone to bury the dead—two of whom were among the doctor's men—and he agreed that all that Santana had said might be true.

The doctor, while listening carefully to the narrative, had been giving more thought to the immediate conditions to be faced and the probable result of this conference. The Indians' attitude at the moment appeared friendly, but their reputation was for cunning cruelty. He must choose between Santana's apparent good faith and his reputation. There was still a possibility of saving their lives by abandoning the property in a hasty retreat to Tularosa. But this involved a trip of twenty miles on foot, while the Indians had horses, and every foot of the way they would be subject to an ambush, which might well have already been prepared, considering the disabled signal and the Indians' surprise approach. Further, to make such an attempt it would first be necessary to destroy the Indians present, which also was only a possibility, and start with the handicap of a failed truce. On the other hand, there was, if Santana's attitude was sincere, a probability of helping these Indians to change their ways and thereby save many lives. Hoping for the best, he decided to accept any reasonable proposition the chief might make.

The doctor's incidental accusation of Santana at their first meeting had been unpremeditated, and had he been less impetuous, would not have occurred. But probably this was the incident which became the fulcrum for subsequent relations. Santana knew from the doctor's appearance and his actions that he was not unconscious of his helplessness. Nevertheless, he had not faltered in the hardihood so much admired by the Indians, which increased their opinion of his valor.

The doctor took a few minutes to hear what his men had to say and consider how best to reply, but having made his decision, and determined to make the best of the inevitable, he felt much relieved.

"I think any kind of people who were men would have done as the Mescalero did," he admitted. "Tell me what you want me to do for you; I want to be your friend, and I want the Mescalero to be my friends."

"I want you to tell the soldiers and all the people what I have told you," answered the chief, "and that the Mescalero that are with me are all good people, and that the people who are with Cha are not my people and that not all of them are Mescalero, for some of Cha's people are bad people from other tribes. Tell them that my people want to go back to the reservation, and that I want to talk to the head men of the soldiers about that. And I want you to write it down on two papers and send one to the head man of the soldiers at Fort Stanton and one to Tularosa, where the soldiers feed their horses, so that when they come there they will know that the Indians that are here are good Indians and do not want to fight, for I will not let any bad Indians come here."

"I will do that," agreed the doctor. "And I will tell any soldiers who come here that your people are my friends and are good people. But I think the commander at Fort Bliss should have a paper, too, so that the soldiers on the Rio Grande will know that the Indians in the Sacramentos are not with Cha and are good people."

"Now we are friends," asserted Santana, offering his hand, which the doctor took with more cordiality than he had thought possible a few minutes before. "And," Santana continued, "if any-one wants to do bad things to you or to your people, my Mescalero will help you the same as if you were our brothers."

Santana's proposition was written in full, and each of the three copies was accompanied by a statement of the doctor of the circumstances leading to his action as a mediator for the Indians.[2]

Two of the doctor's men volunteered to deliver the letters, and Santana provided warriors as escorts to see them safely through that part of their journey where hostile Indians might molest them. But all went well, and within two weeks acknowledgment of their receipt had reached The Mill.

AMBUSH

Heavy snows had fallen in the Sacramentos, and logging at The Mill was now confined to the southern slopes of the mountains, where the accumulation was settled and partly melted.

Santana's Indians still remained as located at the beginning of our story, on short rations, and to some degree still apprehensive about being involved with the soldiers. The corn crop had been better than usual, and the doctor had given Santana several thousand pounds of the surplus in small lots and at different times, together with a half-dozen old oxen that had been turned into the fields and were well fattened on the waste.

In reply to the doctor's communication, the commander at Fort Bliss had written that the troops under his command had been ordered to avoid approaching the vicinity of Santana's camp unless it became necessary in following some band of marauders, and in such emergency to communicate with the doctor at the earliest opportunity.

This information had been given to Santana with the advice that should his people meet any soldiers, they should not run away but should raise a white flag and tell of their affiliation with Santana's followers.

Cha and his renegades had become even more active in their depredations since being relieved of their dependent noncombatants. And the available troops had been concentrated in a campaign which had again driven them back to the Jarillas, where it was now proposed to follow up the effort to subdue him with an attack on his stronghold.

Previous efforts to accomplish this had failed for lack of water, and for this assault it had been arranged to send a wagon train to haul a supply and enable the troops to reach the isolated rendezvous in good condition, where they expected to find the hidden supply which had enabled the Indians to live there. Former expeditions had undertaken the assault during the summer when the glaring desert heat had added to the opposition of the waterless plain to reduce the possibility of success. Now the weather was comparatively cool—cold at night—although a clear sky and the clear dry air made the days warmer than comfortable. Occasional storms left water in depressions at certain points, so that if a storm should occur at the right time it would contribute materially to the success of the undertaking; but the campaign could not be delayed to await a storm without the probable escape of the Indians.

A lieutenant with a small escort had been sent to Tularosa, where the doctor had been requested to meet him. The doctor's advice was desired about the advisability of letting Santana know beforehand of the intended expedition and regarding the hope of securing the chief's assistance or cooperation. The doctor thought it best to interview Santana, as some of the renegades might escape and reach the Sacramentos, in which event some understanding might save trouble.

The lieutenant accompanied the doctor on his return to The Mill, and an interview with the old chief was soon arranged. Santana heard the plans for the campaign in detail without comment; then the lieutenant asked him if he would cooperate with the military in capturing the outlaws.

"No," he replied, "you cannot catch Cha that way, and I have told him that if he or his people come to the Sacramentos, I would destroy him and all his people. But I did not tell him that I would harm him at any other place, and he knows that I talk with one tongue. My people will stay in the Sacramentos until the head men of the soldiers come to talk about the Mescalero going back to the reservation."

"Then what will you do if Cha comes here to escape the soldiers?" asked the lieutenant.

"Cha will not come here," asserted Santana. "He is no fool and knows that if he comes where my people are we will kill him and all his people. You say you have four hundred soldiers and he has only one hundred men, but I know you cannot catch Cha."

"If Cha should escape to the Sacramentos and not come here, would you help the soldiers catch him?" the lieutenant asked.

"No," reiterated the chief. "My people will not fight with the soldiers nor against the soldiers or any other people until after I talk to the head men of the soldiers—unless they fight us first."

"Then if Cha gets into the Sacramentos how can we know if we find his people or your people?" demanded the officer.

"I will tell you how you can know," proposed Santana. "The doctor does not have enough food for his people and my people, too, and there is little game near here now, so we have little food to wait for the head men of the soldiers to come. You give us forty cattle to eat, and my people will stay this side of La Luz Canyon and the soldiers can stay the other side of La Luz Canyon. Then if the soldiers find any Indians, they will not be my people. And if Cha's people come to this side of La Luz Canyon, that will be where my people are and we will kill them."

The lieutenant had authority to make a voucher for his expenses, including a reasonable amount to secure the help of the Indians, so he bought forty head of cattle at Tularosa and had them delivered to Santana at The Mill, thus concluding an agreement in accordance with Santana's proposition.

The logical starting point for the expedition to the Jarillas was San Augustin Spring at the foot of the Organ Mountains, some forty miles to the west, where there was an abundance of good water. Twenty miles to the north of the Indians' stronghold there was permanent water, but it was scanty and alkaline (White Water) near White Sands; the only other known supply was in the foothills of the Sacramentos far to the east.

Four companies of cavalry and sixteen wagons, with a pack train and eight scouts, had been assembled at San Augustin Spring. Five of the wagons were loaded with the usual equipment and supplies for the troops, and the other eleven were each provided with five barrels which were filled with water from the spring. This, together with the twenty gallons each carried in kegs on a number of the pack mules, totalled about three thousand gallons for some four hundred animals.

In addition, each man also carried two gallons of water in canteens on his saddle. And it was expected that the Indians' secret supply would be found when their rendezvous was located. But nature did not cooperate to produce the hoped for storm, and the expedition began near the middle of the afternoon on a bright clear day.

There was no road, and although a downgrade and an alkali flat extended for ten miles or so toward their destination, brush and cactus caused a winding route, both tedious and slow. Nevertheless, the sand hills had been penetrated for a mile or more when night overtook them. Supper was prepared and eaten while the stock grazed and had their grain in nosebags while being hitched or saddled for the night march.

The full moon aided in selecting a route, but brush, deep sand, and the steep banks of arroyos made the going difficult. Teams stalled and had to be helped with rope from the saddle horns attached to the wagons; the men were shivering in their overcoats, and the stock was bathed in perspiration before the midnight rest.

Except for the alkali flats and the sand dunes, the country traveled was well grown with native grasses, standing from year to year, cured and preserved by nature into excellent forage. The Indians' stock, accustomed to this feed, had little need for grain, while the cavalry horses soon lost their strength and energy when deprived of concentrated food.

A two-hour rest was taken at midnight, but, although grass was abundant, the stock was grazed in halters with a man attending each three animals to avoid picket ropes becoming entangled in the brush or the straying of the stock. A quart of coffee and cooked rations had been issued to each man at the evening stop so that no fires in the desert might betray their presence to Indian sentinels on the rocky hills, now plainly visible although some fifteen miles away. The stock had been given a two-gallon ration of water and the canteens refilled from the barrels, which somewhat lightened the loads of the six-mule teams. Better progress was made through the morning hours, but a bright sky soon allowed the glaring sun to change the chilly night to an inferno of dry quivering heat.

The scouts were far ahead, and daybreak found them on the highest peak of the Jarillas lying flat among the rocks while their horses grazed in a gulch below them. Canyons, gulches, hills, ridges, cliffs, and rocky slopes lay before them, disclosed by the fading moonlight and the coming dawn. A few stunted cedars and mesquite could be seen, but they searched in vain with their field glasses for any sign of Indians.

As the light strengthened, far out on the plain to the east, halfway to the foothills of the Sacramentos, fifty horsemen were located by a cloud of dust, with as many more loose stock which they drove before them, alternately visible and invisible as they crossed the undulating plain. The Indians were gone.

One of the scouts returned to meet the troops struggling up the gravelly slope to the foot of the hills, while the other began an exploration of the neighborhood on foot. They were sure the Indians were gone but kept to the high points and ridges to avoid the possibility of an ambuscade until they discovered a moist and trampled place in the sandy floor of a gulch which they believed was the location of the Indians' hidden water.

The troops were guided to this location. Pits and trenches were dug in the damp sand, the adjacent cliffs and banks were explored, but not a cup of water was found. Water was again drawn from the kegs and barrels for a ration to the stock and the animals placed under close herd, while the men made a systematic search of the vicinity for a water supply.

The day was consumed in this fruitless effort. The water had been effectually buried or cut off, and no other spot was found where even moisture was apparent. Piles of shards of ancient pottery, along with dozens of old *metates* (grinding stones) that might have been abandoned during the migration of a settlement of several hundred people were found on the gravelly slope to the east of the hills, but there was nothing to indicate where a former water supply might have existed.

Two-thirds of their water supply had been exhausted, and a hard night's ride lay between them and any means of replenishment. Cha had been dislodged from his stronghold, and to that extent the expedition had succeeded, but he had escaped unhurt to the Sacramentos. Santana had decreed his extermination there, but this threat had been modified and was now restricted to the limited area north of La Luz Canyon, leaving several hundred square miles over which the renegades might operate with impunity.

Both men and horses were badly in need of rest, but sixty volunteers were given the mounts remaining in the best condition to follow the Indians and prevent their return to the Jarillas, while the others made their way by White Water and La Luz to rejoin this detail and make an effort to engage the outlaws in the mountains.

The path of the Indians across the plains had been watched until it was certain that their destination was the mouth of Dog Canyon, and for the unencumbered detail this was not a hard night's ride. But there was no water on the plain at this point, so the detachment of volunteers was given a full supply of water from the barrels, and the balance was proportioned to the other stock.

The detail took no pack animals but carried three days' rations on their saddles, and daylight found them deployed about the mouth of the canyon, beyond arrowrange from the cliffs, entrenched behind the scattered boulders and in washes in the ground. Thus, with their long-range rifles they could prevent the escape of the Indians by that route with comparative safety for themselves.

No Indians were seen, and the scouts reported that all the tracks entered the canyon. The springs were located some distance from the edge of the plain, where the water sank into the sand within the gorge. The plain cliffs rose perpendicularly for several miles to the north and south, and the gorge itself, not over a hundred yards in width, in places was much contracted and bordered with high cliffs. After a further reconnoiter the scouts reported that there were no Indians in the canyon and that the stock had been taken out by the trail above the spring and away toward the higher mountains.

Toward midday the heat became intense. A trip to the Alamo[1] would require several hours to water the stock in relays, while the spring in the canyon here was less than a mile away. An hour would suffice to water and return to safety. The officers in charge were experienced men and had failed in one campaign after another, through the wily tactics of the Indians, to engage them in a fight. This was a notoriously dangerous place for an ambush, and within recent years a number of expeditions had met disaster here. That, however, had been while Santana was out with his thousand warriors, and now their opponents were but fifty.

The floor of the gorge was quite accessible for travel on horseback, although strewn with boulders that made the use of vehicles impossible. Sand and gravel spread by the floods lay almost level between these, and the grade was moderate. The spring was located near the head of the gorge, from which a steep climb permitted the passage of stock to the mesa above, except that the entrance by the mouth of the canyon was the only practical exit.

The detail resumed their saddles and rode to the spring. The water was running for a hundred yards or more, and along this stretch the horses were scattered, drinking, while the men were filling themselves and their canteens with the fresh cool beverage.

Suddenly, an arrow from a marksman concealed in the rocks above wounded a man, and other arrows followed in rapid succession. The scouts shouted, "Climb out by the trail," but the officers ordered a retreat by the way they had entered. The retreat became a rout as flight after flight of arrows rained upon them. Men and horses crowded the restricted passages between the cliffs, where falling rocks from the Indians' slings fell continuously upon them with disastrous results. Not an Indian had been seen; not a shot had been fired by the soldiers for lack of a target.

Less than a dozen horses reached the open uninjured; a very few escaped without some minor wound. There were not enough horses in sufficiently good condition to be used to carry the badly wounded, and some with broken arms walked several miles to the mouth of the Alamo before receiving surgical attention. A courier was sent immediately for assistance, and the main force met them the following night.[2]

The Indians made no attempt to follow up their victory but prevented the recovery of the dead. Cha returned to the Jarillas without the loss of a single man, to continue his former occupation, while the government loss was some lives and thousands of dollars.

This was one of the most serious results of the lack of caution on the part of the military and of the lack of appreciation of the advantages the Indians possessed which occurred during the campaign against the Mescalero. But only a few months before this event, a detachment of ten cavalrymen had followed three of this same band of Mescalero into a bosque on the Rio Grande and had been killed to the last man, probably by an overwhelming number of Indians in ambush.

THE TREATY

The commander at Fort Sumner had declined the responsibility of treating directly with Santana and had referred the doctor's communication to headquarters at Santa Fe with the recommendation that an officer with full instructions be detailed to make a treaty with the Mescalero at The Mill. Such an order was issued in December, but the detail did not arrive there until February.

In the meantime heavy snows had completely stopped the logging operations at the mill, and little could be done outdoors. Most of the employees were illiterate, and the plaiting of oxwhips, ropes, bridles, and so forth constituted their principal occupation—aside from gambling. They became restless, and, in spite of a standing order that no intoxicating liquor should be brought onto the place, during the Christmas holidays they secured a keg of whiskey. There were few, if any, among them who were not periodical boozers, but the doctor insisted that they leave the place when they wished to indulge their appetites. At this time, however, although it had been customary for several of them to go to Tularosa for a spree, all had elected to remain at The Mill to assist the doctor in case of emergency.

They had determined to have a few drinks for Christmas on the sly but not get drunk. Although their intentions were good and their loyalty unquestionable, all were beastly drunk before anyone realized what was happening. Some visiting Indians had been invited to partake of their hospitality with the result that a free-for-all fight ensued, in which one of the employees was stabbed and some of the Indians returned to camp with bashed heads.

The doctor, unaided, could not control the crazed men when he discovered their condition and of necessity left them to themselves until their supply of liquor was exhausted.

Some of the corn the doctor had given the Indians had also been misused by some old women and provided the material for a fermented drink they called *tulhiba*.[1] This liquor also had been indulged in too freely by some of the Indians at the camp, so the bruised and indignant visitors, on their return, soon gathered a mob of besotted companions to go to The Mill and avenge themselves.

Santana, however, was apprised of their intentions in time to reach The Mill before them and prevent an attack. He had left orders for assistants to follow him, and the drunken crowd was subdued and beaten without mercy.

The making of tulhiba had been prohibited by Santana as a precautionary measure while preparing for the abdication, and the violators of the order were severely punished; their liquor was destroyed, and they were denied a further supply of corn for any purpose.

The man who had been stabbed was severely hurt, and, after lingering a few days, died. In the meantime the old chief, with the cooperation of the doctor, had investigated the matter and found that the wounded man had not been one of those engaged in the quarrel but had been trying to prevent the trouble when he was stabbed in the back. It could not be definitely determined which of the Indians had actually done the stabbing, for three of them had had knives in their hands when the act was committed. A council of the head men decided that all three had drawn their knives with equally murderous intent and that all were equally guilty, so that which had committed the actual murder was immaterial,

for the intent was "like killing," Consequently, all three were condemned and executed.

When the doctor's men had fully recovered from their spree,
he decided that it would be best to send them all away for a time
and paid them off. They protested their good intentions and gave
their assurances that no such misbehavior would occur in the
future. But the doctor believed they would be useless if the Indians
decided to do violence, and their presence might mean a greater
loss of life, while he could protect the property alone as well as
with them.

This he explained and said, "It is my responsibility, not yours,
and your staying here is but to risk your lives as well as my own. Although you may not get drunk again, some other circumstances
may arise in which I alone could manage better."

They still protested, and several, Jim Walters,[2] Fred Scott, and
the sawyer, particularly, said they would not go and leave him alone
with the Indians. However, the doctor was firm and said he had decided the matter and would ask Santana to have his warriors see
them safely to Tularosa, but they declined the escort.

When Santana learned that the doctor was alone at The Mill,
he moved his own camp and those of twenty or more of his warriors into the clearing about the cabin and was outspoken in his
praise of the doctor's action.

"It may be," said he, "that my people may get drunk and I
might not know in time, but these I can watch and we will stay here
until the soldiers come."

Thus, when the colonel sent from Santa Fe arrived a month
later he found the Indians apparently in possession of the settlement. Only Indians were to be seen around the place, and although
he had made this trip for the express purpose of meeting Santana
in friendly intercourse, he suspected treachery and that the doctor's
people had been destroyed. His retinue comprised a company of cavalry and several wagons besides a pack train. The wagons were

loaded with supplies for the troops and surplus provisions—blankets, tents, and so forth—that might assist in making satisfactory terms with the Indians. The pack mules were for transportation if impassable roads were found. This had been one of the causes of delay, for not only had it been necessary to pack the loads in some places, but the wagons themselves had to be disassembled and transported on mule-back for several miles.

The fact that the Indians appeared to be in possession of the settlement had been reported by the scouts riding in advance of the command, and the colonel halted the cavalcade before coming in sight of the buildings, riding forward with one orderly and an interpreter to see for himself before deciding whether to attack the Indians or retreat. The colonel's force was not sufficient for an attack against the whole tribe, but if the Indians were holding the men prisoners he considered it his duty to make sure they were released if possible.

While the officer was examining the settlement from a concealed position he observed that there was no appearance of conflict and that the buildings seemed to be intact: he also noted that there were few Indians around the place. At this point, the doctor himself came out from one of the cabins and in a few minutes all was explained.

The colonel's party, besides the enlisted men, included a captain, a first and second lieutenant, two scout-interpreters, and several citizen teamsters and packers, besides a contract surgeon, an old acquaintance of the doctor.

The cabins were placed at their disposal and occupied by the officers and the soldiers' kitchen. The enlisted men had tents, so all were made comfortable. One of the cabins was set aside to be used as a meeting place and furnished with a large table and a number of benches. All the cabins were provided with large stone fireplaces. Since there were no windows, the fires fueled by piñon logs also served to light their interiors.

Santana was instinctively cautious, and in arranging for the interview considerable time was spent in introductions and preliminary talks of little importance but which provided an opportunity for him to get his men together and decide what kind of men they had to deal with. He declined to be hurried and for a whole day put off the discussion of the central question. Instead, with several of his subordinates Santana talked to the doctor for a couple of hours to get his idea of the colonel's character.[3]

Santana and the doctor had been having long talks together since the other men had left, and the chief appeared to have acquired an almost unlimited belief in the doctor's wisdom and friendship as well as admiration of his valor, which the doctor had encouraged by opposing some of Santana's pet ideas. Now the old chief insisted that the doctor attend all the talks, advise him in case of need, and speak for him should any controversy arise.

The early part of the day the conference began was clear and warm, and the door, through which the winter sun provided light, stood open. Besides the dozen or so Indians squatted about the room, which Santana said were to tell everybody what was said, there was quite a congregation outside.

The colonel had his officers present for consultation and to lend dignity to his retinue. One of the scouts, a Mexican who spoke both Mescalero and English, acted as interpreter.

The written order authorizing the colonel to make a treaty with the Mescalero, subject to the approval of the War Department, was produced, and Santana handed it to the doctor for his approval, then to the interpreter, who could not read it. Thereupon Santana asked that the doctor do the reading, for he was his friend, and the interpreter should translate for them. This took considerable time. Since the list of what the government proposed to do for the Mescalero in compensation for their remaining peacefully on the reservation was long, Santana agreed that the colonel might tell them these things, which everyone expected the Indians to comment on as each was read. However, this was not the case, for the Indians listened in silence while the Colonel read from the memorandum.

This included a hundred items or so, stating the kind and amount of each: rations, clothing and supplies of various kinds; protection by the troops for themselves and their property from their enemies; seed and feed for their horses, as well as the necessary implements, should any wish to cultivate land; teachers for any of their children that would attend school; and instructors in farming, mechanics, and so forth, for any who wished to learn a trade. This concluded, Santana said they would think about what had been proposed for one day and then tell the colonel what they thought of it.

The afternoon was well advanced. The sky was overcast, and a cold east wind had dispersed the outdoor audience by the time the meeting broke up; it was the usual February weather, and before night set in the fleecy clouds had darkened and snow was falling. The storm lasted through the night, and snow lay a foot deep around the clearing when the dawn broke clear again.

The colonel had each Indian of Santana's camp given a blanket and would have given them shoes, but they declined them. The wind was keen, and the bare buttocks of the warriors distressed him so that he tried to insist on their wearing pants, which he offered to provide. "No," said Santana, "we are accustomed to this way of dressing just like you have your face bare."

The head men, who had attended the meeting as Santana's associates, had returned to their various bands to report what had occurred, some going as far as ten miles, and were late in returning to The Mill on account of the snow. Santana refused respectfully but positively to resume the business of the treaty until he had heard from each division of the tribe. And after all his men arrived the Indians consulted among themselves for an hour or so before coming into the cabin where the colonel and his officers

Mescalero Agency, 1886. Courtesy Rio Grande Historical Collections, New Mexico State University Library.

awaited them. When all were again assembled it was past noon, and a cold wind and the snow made it necessary to close the door for comfort, so lanterns were brought to assist in the illumination.

Only a few notes of the first meeting had been kept by one of the lieutenants, for the apparent indifference of the Indians had led the officers to believe they were not very interested in the proceedings. The colonel also had the impression that they had understood little and cared less. The list of items was long, and a number of items, which the colonel thought of little importance, he had omitted to mention. Those he had read he had checked while those omitted he had not, so that Santana's procedure caught him unawares.

Santana began by taking up the various items from memory in the exact order he had heard them read from the colonel's memorandum the day before and commented on each item. A number of the proposed supplies he said were of no use to an Indian; others were of little use, and Santana's band would rather have a greater quantity of other items instead.[4]

When the items the colonel had not read and checked the day before were now mentioned, in every instance Santana replied, "You did not tell me that." And when the list had been completed the old chief said, "These other things that you did not tell me yesterday I will think about for a day and then tell you what I think of them," and would not continue but insisted on an adjournment.

On this day the items approved as originally proposed were few, and the amended list was much shortened by Santana's request. The colonel was quite at a loss to remember Santana's comments, which he considered advisable to include in his report to account for the changes. Consequently, when the conference was continued on the following day, he had the lieutenant take down the entire proceeding in shorthand for his later reference.

The third day was a long session, and the original list was taken up again item by item with Santana's comments all recorded. Then a new list was made, which Santana approved, saying, "Tomorrow I will tell you a list of what the Mescalero want."

The Indians' list proved to be not additional supplies demanded but related to privileges that Santana thought essential to the contentment of his people on the reservation, and without which he insisted they would not stay. It amounted to a modification of the unconditional promise to remain on the reservation. This he explained was because they had been on the reservation before, and he knew the Mescalero could not be made to stay there under such conditions as had been imposed on them at that time. Then he insisted that what he said should be written down in the same manner as his comments about the list.

Santana divided the year by moons and explained what was required by his people in each season. He asked that they be permitted to leave the reservation in such number and for such lengths of time as was necessary to secure the articles or accomplish the purpose named, and he devised a plan whereby the soldiers should know that the absentees could not comprise a war party. All these matters he had considered in the light of their former experiences and now set them out with certainty in logical order. Specific requirements for the *haheh* (dance of the adolescent girls) he explained would have to be supplied by the soldiers because the Indians had no wagons. To drag the poles so far on the ground would spoil the tops and make them worthless for the ceremony, which could not be neglected.

The colonel suggested that the government provide a wagon for the head man of each band so that they could haul their own poles and other things as might be needed. "No," said Santana. "If the wagons belong to an Indian, and any of that Indians' people die, they would destroy the wagon, and then there would be no wagon when the poles must be brought." It was arranged by an agreement that a government wagon and harness would be lent to the Indians whenever their needs required it.

A week had been employed in arranging and approving the details before the formal treaty was written out. Then another week was consumed in providing a census of the tribe, with names and a guess at the ages of the individuals, and their family relationships. Arrangements were made to have cattle furnished for the Indians' food, and they were promised a supply of the other articles as soon as the weather permitted a train of wagons to get through. In the meantime the Indians were to remain in the vicinity of The Mill.

Waiting at the "meat house." Four beeves were killed weekly, skinned, and hauled to the agency. The meat was "hung" on Friday evening and issued on Saturday morning. Blazer Family Collection.

HUNTING

Now that the Indians were relieved of their anxiety and no longer anticipated molestation by the troops, parties of hunters made trips to the foothills and the plains, where the game had been driven by the deep snow in the mountains; meat was abundant and cereal food in little demand. February with its fickle weather was past, and the strong winds of March were helping the bright sun to clear the snow from many of the high ridges and summits of the Sacramentos.

The deep canyons of White Mountain, however, which had been full of drifts during the winter, still retained their accumulations to great depths and were little affected, as yet, by the approaching spring. Here the surface crust of snow still remained only a few feet below the tops of the adjacent ridges, which converged toward the twelve-thousand-foot peak of "Old Baldy."[1] Below the surface crust in these canyons the frosty flakes still retained their unstable consistency in layers of varying depths, alternating with other crusts submerged by the recurring storms of the past winter.

Bands of elk were the first game to return to this habitat after their winter retreat to the lower ranges. Snow still remained in places, in deep drifts and large areas, but between these were many open, nearly dry spots where the elk found their favorite browse and comfortable bedding grounds.

The Mescalero ate little elk meat. Coarse and of inferior flavor at all times, an occasional meal, under strenuous circumstances, was all they ever used. However, they made considerable use of the hides and other parts of the elk. The hides of the old bull elk, taken at this time, were thick and tough, and did not get hard when dry, like those of most cattle. Such hides were little affected by moisture, making them especially desirable for moccasin soles. Also, the long tendon from the spine made bowstrings of sufficient length without splicing.

Killing elk with arrows was all but impossible while they were roaming free, and very few were secured in that way. Instead, organized bands of elk hunters provided a large part of the Indians' requirements. Taking them in snow traps was their method.

This method of hunting was attended by considerable danger to inexperienced hunters. A miscalculation as to the strength of the snow crust was the principal danger. If the crust were too soft, the hunter might easily find himself floundering in the broken crust with a thousand pounds of elk in close pursuit, elk with four-foot antlers and beating hoofs; on the other hand, if the crust proved strong enough to support the weight of the animals, their escape to another ridge was certain. Thus, it is apparent that weather conditions limited the time that elk could be taken by this method, and experienced hunters were in demand, not only to secure the desired hides but as instructors for aspiring amateurs.

A lifetime of experience was not too much for a successful leader, and many tales were told of too confident amateurs responsible for the loss of lives in premature efforts. As in other specialties, experience was a prerequisite for success, and the conceded experts were all past middle age. Also, elk hunters had to have a natural aptitude for estimating conditions. Taking no part in the actual killing of the elk, they watched every move of their subordinates from some point of vantage, directing them by signs, or, in emergencies, shouting warnings or directions. In this way they earned their share of the proceeds of the venture.

Among Santana's Mescalero at this time K'ah Tensakes (Crooked Arrow) was the most successful elk hunter. He had made a study of the animals' habits, and on one occasion came near losing his life by getting too familiar with an old lone bull. He had located an unusually large bull that had been driven from the herd by the younger males and ranged by itself. Such elk, being old and unusually fat, are reputed to be slow but very wary, and K'ah Tensakes, then a man in the prime of life, set himself the task of taking him.

As he told the story in later years: "I had a horse that outran anything in the tribe, and I knew I could eventually catch this elk, but he always saw me far away and always grazed in open places where I could not get close to start a race.

"Then I said I would get him anyway, but other men had found him, too, and chased him, though none could catch him. Then I told them all to let him be so I could catch him. But it took me two years to do it, and they called it my elk, and no one bothered him. Whenever I saw him, I rode slowly toward him until he would trot away. But in a year he only trotted from one open place to another and grazed until I came in sight again.

"Then in one year more he would only trot away when I came close, and when I would stop he would stop. And when there was a little snow and the elk was very fat I was near him, but I had been hunting all day and my horse was tired. Then I stopped, and the elk stopped near some thick brush by a tree. I tied my horse where the elk could see him and went into the timber on foot; the elk began to eat the brush, and I went way around and came back from the other way. The wind was right and he could smell the horse, but he could not smell me. I crawled in the brush very close, but the brush was too thick to shoot my bow. I stood by the tree and shot him with my best arrow from right in front where it would go into his heart, but he did not fall down. I took my knife to cut his throat and went closer, but when he moved he came at me and put down his head. I got hold of his horn with this hand (indicating the right) so that when he tried to gore me I held on and tried to catch the other horn with the other hand. He fell, and his head was on me and I went like asleep for a long time. Then it was dark again, and I could not move the elk's head because I was hurt. But in the morning my wife and some other women found the horse, and then they found me and took me home. And this finger was like it is."

The little finger of his left hand stood out at nearly a right angle from his hand, stiff and shriveled. He thought the elk's horn had struck between his fingers and against his head and stunned him.

K'ah Tensakes was teaching other members of the tribe about elk hunting. His class of twelve men and boys included Ntsaaze, Santana's son. They had been under his instruction for varying lengths of time, and he rated them according to their competence, assigning to each certain duties. He insisted on absolute obedience under every condition and a complete knowledge of the "universal sign language,"[2] besides his personal code of signals, as fundamental requirements so that when silence was necessary his orders would be understood.

They had located a band of elk near the main divide of the Sacramentos. After pushing them for several days up the ridge between Ruidoso and the Tularoso watersheds, they had them on the ridge between Rinconada and the Carrizo Creek. There were seven old bulls and twenty cows and younger animals. To the right and left were deep valleys where the snow was rapidly melting, but ahead the ridge they were on rose rapidly toward the twelve thousand foot peak of Old Baldy, and the valleys on either side became gorges which the drifting snows had filled level with the ridges on either side. There the higher elevation had retarded the effect of the coming spring, and the surface of the snow lay only a few feet below the wind-swept summits, so that for a few days yet a satisfactory "snow trap" might be found.

The proximity of the Indians, continually in sight but remaining at a distance, had accustomed the elk to their presence and overcome their wariness to the extent that they did not stampede unless their herders approached the sentinels within a hundred yards or so. The hunters were deployed in a semicircle, in such a manner that the quarry could move only up the ridge without approaching some of them, and thus every move the animals made was toward their destruction.

As the Indians followed their movements, the snow lay deeper, the drifts higher, and the cold became more intense, while the clear spots were constantly contracted; consequently, there were few connecting lanes between them when the snow-filled gorges finally were bounding them on either side.

A light snow followed by a bitter cold morning brought the hunt to a climax. To the left, the slope leading down to the Rinconada[3] was not well suited to their purpose, and the Carrizo Gorge was a considerable distance from the bedding ground of the elk but might be reached while favorable conditions continued. K'ah Tensakes directed his men to flank the band and drive them eastward, while he with one man went to the proposed trap to test the snowcrust.

The first rays of the rising sun glistened on the new fallen snow as he thrust the shaft of his lance into the drift at the edge of the fill. The new drift was deep here where the storm had swirled about the projecting treetops; but farther out the old crust was almost bare and the cold had strengthened it. Here it was too strong, and the heaviest buck could cross it safely. He signaled for his herders to move slowly, for the sun was bright and in time would weaken the crust.

After repeated tests, past noon the signal was given to stampede the herd. Most of the cows with their yearling calves crossed safely as well as most of the two year olds that followed them, while the bulls reluctantly brought up the rear and from time to time turned to threaten the yelling Indians behind them. All the old bulls, and the younger animals that broke through the crust, were stabbed to death by the long lances of the hunters standing on the adjacent crust, while the elk floundered helplessly in the snow.

A cow and a yearling were down in the edge of one of the soft spots, near a fir top that projected through the snow, and Ntsaaze and Tuja, two of the younger Indians, approached her. A young bull charged back to her defense, and as he came near the crust gave way with his weight so that it was broken before and behind the boys. The bull gained a footing on a shelving bank while they sank to their armpits between the animals, not twenty feet apart. K'ah Tensakes shouted from his safe position on solid ground, "Hide under the snow," as others farther out came, testing the snow, but too slowly to help the endangered youths, for every effort they made to extricate themselves only broke the crust. The bull turned upon the newcomers and was killed, but the cow overtook Tuja and trampled him to death beneath the snow. This action gave Ntsaaze time to burrow under the crust, and he was saved.

At this time of year, white-tailed deer, although more timid than the larger black-tailed deer, followed in the wake of the elk, as their favorite habitat cleared of snow, and were accompanied by their ever-hungry enemies, cougars (mountain lions). Thus, there were three important game animals whose hides were in prime condition at this time for the Indians' supply of clothing.

The hides of these animals were needed in great numbers as each individual needed one or more for comfort. Soft tanned, with the hair on, deer hides made warm, light robes, with the furlike coat not yet beginning to shed. And although the meat was tough from the winter's hardships, it retained the pleasant flavor peculiar to that animal's flesh, with an abundance of fat accumulated from feeding on the grasses preserved by nature on the plains. This suet, which as the new growth of browse became available, disappeared, was very solid at the end of the winter season and could be saved for future use.

These deer were very timid, and the sight or scent of an enemy usually precipitated a flight of miles without a stop. They ran in herds of from a dozen to a hundred, before the mating season, and were easily taken with the Indians' arrows when suitable range could be attained—which was difficult and tedious.

Returning to their favorite haunts in the high mountains, as they did with the first favorable weather, these deer were often overtaken by storms and took shelter in protected spaces beneath the drooping branches of fir trees. The winter snows slid down the compacted foliage of these trees and built up a circular drift about their margins, frequently reaching a height that embedded the tips of the lower branches, protecting the dry, needle-covered ground beneath the tree from the wind. And the enclosed space was sometimes filled to capacity with the deer that had pawed their way through the snow drifts. Such retreats were entered at the beginning of a storm and successfully defended by the deer against all their enemies except man. The Indians, however, found such gatherings well suited to the mass slayings necessary to provide for their requirements. The tracks of the deer betrayed their presence, until obliterated by the storm, and the Indian hunters were always on the alert to discover locations.

When a "deer tree" was found, word was passed around until a considerable number of Indians were gathered for the assault, which had to be made before the storm abated and usually involved considerable hardship. The hidden deer would lie quietly until actually menaced, which made it possible to surround the tree by as many archers as could find room to shoot their arrows from the surrounding drifts through openings in the branches of the tree. Others stationed themselves in positions where the escaping deer would make good targets.

The opening made by the deer for their entrance was small, and when a large herd was caught many were often killed or injured in their efforts to escape. Occasionally, an over zealous hunter broke through the branches of the tree and met a similar fate. In this way a large proportion of a herd was often secured by a well-planned *hazhah* (hunt).

After such a hunt, the warm shelters where the deer had been found were well suited for the preparation of the carcasses for transportation to the camps, and this labor fell to the women. But a few men usually remained with them, and the entrance, often much enlarged by the surviving deer in their efforts to escape, was built up with brush. Here a dozen or so women made a frolic of the job, and any carcasses falling in the open were brought into the enclosure for protection. The skinning and slicing of the meat was sometimes carried on for days while a little fire warmed the chilled fingers of the butchers and encouraged gossip.

At such times the cougars usually lay hidden in the nearby trees and other concealed locations where they could pounce upon unwary deer. But driven back by the presence of the Indians, hunger soon made them dangerous to any living thing coming within their reach. Consequently, the area outside the enclosure was a danger zone, and the bones and offal from the deer, thrown out, became bait and attracted the cats within range of the Indians' arrows without exposing the archers to attack.

The cougar hides might be classed as a luxury, for the affluent soon became their possessors; supplemented by contrasting skins, they made beautiful robes. Quivers for bows and arrows were also made of these hides, usually the property of important warriors; such quivers were elaborately decorated with beadwork and abalone shell, and stained buckskin covered the exposed surfaces of the flesh side of the skin.

Free women did a large part of this work and thereby provided for themselves the food and material for their clothing.

HAHEH

As the time approached for the April full moon, settled weather made conditions favorable for the *haheh*[1] (dance of the adolescent girls), which had been long deferred on account of the uncertain conditions of the tribe.

A government mule train had arrived at Fort Stanton with supplies for the Indians, and a detachment of cavalry, with a lieutenant in charge, was camped at The Mill in readiness to convoy the Mescalero to Fort Stanton, where they could more easily obtain rations. But this move had been delayed to allow time for the new grass to recuperate the limited number of horses available for the trip.

A few tipis had been made of cowhides, and a large number of canvas tents were in evidence. The Nogal country had been deserted, and the tribe was established along the upper reaches of the Tularoso, in a much more compact camp than before. The valley and adjacent hills were free from snow, and small green leaves were beginning to impart a verdant hue to the landscape.

The feast ground was ready with brush shelters for the food, where iron pots the soldiers had brought were redolent with cooking game and fragrant herbs.

Piles of flat soggy tortillas were growing as the issued skillets and Dutch ovens were emptied on the canvas sheets, spread upon the ground for their reception. The usual supply of little walnuts, acorns, and piñons was lacking, for the small store of them the Indians had been able to gather between moves had been exhausted while food was scarce. But dried peaches, prunes, and raisins from the government stores had been substituted. A bountiful supply of the inner bark of the sugar pine was at hand for gourmands needing a laxative, and *chuchupate* (wild angelica) roots were available for more immediate relief of the pain in overloaded stomachs.[2]

This dance, like all the Mescalero's dances, was based on tradition and celebrated as a religious ceremony. It was one of the most rigidly observed of their pious functions. Every precaution was observed to exclude the bad thoughts induced by Chete Neh (the malignant influence), and visitors—even those from enemy tribes—were welcomed on these occasions.

All Mescalero girls arriving at puberty became *ch'eeke* (young women). The female children of the tribe were the property of their fathers, slaves in fact, to be sold, given away, or otherwise disposed of, as and when the father wished. Fatherless girls were the property of their mothers, or, in her absence, the girl's nearest male relative. But as ch'eeke their abuse or neglect by anyone was severely punished. At this stage of development, the ch'eeke were each provided with a *yadeche* (priestess-chaperone), appointed by the medicine men, usually a near relative of the girl—aunt, grandmother, or the girl's mother occasionally when she was of mature age and unquestionable character. Their duties included the instruction of their wards in the ways, functions, obligations, and etiquette of women. Any violation of the authority of a yadeche was punishable by death, which she might inflict in the exercise of her duty with impunity from the law. She also was liable to any punishment the head men considered appropriate for failure to satisfactorily perform her own duties.

The traditional, divine requirement was that the ch'eeke should not be touched by any man. This period was completed by the purification of the haheh and one day with Eyata (something above the sky). If this requirement was not met, the penalty fell on the priestess and her ward with mitigating circumstances considered for the priestess. On the ch'eeke, however, fell the extreme penalty if she was touched by a man. She was disgraced and defiled. No accident or other excuse could be accepted. She was no longer a member of the tribe—an outcast. In such a circumstance, should she so elect, however, the ch'eeke might be marked by permitting the end of her nose to be cut off, whereby she acquired the privilege of remaining with her people but as the property of everybody; immune from the law, she might use anything she could take but could own nothing and was subject to the use of anyone under the same conditions. Otherwise she must leave the tribe or die.

The haheh might be compared to a coming out party in white society, and made public announcement that the ch'eeke was now a woman of marriageable age and ready to be disposed of by her father, or in his absence, her nearest male relative. It was celebrated during the four days and nights ending with a full moon.

The parents' ownership of their girls ended with the appointment of her yadeche, when she became the property of the tribe; but the approval of the candidate was necessary to his permission to "catch" a newly made woman while her spirit was with Eyata, between sunrise and sunset of the day after the ceremony.

With the owner's approval, any man might catch a newly made woman during that time. But, being a matter of public interest, a suitor had to be publicly announced by the owner. Such proclamations were usually secured by substantial payments to the owner, who was not restricted to the acceptance of a single offer. Thus, when there were rival applicants for the same girl, the bargaining became of the nature of an auction, often lasting for years, and deferred payments subject to the bidder being able to catch the girl were common. In such cases the girl had a possible chance of choosing between rival suitors by jockeying the race in favor of her preference; otherwise she had no control over the outcome.

From sunrise to sunset of the fifth day the purified spirit of the ch'eeke remained with the Deity above the sky and acquired her soul.[3] Children and the mentally and physically defective were believed to have no souls. The successful suitor became the husband of the girl he caught during this time, at the setting of the sun without further ceremony. And all ch'eeke finishing the dance became *isdza* (women). Those caught were the property of their husbands, and those not caught were free women, rulers of their own destinies, with no one else responsible for their protection or support.

The ceremony of haheh was celebrated in a tipi called a *kotulh* (a tipi of special design where the ceremony of haheh was carried out). The cover was of buffalo hides of the shape and dimensions of a common shelter, but erected on poles some six feet longer than those usually employed. The poles had to be of pine and a tuft of green branches left at their tops to project above the smoke hole and prevent the "evil spirits of the air" from entering there. The longer poles elevated the lower edge of the tipi cover to allow a clear view of the interior. A screen of green oak and willow brush standing imbedded in a trench around the western half of the kotulh and extending five steps east from the opposite tangents intercepted the evil spirits of the earth from the U-shaped enclosure with the kotulh in the curve and facing east. Thus open toward the rising sun and exposed to the sunlight it would preserve the purification of the kotulh during the daytime.

At a distance of ten steps east from the ends of the projecting screen a bright fire was kept burning when the sunlight failed, and all during the night, in the belief that evil spirits would not pass green leaves nor enter a brightly illuminated area.

About the middle of the afternoon, before the beginning of the dance, the girls and their priestesses gathered at the open end of the U-shaped enclosure and made fire with the conventional firesticks, all taking turns in the operation while reciting the prescribed incantations. From this fire each priestess took a brand,

Kotulh (*sacred tipi*). Blazer Family Collection.

symbolizing the sins of her ward. These were placed in the *kukeh* (firepit) dug in the center of the kotulh, and all other furnishings were provided at this time.[4]

These preparations completed, the purification of the bodies of the ch'eeke began in a nearby tipi. Each girl was bathed and anointed with sacred unguent by her yadeche and clothed in her ceremonial suit. The medicine men and the girls then gathered in the enclosure, where everything, themselves included, was sprinkled with the pollen of cattail flags *(hoddentin)*. The fire in the pit was fed with fuel provided by the medicine men, so that the sins of the girls should be fully consumed before the dance began.

The big fire, outside the enclosure, had no significance except to provide light for the ceremony and for the public feast—always a feature of the haheh. It was lighted whenever the sunlight failed to illuminate the purified enclosure, and an abundance of resinous wood assured its replenishment.

All this was provided by the parents of the dancing girls or other interested relatives and friends. The abundance and quality of the fare, free to all comers, indicated the wealth and generosity of the sponsors. Poor girls participated with their most affluent companions in the ceremony, and widows or free women having ch'eeke in the dance contributed their services, or whatever else they could for the glorification of all.

At sundown the medicine men took their places in the ko-tulh, seated on robes provided for their comfort, to the east of the firepit, and began their chant in concert, accompanied by the staccato clatter of their deer-hoof rattles.

The girls faced them, seated along the western edge of the enclosure, but the dance did not begin until the firelight cast distinct shadows within the kotulh. Then they began to move, using the Mescalero woman's dance. Alternately on their heels and toes, with a rigid swinging movement of the body, turning slightly from right to left and back, their clenched hands elevated to the level of their heads, and loose hair flowing free, they moved a distance to the right or left in unison with the chant and the click of the rattles.

The songs were chanted prayers in verse or rhythm, supplications to Eyata, and directed to a subdivision or part of "something above the sky" in direct control of a natural provision for human existence and happiness; there was an intermission after each song. Professional mourners, employed for the purpose, raised their voices out in the darkness, bewailing the past childhood of the dancers at each intermission, to distract the attention of evil spirits from the vicinity of the kotulh.

The first night was devoted to petitions for things necessary to life—food, drink, strength, and so forth—specifying many different items with a stanza or verse for each.

The second night's petitions were for shelter and protection, in similar manner. The third night they were for immunity from death by natural elements, such as cold, heat, lightning, and for many children to enjoy similar immunity.

The first three nights passed easily. Lengthy intermissions left time for rest between dances, and the prescribed songs were usually finished soon after midnight. All then rested until sunrise permitted their return to the dressing tent for refreshment.

The fourth night, however, was a recapitulation of the preceding three, and from dark to daylight there was little opportunity for rest. The girls in their heavily ornamented costumes had to be in prime health and condition to finish without becoming exhausted.

The dancing in the kotulh was timed to be completed at dawn of the fourth morning, and at that time preparations began for the final set determining the future of the newly made women, while they rested until sunrise.

In the meantime, throughout the four nights while the ceremony was being celebrated in the kotulh, and during the

Three Mescalero girls dressed for puberty rites. Blazer Family Collection.

intervening days, feasting and merrymaking continued about the big fire outside. For the double purpose of entertaining the crowd and enticing the evil spirits from the vicinity of the ceremonial, the sponsors secured the services of professional dancers. Voluntary clowns, in grotesque masks, offered their buffoonery for the amusement of the audience.

The professional dancers were men organized in troupes consisting of any number and trained to move in unison, as a ballet. Each troupe was made up, uniformly, in headdresses and characteristic designs painted on the parts of their naked bodies, intended to identify the members of the different troupes. The designs were also used traditionally to lure away the evil spirits which might be lurking near the haheh.

All professionals wore buckskin skirts and high-topped moccasins, such as in common use by women, to further confuse the spirits and the audience. Their headdresses were light, trellis-like frames of wood, attached to the crowns of buckskin helmets extending below the chin, where they were gathered and tied for stability; they were provided with small openings for vision and breath, forming a mask to conceal the identity of the wearer.

One or several troupes of dancers were employed as the affluence of the sponsors determined, with combinations of makeup for two or more kinds of spirits when the number of troupes was restricted or when the number of dancers in the various troupes was limited.

These troupes performed in concert or alternately according to the stage of the ceremonial. They all used the man's dance step, a low jump alternately advancing and retracting the feet and coming down with a stamp, while the hands carrying symbolic charms described traditional events in pantomime. At the conclusion of each act the dancers trotted off into some deep shade where the evil spirits that might have been attracted would follow and be removed from the vicinity of the haheh.

The final ceremony was celebrated at sunrise after the fourth night of dancing. While the ch'eeke rested, the "devil's pit" was dug across the opening of the sacred area—figuratively—by marking it out on the ground with a stick, and all evil spirits that lingered near retreated there to hide from the light of the rising sun.

The mothers of the dancing girls then performed the last service required of them, by bridging the pit—spreading rawhide over it. And the last responsibility of the yadeches was to cover this with a buckskin.

The medicine men then outlined—with pollen—four footsteps on the buckskin, leading to the symbol of the sun, also strewn with pollen and indicating the last stand of each ch'eeke under the protection of the haheh.

Each adolescent's medicine consisted of an elaborate basket designed and woven by the girl's mother or a friend and furnished with a number of articles required by tradition, which included an eagle feather. These baskets were kept near their owners throughout the ceremony, and during the last night the songs were tallied by the medicine men, who set a small stake beside the firepit for each girl at the end of each song. When all were finished each girl's stakes were added to the contents of her basket; then her medicine man, holding the feather by the quill and the girl grasping the barbs, led her across the four footsteps to the symbol of the sun, completing her transition from ch'eeke to isdza. This completed the ceremony required by tradition, and the spirit of the newly made woman left her for its day with the Deity above the sky. In the meantime her earthly form was not responsible for its actions. Nothing she did between sunrise and sunset was punishable under the law. But under man-made law, she must make four "ventures into the future"—symbolically—by carrying her basket toward the rising sun, providing a public opportunity to be caught.

First, the girls carried the baskets only a short distance. In their absence the bridge was removed so they might not return to their childhood; and the kotulh was dismantled, except for four poles left standing to be thrown down as the ventures were completed, one of which was let fall each time the girls left their baskets and turned back.

Second, they took up their medicines where they had been left and moved them farther away. In the meantime the brush screen was removed to permit their accepted suitors to assemble behind the pit, to be identified as suitors by their fathers, and to indicate the woman of their choice before the public, so that no misunderstanding could occur later.

Third, while the girls were moving their medicines still further away, the pit was obliterated with branches from the screen to allow the candidates to follow the woman of their choice when she abandoned her medicine for the fourth time, which was the signal releasing her suitors.

Fourth, the girl might carry her medicine to any distance she saw fit, but must leave it toward the rising sun and in sight of the obliterated pit, and all approved candidates for each girl were released to follow her when she did so. Each candidate must secure the feather, or some other article, from his girl's basket and touch her with it before sunset to make her his wife without other ceremony at that time. In this manner, one after another, the newly made women were disposed of, until all were married or sunset confirmed their spinsterhood, making them free women.

While this last act was in progress all matrimonial matters pending among other members of the tribe were subject to public adjustment. New alliances were confirmed by a woman joining the throng around the big fire where she began the woman's dance-step. There, she was joined by the man with whom previous arrangement had been made, and a medicine man then cast a robe about their shoulders, making them man and wife before the public. This gave the man full possession of the woman and whatever property she owned but not of any children she might have.

Divorce was likewise granted before the public. To divorce, a couple presented themselves at the big fire holding a strip of robe between them, which was severed by a medicine man, dissolving all obligations between them.

The foregoing description of the haheh is only a sketch which may leave the impression that the Mescalero's family relations were heartless and cruel— this was not the case. Affection between husbands and wives, although plural wives were common, was usually marked, although it was common for men to have more than one wife and this led to preferential treatment to some degree. Mothers especially were notably indulgent with their children, while fathers treated them with a more distant regard; but physical punishment was seldom used. No outside interference was allowed in family relations, and cruelties might be perpetrated without punishment. However, this resulted in a lowering of the perpetrator's standing with his fellows.

DATLIH'S ROMANCE

The haheh of the April moon in 1868, which the Mescalero celebrated in the upper reaches of the Tularoso Canyon, was an unusually grand event, although the attendance of visitors from other tribes, which was often a feature of such occasions, was prevented by existing conditions.

The tribe had been scattered and on the move for several years. And although the requirements of the haheh might be met, in compliance with the traditional ritual, and ch'eeke became married woman in good standing, such ceremonies were subject to review by the medicine men. At this time sixteen ch'eeke were found worthy and took part in the dance. Two women, however, were declared defiled; one fled to the troops at The Mill and was sent to Santa Fe, and the other committed suicide, so there was no execution.

Among the sixteen ch'eeke to take part in the dance were Katsuue, Santana's daughter, and her intimate friend, Datlih. Santana was affluent and had no need of remuneration for his consent to the suit for his daughter's hand. So when Katsuue had declared her preference for Shash (Bear), a likely young warrior, more than a year before this time, he had accepted Shash's offer of two horses and promised Katsuue that no other suitor would be accepted.

An older man that everyone disliked had offered more afterward, but the old chief had explained the situation and he had transferred his affections to Datlih. She was not so fortunate as her friend. Her mother was a widow with a younger son and daughter, and this situation had kept her and Datlih hard-pressed to find food and clothing for the four. Datlih had a decided preference for one of her suitors, Iti (Noisy). Her uncle Iyane (Cow), her father's brother, was her nearest male relative and the one to decide on the suitor to be accepted. Her mother would receive the dowry, but the guardian did the business.

Datlih was a fine young woman, fifteen or sixteen years of age, strong and good looking, who would make a valuable addition to any man's establishment, but with a mind of her own. There had been half a dozen or more offers for her. Although horses were scarce and few of the young men had even one to offer, they offered furs and robes, for Datlih was in demand. Consequently, old Iyane was overwhelmed with the business of deciding among the suitors until Tatsu (Plenty) became one of them.

Tatsu was a gambler and would have been known as a confidence man in a white community. His reputation for trickery in the various games of chance had earned him the scorn of his fellows, although many of them still opposed him in the vain hope of getting even. He was short and tended to be stout, while a game leg gave him a decided limp. Little inclined toward physical exertion, he had been adding to his girth for years; but he was still active on occasion, even taking part in footraces, which he seldom won. They often led to matches of some other nature in which he regained his losses, and usually more.

Tatsu already had four wives, whose lives he made miserable with his exactions and fault finding. But he had decided to add a younger and more attractive wife to his household, and his ideal was Datlih, when the more desirable Katsuue became unavailable. However, in competition with an able-bodied opponent he would have little chance of catching her in a race against her will, which he soon discovered was her state of mind.

As a child Datlih had idolized Iti; and he had shown his

affection for her as a ch'eeke, giving her yadeche a beautiful catskin robe for the girl, to replace the old buffalo hide which had served her for years as her only wrap and bedding. Iti had offered the only horse he had for her and when his bid was raised by a competitor with a better horse, he proposed to add a number of untanned furs to his offer.

One of Iti's friends had been very sick for a long time, and Iti had been providing for his family besides helping in other ways. This friend's condition had become so serious recently that his tipi had been moved to a distance from the camp in anticipation of his approaching death, in order to avoid the necessity of moving camp. When Iti called to minister to his friend, their conversation turned to the progress of his suit. And learning of the result of Iti's offer, the friend gave him a very superior mare he owned, saying that his other horse would be good enough for his mourning and that the mare was worth more than any horse that Tatsu had.

By this fortunate turn of affairs Iti had been enabled to make a much better offer than any that had been proposed, and the mother, as well as the girl, was well pleased to have the uncle accept the offer. Tatsu, however, had more horses, though none as good as the mare; but when he found himself outbid he offered the pick of any three horses in his herd, on condition that no other offer be accepted. This would leave him the only competitor in the race, and Datlih's own resources the only obstacle to be overcome. This proved too great a temptation for the mother in spite of the daughter's remonstrances; she made her selection of Tatsu's horses, and Iyane closed the deal.

By this arrangement Datlih had to begin her womanhood with no alternative but a despised husband or if she could evade him for a day, become a free woman and choose her own man. She had no doubt she could escape him for a time, and, if she could conserve her strength, might reach some hiding place where he could not find her. But she knew the dance would leave her nearly exhausted and that the man was not of a disposition that would prevent him from taking advantage of any scheme he might contrive in pursuing her. Neither was he barred from using any means of catching her, short of personal injury or the assistance of another person.

Also, her mother was poor and needed the horses in the struggle for existence in which Datlih would no longer be able to assist. As a free woman she could continue her assistance, but to do so she would have to forgo marriage, maybe for years until the younger children were old enough to care for themselves. Nevertheless, she had decided that she would not be Tatsu's wife if she could avoid it.

Datlih visited her friend Katsuue while their costumes for the dance were being prepared. It was required that the *ede* (upper garment) be made from a tanned deer hide without blemish. At the center of this a T-shaped incision was made, producing a triangular opening for the passage of the head; two triangular flaps folded down upon the breast. The skirts were of the usual style worn by the women, made of two small buckskins forming the front and back and reaching to the knees; from there the skin of the deer's legs hung at the outer side of the lower leg as tabs, without the hair being removed.

These two garments comprised the costume and were ornamented according to the taste, affluence, or ability of the owner. The triangular flaps at the neck were always emphasized, at least by some bright satin or print, and usually completely covered with beadwork. To this was commonly added one or more rows of fringes made of strips of buckskin, often six or eight inches in length, sewed across the front and back of the ede and slashed into narrow strips. Tassels were also constructed in the same manner and worn pendent from the back of the shoulders. Similar ornamentation was used on the skirt, and small scraps of sheet metal formed into deep cones and pinched onto shorter fringes were worn to add a tinkling sound to the wearer's movements. In addition, various accessory ornaments were worn, such as strings of beads about the neck, breastplates of beads, shells, bones, and so forth, in some cases amounting to several pounds in weight.

The ede was worn by passing the head through the opening in the hide so it lay loosely on the shoulders, allowing the garment to drape about the body and the upper arms and hanging loose over the hips without it being joined in any way at the sides. The skirt fitted closely about the hips with little fullness at the lower extremity.

Moccasins were not an essential part of the traditional costume but were by custom generally worn. The soles, preferably of elk hide, were cut larger than the soles of the wearer's feet. The vamps, cut from the hide of the deer's neck, were of equal size, and when the pieces were stitched together at the edges the inserted feet rolled the surplus width to raise the seams from contact with the ground. The legs, in a single piece with the uppers, and of soft buckskin, reached up to the thigh and were supported from a belt when extended. But they were commonly rolled down to just below the knees then up from the ankles and the surplus tucked in above the calves to substitute for garters.

Katsuue complained of the great weight her costume had acquired. "Tatade [father] has given me so many juu [ornaments] that I hardly know how I can use them all, and he would be offended if any of them were left off," she said. "It is a load to carry, but he says I will not have to run very far for he has accepted but one man for me, and he is the one I want."

"I don't have that kind of trouble," asserted Datlih, "I only have a handful of beads that I have put onto the neck tabs of my ede, and Bima borrowed a buckskin to make fringes. Iti gave her a fine big deerhide last spring, and I tanned it with the hair on the legs and made many besh dilhentee [metal jingles] that would make a lot of noise. But I thought then that Iti would get me for he had offered a very fine mare. And now Bima has gone to select three of Tatsu's best horses, and he is to have the only chance to catch me."

"It does not seem right," remarked Katsuue, "that the men can have the women they want whether the women like them or not. But there are many things that Eyata's law says are right that I do not understand. And sometimes a woman can get away when she doesn't like a man."

"That is what I have been thinking about, too," Datlih admitted. "Tatsu is old and fat though he can run fast for a little way. I can run faster and longer if I am not too tired from the dance, so if he does not do something *bytah* [foxy] I can get away and hide. But I want Bima to have the horses, too, and do not know what to do."

"I think your mother did wrong," decided Katsuue, "when she knew Tatsu was a bad man and that you do not like him to let him have the only chance, and you should not think much about her. Remember that Tatsu would make you miserable as long as you live."

Both the girls' yadeches also thought Datlih justified in sacrificing her mother's interest to her own well-being, and the four went to look over the course the girls would run.

The location for the haheh had been selected, and the scattered bushes were being cleared away from a slightly elevated spot at the mouth of a side canyon, where the kotulh was to be erected. To the east the main canyon led in a somewhat southerly direction, making the course the girls would run cross the level floor diagonally toward the foot of the mountain three hundred yards or more away. On this stretch a small herd of ponies was being close herded to clear and trample the tall dry grass to an open lane. An easy incline from the canyon's edge reached some distance upward to the steeper ascent and was overgrown densely with small oak brush. Somewhat to the south of this lane a small group of pines grew at the edge of the canyon where the scrub oak was taller, and the mountainside above was covered by large pine trees.

No hiding place could be seen nearer than the forest on the mountainside, for there was no cover leading from the thicket in the canyon bed. "I do not see a chance to get away," said Datlih, "for I will be too tired to go much farther when I get to the timber." "I wish I could do something to help you get away," said Katsuue, "and I will if I can."

"I expect him to do any mean thing he can, and if he goes for a horse I may be able to get to the timber and hide before he gets back. I will get a club if he doesn't, and maybe I can fight him off till sunset if he follows me on foot, for I will get away from that old toad if I can," decided Datlih.

When the dance was finished, the girls had a half-hour or more for rest while preparations were made for the final act of the ceremony. Datlih maneuvered so that her place was next to Katsuue and whispered, "Don't run very fast."

The three ventures were made, and Datlih started on the fourth and last at a moderate gait. Katsuue said, "Wait a little," and as she was released fell as if exhausted so that her padded calves tripped Tatsu as he ran.

No doubt Tatsu's game leg contributed somewhat to his somersault, for his limp was worse as he regained his feet amid the jeers and delighted shouts of the onlookers. Scowling and cursing the girl and the watching throng, he reached Datlih's basket and with the necessary feather veered to the right toward the thicket and the clump of trees.

Datlih held her course toward the timber, but over her shoulder as she ran she had seen her suitor's discomfiture to her encouragement. However, another hurried glance detected his change of direction, and a look at the thicket from her higher position disclosed a horse's head above the brush; she suddenly understood his scheme. He could easily overtake her on horseback, and she, with equal certainty might escape him by the same means. There was not much distance in favor of either in a race for the horse, she handicapped by the knee-high brush and he by his lameness and the tall grass. But she had to best him to be able to untie the horse. Datlih ran as she had never run before, leaping over the obstructing brush like a fleeing deer, and had the horse untied when he arrived. As Tatsu grasped the end of the rope, the startled animal jerked it from his hand, bounding away under encouragement of the thumping heels of the rider.

Datlih reached the mountaintop, from where she could see the dispersing of the merrymakers at the feast ground far below. Packed horses were moving off in every direction. Women and children with bundles on their backs could be distinguished but were too far away to be recognized. A lone figure moving across the flat, which she thought to be Tatsu, did not join the crowd but passed from view behind a timbered ridge, so she believed herself safe and tarried to watch the scene. Brush piles were burning, and all vestiges of the late ceremony were being destroyed that nature might the sooner obliterate the signs of activity and resume her way.

Datlih rode on, crossing the high summit and down a deep canyon to a spring. Tatsu had carefully provided for his comfort; two good robes spread over the saddle made a soft seat. In the rawhide containers at the saddle horn she found abundant provisions for the day. A water gourd also had been supplied; however, she did not drink from that but of the cool sparkling water from the spring. And when her hunger was appeased, she spread the robes in a grassy spot on the hillside and lay down to rest.

She had picketed the horse in an open glade farther up on the hillside where by the timber, and from the slight elevation where she lay she could see anyone passing on the trail in the bed of the canyon below. She was at least five miles from the point of her escape, and although there was but little chance of her being followed here, she intended to remain alert. But instead she fell asleep.

When she awoke, it was past mid-afternoon. The warm sun bathed the mountainside, but the evening shadows were deepening below. Her immunity from punishment would cease with the setting of the sun, and Tatsu's horse and equipment was still in her possession. He might have given up his pursuit of her as a wife, but his vengeance was another matter.

She placed the robes and other articles on the saddle and secured them with the rope, then gave the horse a sharp cut over
the rump and started him down the trail into the main canyon.
This trail led from the main camp near its mouth up the north
fork of the Tularoso, where, near the summit, Iti and some of his
cronies had temporarily established themselves because it was convenient for hunting.

Iti had not attended the haheh. Morose and disappointed at
the failure of his plans, he had avoided the festivities and a meeting with his successful rival. He had been alone for a week while
his companions celebrated the ritual. Now it was over, and there
would be remnants of the feast in his mother's camp; her consol-
ing sympathy would ease his mind. But as he rode toward camp
this evening his humor was homicidal, and a meeting between him
and Tatsu could easily have been fatal to one or both of them.

Datlih could see Iti from where she was, and as the sound of
the trampling hooves reached him he sprang from his horse behind a tree; then after a few minutes he concealed his mount and
renewed his vigilance. She could not account for his actions unless he had seen Tatsu. Had he followed and failed to find her? She
would remain hidden until the sun was fully set; then she would
make her presence known to Iti. She had feared to meet Tatsu, for
in his wrath he might attempt anything against an unprotected
woman. Of Iti she had no fear, but she thought he might be temporarily in such mood that he would not listen to what had
happened since the haheh so had not called to him.

The sound of a horse entering the trail before him interrupted
Iti's reflections, and not twenty steps away was Tatsu's horse. Concealed by a tree trunk he observed more carefully. There was no
rider, but the horse was saddled and bore such equipment as might
be needed on a short trip. It was apparent that the horse had
been intentionally liberated for the equipment was securely tied
to the saddle. There was no reason to believe that the owner

would deliberately put himself afoot several miles from home while able to make such disposition of his property, nor that anyone else would go to that trouble if they had done so.

Iti remained concealed; it might be that Tatsu was in the same mood as himself, and there was no knowing what fantastic scheme he might conceive for his undoing. With bow in hand and ready arrows he awaited the fast falling darkness.

Without a warning sound Datlih appeared before him in the trail, walking briskly toward the camp. Was this a lure? She would not choose to do such a thing of her own free will, but Tatsu might have deceived her or compelled her to act in this fashion. He still waited, until she was out of sight around a bend in the trail, then, remounting his horse, he soon overtook her.

Datlih told Iti what had occurred. His homicidal mood changed to cynicism as he berated Tatsu, and they soon agreed to spend their future as man and wife. They were not yet married, however, and Datlih was a free woman. So the mother-in-law hoodoo was not in effect, and riding double they went first to the feast ground for Datlih's medicine and then to her mother's camp.

The bright moonlight revealed her mother's raving, and she vowed vengeance on her undutiful daughter, whose arrival brought a flood of tears and such a tongue-lashing as few girls of any race receive. But when she attempted to administer corporal punishment, Iti interfered.

They could not be married, according to the custom of the tribe, until the feast of the haheh was again celebrated. But in the meantime living together as man and wife was no uncommon practice, and they did so in a tent provided by the military, which they erected near the mother's tipi. In a short time Datlih's mother became reconciled, for Iti was a good hunter and Datlih as a free woman owned what he gave her, which she contributed to the welfare of the family.

CONFLICT AND COMPLICATIONS

The various bands which had become widely scattered after their flight from the Bosque Redondo gradually drifted back to their old haunts in the White and Sacramento mountains. The change in government policy beginning in 1867 brought a new type of Indian agent, one that invited the starving Mescalero to come in to Fort Stanton for rations and subsistence.

Santana knew that to be content his people must have work, which he had proposed to provide for them along the lines of their usual occupations. His plans, however, had been frustrated by the advice of a committee of the Indians' rights people, who recommended agriculture as employment. Attempts at farming had been tried at various times,[1] and arable land was broken and planted near Fort Stanton. It had also been attempted on the Peñasco, in La Luz Canyon, and at the Bosque Redondo—all with little success. Now, an agent provided for their immediate supervision.

The Indian Service, at that early time, was under the War Department, although it was not a branch of the military; and the agent, in matters pertaining to the Indians, was the ranking authority. The colonel in command at the fort had orders to provide such military assistance as he might consider necessary in support of the agent; and occasionally the extent of such support was disputed. Given the situation, the agent was very hopeful that his wards would take kindly to the agricultural pursuits proposed, but this proved a vain hope regarding the men, and he had given his attention to providing employment elsewhere for the women.

Generations of warfare and hunting, in which the able-bodied men had been constantly engaged, required that they be always ready to resist an attack or other emergency. Consequently, the exhaustion of manual labor had been found detrimental to the best interests of the tribe and was considered unwarrior-like and a reason for contempt. All duties involving manual labor were performed by women, the aged or other persons not expected to assist in the protection of the community. The agent was not prepared to accept this long-established attitude of the Mescalero.

Had the agent been content to allow the women to do the farming as Santana proposed, it is probable that a few years of experience would have accomplished his desire, at least to some extent, and men would have taken over a part of the drudgery. But he insisted that the able-bodied men do the work. They had no immediate need for wheat or corn, which they were encouraged to plant and produce for sale, for in large measure money was of little value in their estimation. It would buy many things they wanted, but their appreciation of values was undeveloped so most of them would pay a dollar or two for a bright-colored cotton handkerchief or a bunch of beads and brag about their bargain.

Their rations provided more flour than the Indians were accustomed to using, and their ponies did well on the abundant grass without the toil of farming. A few old women were interested to the extent of raising corn for tulhiba. But aside from this and a few pumpkins, squash, and melons which they desired for food, the farms were used mostly for corralling their stock, and the little patches the old women planted had to be fenced off to protect their crops.

The young men grew restless and spent most of their time gambling, which caused endless rows and resulted in several fights that ended in fatalities. The agent objected to their "eternal games" and made several arrests of owners of gambling paraphernalia. But a proposal to destroy the equipment met with such strenuous opposition that the crusade was given up and the prisoners released. The instinct for gambling was highly developed in the Mescalero, and the old chief himself saw no harm in it aside from the quarrels it caused. His orders against it, which the agent insisted he should issue were lukewarm and their only effect was to restrict publicity to some extent, which did not satisfy the agent.

The agent was a good man, but his knowledge of Indians and their ways appeared to have been acquired from some poetical source rather than from practical knowledge. His representations had been, to some extent, responsible for a strong sentiment in the east that influenced the authorities in Washington in favor of breaking up tribal relations and "barbaric customs" among the Indians. It was thought might be easily accomplished when amicable contact had been made.

To this end two missionaries had been sent to the Mescalero, and through military cooperation they were to receive every protection and assistance. This the agent thought entitled him to such support as might be required to stop the gambling by force, but the post commander had a practical knowledge from years of experience on the frontier and refused to use his troops for the purpose. The post commander had given the agent a detail of soldiers and several scouts to act as interpreters, as well as to instruct the Indians in farming. They now outnumbered the Indian farmers, but the commander had given orders that no guns should be carried in this service in order to avoid the appearance of using force. They were allowed only pistols for possible emergencies.

The missionaries had made frequent visits to the camp, accompanied by interpreters, and had made some headway toward learning the Mescalero's language and becoming acquainted with a number of the Indians. Such instructions as they had offered had been received with some degree of interest and toleration, but as yet there had been no apparent results.

Most social activities of the Mescalero were based on tradition, and ancient customs were observed with extreme care. Their game of *gunesnane-tu* (ten-hundred), sometimes called the hoop and pole game, was subject to numerous rites and restrictions; and this was the agent's pet aversion.[2]

Two men were matched to play, usually for wagers between themselves, but for championship or sport alone at times. All men might participate by making side bets on the players, and in such case the outside participants might select a referee; or, when the game assumed importance, two or more were selected. Women might bet among themselves but were not allowed in the immediate vicinity of the course; and no person nor animal was permitted within the course, except the players. The referees were given unlimited authority over all matters pertaining to the game and were the court of last resort in case of controversy.

Several of the elderly men were addicts to this game and had elaborate paraphernalia, the construction of which had cost them many hours of labor. This they set up in a suitable place about the camp with prescribed ceremonies. The essentials of the game were a long pole for each of the players, a hoop, a strip of level ground, and two grass goals. The poles were made up of three lengths of hardwood, preferably oak, each about five feet long. The bottom section was of a diameter over an inch and tapered evenly to a central length also tapered to match the third, of which the point was a half-inch or less in thickness. Thus the three sections were tapered continuously from end to end, with the scarfed joints secured by four wrappings of sinew. These wrappings also served as markers to count the game.

The hoop was made of oak, about fifteen inches in diameter, of round sections, and also closed with a scarfed joint wrapped with sinew. The hoop was bisected by a buckskin cord supporting in its center a bead, the indicating counter. The goals were heaps of grass, elongated and placed transversely ten steps apart to obstruct the ends of the course in such manner as to check the momentum of the rolling hoop and cause it to topple over.

The two players, each armed with his *shapaz* (hoop pole), stood together at a goal, their poles extending along the ground parallel to the course, and one rolled the hoop between the poles. Reaching the opposite goal, the momentum of the rolling hoop was checked; and each player launched his pole, spearlike, with the object of causing its unwieldy length to lie in such position that the bead counter in the hoop would register on one of the circular notches near the butt of his pole. This would achieve the highest possible score, winning the game at a single throw. Registering on any part of the string, the hoop, the sinew wrappings, or on any part of the naked pole also counted in the score, and the first person to score a thousand points was the winner.

Great dexterity was acquired by practice in the casting of the poles in such manner that the roller's skill would be frustrated by his opponent's pole striking the hoop as it fell, while the roller's object was to avoid such result and win the tally for himself.

At this game Indaa Chatsuzhez (Dark Eyes) was one of the professionals, and Tatsu, the gambler who had failed to catch Datlih, was matched against him for heavy stakes. So far a draw game had heightened the excitement. A horse each, wagered between the players, was not an unusual occurrence in a game such as this, but a draw game was exceptional. It showed such equality in the players' skill that the stakes had been doubled, and the deciding game was to begin early on the following morning.

Santana had ignored the initial game, which had been deferred until after the agent had made his morning visit to the camp. But it was impossible to ignore the upcoming game since the tribesmen had spent the night in controversy making bets. And sunrise found half the tribe involved in the betting despite Santana's efforts to stop the game. The men were staking their horses, robes, blankets, their fancy dress, and even the women—every conceivable thing that was of value. The fields were deserted, and the agent would be in a great rage when he discovered the condition of affairs; but there was nothing more that Santana could do. And if the agent undertook to stop the game by force, there would probably be a general revolt.

Santana was sincere in his conviction that the day of the Indian was over, insofar as their free, nomadic existence was concerned. To survive, they had to adapt their activities to a largely unknown future, in which they had to adopt the ways of new and—at least to some extent—foreign neighbors. His point of view had not changed, nor had his Indian characteristics been altered; but his keen intelligence enabled him to anticipate the future to some extent, and his instinct for the preservation of his people was paramount in all his reasonings.

In the past, Santana's behavior had been domineering, fearless, even heartless; he had permitted nothing to stand in the way of the achievement of his ends. Politic and conciliating on occasion, he was cautious and calculating always; he was affectionate with his friends and supporters, but adamant in his decisions. He had attained his power, during the height of his efficiency, by relentless punishment of opposition, assuming the authority of life and death, judge, jury and executioner in one, always, as he believed, for the best interest of the tribe as a whole. Age and experience had taught him when he must curb the exercise of his authority, and this hoop and pole game was such an occasion.

Mounting his horse, Santana rode off toward the fort to meet the agent before that officer should reach the camp on his daily visit, to warn him of the precarious conditions that awaited him. He met the agent, with his guard and interpreters, nearly halfway between the camp and the fort, and made known the condition of affairs. He explained that, due to the religious aspect of the matter, interference would no doubt result in mass opposition, which if undertaken by himself would destroy his influence and probably lead to his death. His people were in a state of religious frenzy and would tolerate no interference from the agent or the military. Instead, they must be permitted to finish their present debauch or any good that had been accomplished by Indians' surrender would be lost.

The agent, with the docility of his wards in mind, who had submitted to punishment on numerous occasions, did not realize that it was to Santana and not himself they had submitted and believed the old chief to be opposing his authority. Consequently, his only reply was, "I am supposed to stop all this, and it is as well to nip it in the bud as to have it to contend with later." He then rode on without paying further attention, although Santana rode beside him for a time, protesting. But receiving no satisfaction, he turned back and went on to the fort as fast as possible.

The agent rode on, past the deserted fields and through the camp where but a few Indians were to be seen. He arrived at the game while the players and the referees were engaged in an argument over the tally of a previous roll. Then he undertook to lead his men across the consecrated strip of ground between the goals, but a great cry went up and a dozen Indians stopped them. The agent's men were dragged to the ground without ceremony, but with no further injury than a few bruises, and their pistols were taken from them. Then they were quickly bound hand and foot and removed to a distance from the game.

Here several old women were set to guard them with menacing clubs and drawn knives, while ropes were being stretched along the gaming course to determine if any of the intruders' tracks had desecrated the area. No tracks were discovered within the confines of the game. However, had there been tracks, no amount of argument would have arranged for a continuance of the contest until the area had been purified with the desecrators' blood, and an ensuing riot would have included the death of the agent and his party.

At the fort, the commander's confidence in Santana was such that when the situation was explained and the old chief expressed his anxiety for the safety of the agent and his party, the commander, with his orderly, accompanied Santana to rescue them. They arrived in time, and, although they found the whole population in a turmoil and the game suspended pending a decision as to what should be the fate of the prisoners, Santana leaped from his horse and, grabbing two of the frantic guards by their hair, cracked their heads together. As they fell he grabbed for two others; these, however, had taken the hint and were beyond his reach, running as for their lives, while the crowd forgot their wrath and set up a chorus of shouts and jeers in derision of the discomfited guards.

Santana cut the prisoners' bonds. Their horses, which were tethered nearby, were mounted as quickly as their numbed limbs would permit; then, accompanied by the commander, they made no delay in their departure. The game was resumed and concluded without further mishap, and nothing further was done about the interruption.

Santana's knowledge of the humors of his people and his timely arrival no doubt saved a much more serious consequence of the agent's untimely valor. And he told the commander afterward that if he had done that a half-hour sooner they would all have been killed, but just then they did not know what to do and were glad to have the matter decided for them.

This game was noteworthy, not only because the incident materially modified the agent's enthusiasm and discouraged the missionaries but because it delayed the breaking up of the Mescalero's tribal relations for many years. Further, the final result of the game itself became an oft repeated tale. Tatsu lost, and peevish from the fiasco of the recent haheh, which had made him the object of constant ridicule, he challenged his opponent to another round and wagered the four horses he still owned against the stakes of their recent game. His challenge was accepted, and the other Indians joined in the excitement until there was little property in the tribe that had not been wagered. Indaa Chatsuzhez won again, and Tatsu, now frantic with the jeers hurled at him, bet his four wives against the eight horses and lost.

A dozen or more other wives had been wagered on side bets, and half the tribe was reduced to their breechclouts for clothing, with many devoid of their food supply until the next Saturday when they would again receive their rations.

When Santana's followers had left the Sacramentos, he had renewed his threat to Cha, sending a trusted messenger to tell him that he would not only hold him responsible for any attack his renegades made against his friends on the Tularoso, but if they returned to the Sacramentos his band had to protect the mountains from the invasion of any other tribe. It was not long, however, until the whole country was infested by the outlaws. Several trappers had established themselves in the White Mountains and in the Sacramentos. Some of these were murdered and others driven out. But the Tularosa people and the doctor's men at The Mill were not molested, nor had their stock been bothered.

The constant depredations within a few miles of them on every side would have caused the abandonment of The Mill had it not been for a detail of soldiers stationed there to protect the industry while lumber was being made for military use; convoys of troops escorted the ox teams transporting the lumber to the various forts.

This condition prevailed until late in the summer of 1869, and in the meantime an adobe house had replaced some of the cabins. The Indians were known to have secured some of the heavy Sharpe rifles used by the buffalo hunters on the plains, which were of sufficient power to penetrate any ordinary log wall. Consequently, the walls of the new building were made three feet thick, and the upper half-story was also provided with portholes temporarily filled with clay that could be easily removed in a few minutes in case of necessity. An observation box on the roof was also built to be used as a lookout in case of alarm.

In the winter of 1869–1870, during the time the doctor was absent, a strong band of Comanche invaded the Sacramentos, driving the other Indians from the locality of The Mill. After committing numerous other depredations, they besieged the house. No one was killed, for the attack was made in the early morning before the men had gone to work. But the mill was burned, and all the stock driven off, leaving the partners destitute.

In 1870, Santana was successful, to some extent, in his efforts to have his people take up farming. Some crops were raised, largely by military details, but the Indians were induced to accompany the soldiers, and they did a small part of the work. The corn produced was bought for the cavalry at high prices to encourage the farmers. To Santana's great relief, no considerable amount was available to be made into tulhiba. The making of basketry and beadwork, which occupied some of the women's leisure time, was encouraged by a ready sale which added to their earnings. But the traditional objection to the men doing manual labor left them generally unemployed.

The treaty stipulations for absence from the reservation were liberally construed by the authorities. Thus, it was seldom that the various expeditions off on passes did not amount to from a dozen to a hundred individuals. Such journeys helped to dissipate the surplus energy of the young men.

Santana assumed the right to dictate who should have the passes for these outings, which soon acquired the aspect of a picnic, and used them as a regard of merit. Thus he rewarded fidelity, punished misdemeanors, and permitted the tribe as a whole to exercise the religious functions necessary to a degree of contentment in their idleness. But the drunken rows, which sometimes threatened serious complications, caused him a great deal of trouble and worry.

Most of the settlements supported a *tendejon* (a combination of general store and grocery) and at these the Indians off on passes found means of indulging their appetites for liquor.

Bootlegging on the reservation was also a matter of serious concern, but more within reach of his authority. And as means were found for the mysterious disappearance of some of those engaged in the business, it became less popular.

A few killings occurred at the settlements for which the Mescalero were blamed, and the old chief was required to apprehend the culprits when they returned to the reservation. In this he succeeded in a few cases, but it soon became a common thing for Indians getting into trouble not to return, and Cha's renegades increased accordingly.

During this period several choice locations had been settled by Mexicans and a sprinkling of white men, mostly ex-soldiers discharged from the California Column when that organization was mustered out at the close of the Civil War. Many of these had taken Mexican wives, and one or more of them were usually the leading citizens in these settlements. Their status was generally that of owner, in effect, of the community property. The land, as yet unsurveyed, was subject to what was known as squatter's rights which held that an acreage gainfully employed by the squatter was his until the government survey determined the legal boundaries and gave the occupant a preferential right to acquire title under the homestead law. These whites were the influential citizens, commonly having appropriated several times the amount of land they could finally secure title to in their own right. But with the following of "relation"-in-laws to file on the surplus, they were quite safe in making considerable improvements without any real subdivision of their holdings.

The governor and other officials of the territorial government were appointed by the president, and it was seldom that a jury could be found that would convict a defendant against the wishes of these men.

In 1871–1872, the authorities decided to increase the effort being made to control the hostile Indians in this section of the country, and several companies of infantry were brought in to relieve the cavalry of garrison duty and assist in the repair and re-occupation of several forts that had been abandoned for a number of years, one of which was Fort Stanton, located in the White Mountains.[3]

A regiment of cavalry had taken the field with mountain howitzers and gatling guns, and four companies of these had arrived at Fort Stanton in passing through the country. The military had made several attempts to secure Santana's help in capturing his brother, Cha, but he had refused to cooperate with the soldiers and insisted that the troops did not know how to fight Indians and could never catch Cha.

Santana, steadfast in his desire for peace, was unable to understand why the desertion of a few of his followers should cause several of the higher military officers to question his sincerity. He had succeeded beyond his expectations in keeping his people on the reservation and was impatient with their faultfinding. The military had failed to grasp the difference between their point of view and that of the Indian, interpreting Santana's assertion that he wanted peace and his refusal to aid in arresting Cha as inconsistent.

They had explained to Santana that they proposed to capture as many of the outlaws as possible, give them a fair trial in the court, and punish those found guilty in such manner as the law prescribed. This was according to the orders from Washington, where the influence of civilization had replaced the idea of extermination with that of conciliation, which had been anticipated by Santana's own choice. But the Washington authorities believed that a thousand well-equipped and trained soldiers could easily capture a hundred savages.

"I can bring them all in," said Santana in reply to their proposition, "or kill them with my own men. But I cannot do it with the soldiers, for the soldiers do not know how to fight Indians. And if the soldiers found them, the Indians would be afraid and run away so that all would have to be killed to catch them. And if the soldiers did catch some, they would put them in the guardhouse for a while and then let them go. Then if my people had helped to catch them, those they let go would be mad at my people, and we would have to fight them again. And the soldiers would not let us kill them all, so the fighting among ourselves would be forever."

The officers thought this counterproposition to be only another of Santana's inconsistencies and refused to sanction his leaving the reservation with the expedition he had proposed.

The officers' expectations of capturing Cha and his followers were based on the effect they believed the increased number of troops and new guns would have in convincing the Indians of the futility of resistance, and thus securing Santana's help. To this end the old chief was invited to bring some of his head men to a feast and witness target practice with the new guns. Some twenty of them came, and when well fed they were shown how the big guns were operated. A Gatling gun was turned onto a willow thicket a quarter of a mile away, which was mowed down in short order. A howitzer was then brought to bear on a large rock still farther away, which was blown to bits. The officer in command of the troops then gave a short talk and asked Santana what chance the Indians would have against such an assault.

"None," admitted the chief, readily, "but how can you make the Indians wait till you get ready? If there had been a few Indians in the willows they would have been killed if they had not lain down, but they would not wait for you to shoot that much. Then you would have to get another mule-load of cartridges and they would be gone. And if there was some by the rock I expect they would be killed, but they would not stay there when they saw the soldiers bring the gun and fix it."

The demonstration at the fort was a complete failure insofar as the desired effect on the Indians was concerned. The only result was that the Mescalero became alarmed when they realized the exposed position of their concentrated camp, on the open plain where it would be subject to almost instantaneous destruction by the use of these new arms. Consequently, an uneasiness resulted that threatened a general exodus. Santana himself went to his friend the post commander for confirmation of the promise that his people would not be molested so long as they remained peaceably on the reservation. This assurance was, of course, given, and the big guns were sent on their way to another fort a day sooner than had been intended.

That satisfied the old chief; however, he was unable to convince the tribe that this was sufficient, and a council of the head men demanded that they should be given a reservation in the mountains. This was not allowed but led to the camp being permitted to spread over a greater area, and only a few days was required for the tents and tipis to be scattered along several miles among the trees on both sides of the river .

Although this increased area was desirable, at the same time it reduced Santana's opportunities for personal observation of his tribe. Consequently, the bootleggers of liquor became more successful so that it became necessary to deal with the customers as harshly as with the sellers. Rewards were offered for information leading to the conviction of the bootleggers, and a few were convicted and given long terms in the penitentiary, which somewhat reduced trouble of this kind. Santana arrested all he found intoxicated and turned them over to the authorities at the fort, where they were given terms of manual labor under guard.

AN EASTERN TOUR

The campaign against the renegades was in full swing, and the Mescalero who occasionally deserted from the reservation were not joining Cha's band but remained in hiding in the mountains. They were careful not to attract attention to themselves, although they occasionally found ways to communicate with their relatives around Fort Stanton.

A few of these deserters had returned to the reservation, and Santana had reported their presence to the commander at the fort, with the suggestion that they should not be arrested, hoping that others would follow their example. His idea was approved, and, although some of them were under indictment in the court, they were permitted to remain at large with Santana's caution to avoid being seen by the officers.

Nearly a thousand soldiers, in the field for several months, had captured half a dozen of Cha's followers, and were supposed to have killed some others. Also the fact that no Indians had been found for some time gave the impression that they had been harassed beyond endurance and had gone back to their stronghold in the Jarillas. Santana's cooperation was still very much desired in the campaign against the fugitives, but he refused to be identified with the soldiers. He had offered to undertake the job provided the soldiers were withdrawn, and when the mountains were rid of the hostiles, his people would be allowed to go back to their old haunts in the Tularoso country and live there on the same terms as on their present reservation.

Still persisting in the idea that the Indians would be overawed and yield when they realized the great odds against them, the authorities in Washington ordered that Santana and a few of his influential men be taken to the capital and shown the resources against which they had to contend.[1] Whereby it was believed that this would make the old chief change his mind and find means of assisting the troops to subdue the renegades.

The Indians' point of view was so different from anything conceivable to the white authorities that, at this time, Santana's greatest concern was the fact that the military was intent on capturing the offenders rather than exterminating the tribe. As with all people, self-preservation came first for the Mescalero. Their absolute belief, however, that "might makes right," coupled with predestination, made them unyielding.

Certain basic principles were fixed beliefs among the Mescalero. The destruction of enemies was considered in no way a sin but the neutral struggle for existence, in the same category as killing a beast for food or raiment. Moreover, to be killed by an enemy was a personal misfortune, not a matter noted by the Deity such as the destruction of a people. It was so common an end that it was expected; its occurrence was one of the normal events of life, just as birth and puberty.

To be killed—or injured—by an associate was a sin against the individual killed or injured, not against the Deity, for the act was a pursuance of the divine law. No sins were to be punished after death. All punishment was physical, earthly. Bad thoughts rendered the individual subject to the domination of Chete Neh and prolonged the spiritual existence on earth after death. And the mental attitude of the individual at the separation of the soul from the body—death—determined whether Eyata or Chete Neh would control the destiny of the soul.

The soul, spirit, was an attribute of maturity. Children had no souls, no responsible thoughts, good or bad. The mentally undeveloped and the physically deformed had no souls of their own but after adolescence were available as the habitation of the spirits of the people of Chete Neh's people. Consequently they were feared, shunned, and sometimes killed by terror-stricken individuals in fear of their evil abilities.

Santana was convinced that his people were physically unable to cope with their new environment, and was straining his wits to prevent their destruction as a people. But physical superiority was not the only strength that might be resorted to; mental ability, ingenuity, and resourcefulness might also determine the survival of a people. It was not a question of the resources of the white people opposed to the Mescalero. He was already certain that their triumph was only a matter of time. The menace, which had been encroaching for so long without being recognized, now appeared to be unlimited. His objective was to understand these people and learn why they were not intent on the extermination of the Mescalero. Had the conditions been reversed, his only thought would have been the destruction of any of them that could not be absorbed by the Mescalero. No individual hatred or revenge was involved in this idea but a precaution, that the enemy's strength should be made inferior to their own by learning the source of their advantage, enabling the Mescalero to meet them on equal terms.

Santana was very much pleased with the prospect of seeing with his own eyes what the source of the apparently inexhaustible immigration was but at the same time he believed that his presence with his people could alone ensure that they remained on the reservation and at peace. Santana talked these matters over with his friend the post commander, who helped arrange several details that they hoped would ensure present conditions in the camp while the head men were absent. Roman was made Santana's representative.

A lieutenant was detailed to have charge of the expedition to Washington, and three ambulances provided transportation for the chief and eight companions of his selection for the first leg of the journey. A detachment of cavalry and four escort wagons conveyed them to St. Joseph on the Missouri River, where they were to take a steamboat to St. Louis.

The Indians wore their usual dress, consisting of buckskin shirt, leggings, and moccasins, with no head covering of any kind. Their hair, in two queues gathered back of their ears and wrapped in bright-colored yarn, rested on their shoulders. The agent had provided each with a new red blanket, which they wore largely for ornament.

Each Indian had provided himself with a baggage fold, such as were commonly used for the protection of their "fancy dress" and more valuable possessions. These were made of buffalo hide with the hair removed but not tanned, and folded while damp and allowed to set. They were closed lengthwise by the edges of the hide folded back to lap along the center and then crosswise, forming an envelopelike receptacle, about eighteen by thirty-six inches in size.

Each *sazh* (hide trunk) was decorated in various colors with the owners' symbols recording their principal achievements in sign writing, and contained their gala dress to be assumed on special occasions. Each also contained a present for the president, consisting of valuable articles of Mescalero make. These were mostly robes of the finest furs the country produced, blended harmoniously in designs like a patchwork quilt with all the signs done in sinew; there were also beautiful samples of beadwork, arms, and specially designed equipment included in their offerings. Santana's gift was a large robe, the hide of a buffalo heifer, flossed to the grain and soft as silk. This had been surrounded with beaver pelts and lined with soft fur-like skins of antelope fawns, then bound with a border of beadwork and a finishing fringe of buffalo mane.

The length of the trip across the Plains proved a wonder to the Indians. They were all men past middle age, but none had made the trip before. Some of their ancestors had, however, and the phrases "long, long trail" and "many days" had been used to describe such trips. But their conception of the meaning of these descriptions had been vague and unappreciated.

To the Mescalero, the entire journey was through enemy country, but the presence of their military escort relieved them of any anxiety for their safety. A number of bands of, to them, hostile tribes were met on the way with whom salutations were exchanged; and some communication consisting of remarks and inquiries was accomplished by means of the universal sign language, although the very names of some of these tribes were strange.

The geography along the route was of great interest to the Indians. That no mountain ranges intervened was a surprise that provoked hours of talk and speculation. The trip was delayed on several occasions to allow the Indians to ride to elevated positions and view the surrounding country through field glasses. The Mescalero were familiar with buffalo in the Comanche country, and immense herds of the animals were no novelty. But there the high land contours limited their vision to a few miles, while here from an isolated elevation, surrounded by level plain, the range of the glasses disclosed no end of the grazing beasts. The scarcity of timber and the total absence of conifers was also remarkable to them. And as they neared their journey's end, the number of flowing streams delighted them, but the consensus of opinion was that all in all the Sacramento Mountains country was much to be preferred to this.

The muddy Missouri River, the Indians declared, was ten times bigger than the Rio Grande in flood, and the hundreds of freight teams loading from the warehouses were so far beyond anything they could imagine that they walked far out on the prairie to convince themselves that there was nothing wrong with their eyes. Then, when they found the same sights on their return, they concluded there was something miraculous about this for so many mules and oxen would starve to death before they could travel far enough for all to graze.

The Indians were dazed by the crowds of people rushing about the little town of St. Joseph and refused to board the steamboat. Their experience in fording swollen streams in their own country convinced them that no power on earth could combat such a volume of water as the Missouri River and that the boat would be swept over the edge of the world with all onboard.

Consequently, the trip was delayed a day to permit them to adjust and watch the arrival and departure of the boats. To convince the Indians of the safety of the boats the lieutenant arranged an interview with some northern Sioux Indians, who were returning from a trip similar to that of the Mescalero. This began with sign language, which soon proved inadequate and two interpreters had to be employed, to get the Sioux into English and then into Mescalero. But a few hours of conversation satisfied the Mescalero that the white men knew the river and the boats and could manage them. So they agreed to go on.

The boat made occasional landings and tied up at night so Santana's party regained their confidence. But they watched and listened for everything they could understand, keeping the interpreter at their side and demanding explanations of everything. The lieutenant, also, was called on frequently, and even he could not always satisfy their curiosity.

"Is this the biggest river in the world?" demanded Santana of the interpreter. But all that he could say was that it was the biggest he had ever seen, so the matter was referred to the lieutenant.

"No indeed," the officer said in answer to the question, "we will soon see a river more than twice as big as this. And there is a water the other side of Washington where it takes a whole month of travel after leaving one side before land can be seen again on the other." The old chief could not believe this and told the interpreter he thought the lieutenant was lying.

The Mississippi River was reached in the late afternoon of a gloomy day. The sky was overcast with low foglike clouds, and the visibility was poor. The south bank of the river, not far distant, was the only land in sight, and the Indians could see no houses. They were expecting the boat would soon round in to a landing for the night so strained their eyes toward the northern shore while the boat glided out onto the "father of waters." Turning back to the south Santana remarked, "Water, nothing but water; if they have been lying and this is the edge of the world, they must know how to fly away and leave us."

The Indians hunted up the interpreter, and he also seemed to be uneasy but tried not to show it. Santana repeated his observation and insisted on finding the lieutenant. The boat's lights were burning, and all but this group seemed quietly content, which was reassuring. And when the lieutenant was found, he called their attention to specks of light some distance away, which he assured them were lights in the houses along the shore. Then he explained that they were near their destination and would not camp again until they arrived.

The old chief remarked, "Maybe we are just old women, but this makes the hair stand up on my neck worse than it ever did before."

The Indians sought out a shadowed spot and watched for the specks of light to be seen at intervals, until the city lights appeared. The boat seemed to be headed directly for the illuminated area, and the assurance of the lieutenant was again required to persuade them that they were not headed into a forest fire. But when the boat tied up in the long row already at the wharf and they were told their voyage was over, they wrapped their blankets about them and slept.

St. Louis was the first city any of the Indians had ever seen. They had been told of cities, but as with descriptions of the "big water" they thought their informants were lying and paid little attention to the magnitudes described. However, a day of sightseeing opened their eyes to the possibility that the information had been accurate. The most incredible yarn, to them, had been that there were so many people in the cities that all of them could not live on the ground and built their houses on the top of other people's houses. Here they found that not only had that tale been true, but that there were even some houses on top of the second tier.

The boats along the riverside prompted an observation from Santana, "They have as many boats as the Comanche have horses, and some of them are big enough for all the Mescalero to ride at one time." However, overall the stoicism the Indians displayed with reference to the immense buildings, great stock of goods, and the multitude of people was surprising.

Since they were becoming accustomed to big things and strange sights, when they boarded a train they were not fearful at first. "The houses on wheels" were not very big, but the Indians were skeptical when they were told that they would be pulled by an iron horse that could run all day without getting tired. When the train started off with a succession of jerks, they all leaped to their feet. However, the other passengers remained in their seats so they settled down. And when the train gained velocity and steady motion, they were uneasy to know if the horse was running away, but when told that this was its usual gait they concluded it was not well broken and had tried to buck.

The few days in Washington were spent in sightseeing. Their guides led the Indians to such places as it was supposed would impress them most with the power and resources of the government. But the great stores of arms, ammunition, military equipment, and so forth induced no comment, and the Indians' stoicism was misunderstood for indifference by their guides. Barracks and drills of the various branches of the service appeared to be exactly what they expected to see.

They were taken to the museum, where their presents for the president were effectively displayed in glass cases, and were told that they would be kept forever by the president's order, so that people might always see what beautiful work the Mescalero could do. This was quite interesting, and they spent some time comparing this exhibit with similar displays of objects from other tribes.

When the Indians were presented to the president, he gave them time for talk and told them that he would have a paper and a medal prepared to confirm Santana's appointment as head chief of all the Mescalero because he had proved himself a wise man and kept his people at peace.

Then the president explained to the Indians the attitude of the government toward the Mescalero, thus: "The white people are so many that they must have all the country to produce all the food needed for all the people, but they have found ways of making much more food grow on the same ground so there will be plenty for the Indians and the white people, too, who will live in the Indian country. The government does not want to destroy the Indians but wishes that the different tribes should live together with the white men like all were brothers in the same country, and that the Indians learn the ways of the white men so that all will have plenty. And while the Indians are learning these new ways, the government will give the Indians food and clothing so that they will not need to take it from their brothers."

This little speech proved to be much more important than anyone realized at the time, and more effective in the control of the Mescalero than everything the military ever did. The president had, inadvertently, used language that, when translated, reached the Indians' understanding and answered the question that Santana had failed to answer: Why did the troops not exterminate the Indians? He realized that they could, but now he knew from his personal contact with the president that he with his great power was restraining the troops and his people to preserve the Indians. This was logical, proved by their actions as he understood them.

Thus, Santana and his men were convinced that Grant was a great man personally, and as the president, little less than a god. He was a friend of the Indians, and, although he was under the influence of the white man's law, they were ready to support him in any undertaking.

The Indians attended a number of functions, a ball among them, where the gaudy uniforms and the bright, fantastic costumes of the ladies delighted them. A sleight of hand performance convinced them that their medicine men at home were but *iskenyeh* (children) in comparison with this white man. But the promise of a medal by the president proved to be the outstanding incident of the whole trip to Santana. For here he conceived the idea that the medal promised him would be presented with some such ceremony as that he had witnessed. He was of two minds, whether he would prefer that the president journey to the Mescalero country for the ceremony, where his people could witness his triumph, or that he himself should return to Washington for the occasion, where so many more white people would be present. However, he was not consulted in the matter.

The return trip was uneventful. The Indians had learned to trust the lieutenant, and, with few exceptions, believed what he told them. The marvels that had left them half-dazed on their way to the East were still in evidence to confirm their first impressions but were now usually taken as a matter of course. And the delegation reached their camp near Fort Stanton in due time.

PASSING ON TRADITION

Roman, in collaboration with Gorgonio, had organized the classes in traditions of the tribe earlier than usual to entertain the boys and young men, and now that the autumn was advancing into winter and the long, cool evenings encouraged gatherings within the tents, these were gaining in popularity. When the medicine men were not delivering their lectures, tales and anecdotes filled up the time.

"Many tens of tens of tens of winters gone," Gorgonio began his lecture, "all the people in the world were one people, and none of them ate meat, for Eyata had made many kinds of food to grow upon the ground, and no animals or birds or other things ate the flesh of anything that lives, only the food that grew on the ground.

"Then all the people were friends, and all the people, and all the animals, and all the birds, and all the other things that live were friends together. And all were good like Eyata made them. And all lived to be very old, and there were many young, so that the world was filled with people, and animals, and birds, and other things. Then Eyata went far away to make another world.

"And when Eyata was gone far away to make another world, Chete Neh came and gave the people bad thoughts (spirits) for he was bad. But there were too many people for him to give bad thoughts to all. And when Eyata came back, he gave all the other people good thoughts, for they were his people whom he had made.

139

Then Eyata made a law that all things that live must die. And the new world that he had made was only for the spirits of the people who die and not for the dead people. And all the spirits of people who die with good thoughts camp in the new world that he had made and become his people. And all the spirits of people who die with bad thoughts had to stay here in this world and be the people of Chete Neh.

"And when Eyata was gone far away to the new world that he had made for the spirits of the people who died with good thoughts, Chete Neh was here. He made little rain come so that there was not enough food growing on the ground for all the people, and all the animals, and all the birds, and all the other things that lived in the world. And when all the people were hungry, Chete Neh said to his people, "Kill some of the animals and eat their flesh," and Chete Neh's people ate meat.

And when the other people saw the people of Chete Neh eat meat, they killed some of the animals and ate meat.

"And when all the people had thoughts, Matah was very old and very wise and he was iskenyeh and had no thoughts for he had never taken a woman. And Eyata said Matah should be Nant'a (a representative of Deity on earth) and should not die while iskenyeh; and when he was "old to death" he should be young again. When Matah was very "old to death," Eyata made him young again many times, for he took no woman.

"And Chete Neh had no place to keep the spirits of his people who died with bad thoughts, and he made some kinds of animals, and some kinds of birds, and snakes, and lizards, and fish, and other things for the spirits of his people to go into when they died with bad thoughts.

"And Chete Neh told many of the people bad thoughts so he would have more people, and he told Nant'a many bad thoughts. But when Chete Neh told Nant'a bad thoughts, he thought good thoughts, and the bad thoughts could not stay in him.

"And when all the people ate meat since there was little rain to make food grow on the ground, Eyata said, 'It is good, for there are too many of all kinds of things in the world, and animals, birds, and the other things can have plenty of food on the ground when little rain comes if the people eat their flesh.'

"And when Eyata was far away in the world he had made for the spirits of his people who had died with good thoughts, Nant'a wanted a woman. And Chete Neh told him that a ch'eeke was not a woman and had no soul, so that if he took a ch'eeke he would have no soul and still be iskenyeh and not die when he was 'old to death,' and Nant'a did not know that was a bad thought.

"Then Nant'a took a ch'eeke, and the ch'eeke had two boys at one time. And Nant'a had good thoughts and bad thoughts, too, and could die because he took the ch'eeke; and that made her a woman and him a man, and they both had spirits.

"And all the people said Eyata would be angry because a ch'eeke had two boys at one time before she had a soul. But Nant'a said it was his fault because he had taken her, and she did have a soul, and they were his boys.

"Then when Nant'a was 'very old to death' again Eyata would not make him young again for he had both kinds of thoughts. But he taught some very good men to take the bad thoughts from the people of Chete Neh, and how to cure some of the troubles that make people die, and they made Nant'a good again until he died.

"And Eyata made a law that all ch'eeke should be watched from the first sign of puberty until they should be publicly declared *iszhah* (women), and that no man should touch a ch'eekee on pain of death. That is the law now.

"When Nant'a was dead, he was very old, and his sons were very old. And there was no Nant'a for all the people, and the people said the oldest son of Nant'a should be the Nant'a of all the people, but Eyata did not say who should be the Nant'a. However, the people of Chete Neh said, 'Is Lhizhi the oldest son of Nant'a?' for these were the sons of Nant'a that was dead. But their mother was dead, and the old women that were there when they were born were dead, and none knew which was born first.

"And some of the people wanted Lhizhi to be Nant'a, and some of the people wanted Lhitsue to be Nant'a. And when Chete Neh saw that some wanted one and some wanted the other he made each one believe that he was born first and that he should be Nant'a.

"Then Lhitsue told the people that he was born first, for that was what Chete Neh made him believe. And Lhizhi said he was born first, for that was what Chete Neh made him believe. But both lied, for they did not say that they only believed it.

"And Chete Neh made some of the people believe what Lhizhi said and some of the people believe what Lhitsue said so that some thought one lied. And some thought the other lied, and the people of Chete Neh wanted to kill them both, for they thought they did not have bad thoughts.

"But there were more people who had good thoughts that would not let them kill either one, and they said, 'Let these two brothers talk by themselves alone and see which would be Nant'a.' And when they talked alone by themselves, Chete Neh kept the lies in the two brothers' thoughts and told each of them that the other had lies in his thoughts; so when they talked alone by themselves they were both mad, and neither would say that the other should be Nant'a.

"Then all the people that were wise said no one could know which was born first, and they said, 'We will go in the cave, each one alone, and all that want Lhizhi will make a red mark on the rock, and all that want Lhitsue will make a yellow mark on the rock. If there are more yellow marks, Lhitsue will be Nant'a; and if there are more red marks, Lhizhi will be Nant'a.'

"But Chete Neh could see in the dark, and when someone made a red mark Chete Neh made a yellow mark; and when

A traditional shelter (wickiup). *Blazer Family Collection.*

someone made a yellow mark, Chete Neh made a red mark. And when the people brought fire to see if there were more red marks or more yellow marks, they were just the same.

"Then the people were all mad, each with the other. Some went with Lhizhi and some went with Lhitsue, and they fought until they were very tired. Many were hurt but not many were killed, for they fought with their hands and had no weapons. And when all the people were too tired to fight, some went with Lhizhi and some went with Lhitsue, so there were two peoples and two head men, but no Nant'a for all the people, for Eyata did not say who should be Nant'a.

"And Chete Neh saw that when there were more peoples they had more bad thoughts, and he made his people put black on their faces and fight the other peoples, and Lhizhi's people could not know which were Lhitsue's people and fought their own people, too. And Lhitsue's people could not know which were Lhizhi's people and fought their own people, too. So Lhizhi's people put red on their faces, and Lhitsue's people put yellow on their faces; and the three peoples all fought each other.

"And there were too many people in the world who knew all about this. When the other people knew, some put red on their faces and some put yellow on their faces, and some put black on their faces. And all the people who put colors on their faces fought the people who had other colors, and some who did not want to fight put red and black and yellow on their faces and did not fight.

"Other people who did want to fight put other colors on their faces and went with other head men. And some men who wanted to be head men had no different colors to put on their faces, and they fixed their hair different so their people could know them and they could fight.

"Then there were many peoples and no Nant'a for all the people. And all the different peoples were enemies and fought all the other people, and there were not too many people in the world when there was little rain to make food grow on the ground. And when they fought, they learned to use clubs and stones and more were killed.

"And the people of Lhizhi learned to make lances with sticks burned hard in the fire and sharp. And they killed more enemies and made the other peoples go far away. But the people of Lhizhi stayed here and were the fathers of the Mescalero."

This seems to be the fundamental tradition underlying the beliefs of the various sects.

SANTANA'S MEDAL

In March of 1869, Cha's renegades destroyed an ox train near "Round Mountain" on the Tularoso, killing all with it except one boy some twelve years of age. He and a companion a few years his senior had been sent at daybreak to bring in the cattle while breakfast was being prepared, and thus escaped the onslaught of the Indians.[1]

The oxen had been driven to a swamp at some distance from the camp where the young *tule* (a large bulrush common in the swampy areas of the Southwest) was well grown but still tender, while the grass near the camp was too short for good grazing.

The boys had delayed their errand to play and had not heard the fusillade so that when they finally started the herd a part had crossed the ford but a few lingered in the stream. The older boy crossed over to get the stock started in the right direction while Benito was a short distance in the rear to bring up the stragglers.

The Indians, in the meantime, had completed their bloody work at the wagons and were coming for the cattle. They saw the boy ahead and killed him; the other, screened by the bank of the stream, heard his cries and, secreting himself in the undergrowth, escaped their observation, and made his way, about ten miles, to Tularosa, during the day.

There was a detail of six soldiers stationed there in charge of military stores and to serve as couriers. Three of these accompanied a party of some twenty of the citizens who rode out the following morning to investigate and bury the dead.

They had no expectation of finding the Indians still in the vicinity, for the troops were known to be crowding them. When they approached the site of the massacre, however, they were attacked by a large number of Indians and compelled to retreat to an earthwork, which had been constructed near there for such an emergency, where they were surrounded and fought all day. None of the defenders were killed nor seriously wounded, but they lost all their horses. They escaped during the night and reached the town in safety.

Although the dead included none of the friends Santana had warned Cha not to molest, the deed had been committed within the limits of the prohibited territory, and the attack on the party from Tularosa was in direct contempt of his order.

The medal for Santana had just been received by the commanding officer at Fort Sumner, and an orderly had been sent to ask the old chief to call at the office, when a courier from Fort Stanton arrived with dispatches reporting the fresh atrocity on the Tularosa. The commander, of course, supposed the dispatch would be news to Santana, but the orderly had met him already passing the Fort intent on consulting with his friend and adviser with relation to this very matter. Santana had much more detail than the dispatch conveyed.

Santana was in a towering rage, something the commander had never before witnessed, and the interpreter, who had been a captive among the Mescalero and had known him quite well for several years, was visibly concerned.

"Cha has defied me," roared the old chief ignoring the chair placed for him; "he has killed people on the Tularoso and tried to kill my friends." Turning to the interpreter he said, "Tell him quick," and as rapidly as possible related what had happened, which in some measure cooled him off.

"I have just received a paper from Fort Stanton about that," said the commander. "And also a paper from the President at Washington and this medal he has sent for you," he continued, opening the case and sliding the trinket across the desk.

The angry chief seated himself and for a moment lost himself in contemplation of the likeness of General Grant in profile on the burnished silver, but he did not touch it although the angry lines in his face and the snapping eyes gave way gradually to a contented smile, before assuming his wonted immobile expression.

"Where is the President?" demanded Santana raising his eyes from the medal to the commander's face.

"In Washington," was the reply, "but he sent it to me to give to you."

The old chief had fully regained his poise and after a moment of consideration, and searching the faces of the commander, the orderly and the interpreter in turn, demanded, "When will the President come? Cha has killed people on the Tularoso and I must kill him."

The commander realized that there was some misunderstanding about the medal but failed to grasp Santana's idea. But proceeding cautiously with his questions, learned that he expected to be decorated by the President in person, assuming no doubt that some such elaborate ceremony as he had witnessed in Washington would attend the presentation.

Arrived at this conclusion, the commander made a great "to do" of opening his safe, and produced therefrom a document with a great seal upon it which he showed to the chief and said, "This is a paper from the President. He is very busy just now and cannot come for some time, but he wants you to get Cha and says to tell the soldiers to help you."

"When will you give it to me?" asked Santana.

"I give it to you now," replied the commander, touching the trinket between them on the desk. But the old chief was not satisfied, and rising from his chair indignantly demanded. "Where is the band to make music? Where are the soldiers with their new clothes? Where are the women with their pretty dresses? And all the people to see you give it to me and shout?"

When the interpreter finished translating this, without dropping his voice he continued, "Don't answer yet." Then, turning as if speaking to the orderly, said, "The old man is losing his temper and his confidence in your sincerity."

The commander hesitated. He had expected Santana to accept the medal as an ornamental trinket, to be valued only as a souvenir of his trip to the Capital, and had not thought of such a contingency as had presented itself. He was convinced, as were many of his fellow officers in the field, that it would take years for the military, unaided, to subdue the renegades, and that the detention of the main tribe on the reservation was daily becoming more difficult.

Santana's change of attitude, no matter what the cause might have been, which was a matter of controversy, was the only real accomplishment so far, and his whole-hearted cooperation alone might be expected to meet with success within a reasonable time.

The interpreter asked Santana to sit down while the commander thought what to do. Then he asked permission to make a suggestion and, being requested to do so, said, "The old man is very much excited, and, from his appearance and talk, to oppose him at this time would likely cause him to take matters into his own hands regardless of any treaty and go after Cha without concern for the military. This would no doubt be the end of the outlaws, but would probably replace them with Santana and the whole tribe of several times the number of fighting men in their stead. For that reason I would suggest that the old chief be humored if possible, which would please him and make him easier to deal with."

This advice may have helped him to decide, and although the commander realized that he was setting a bad precedent, it was arranged that a dress parade should be ordered for noon of the following day.

The explanation that the President would not be able to attend for some time and wished Santana to be inaugurated as head chief of all the Mescalero, reconciled him to the idea of the commander substituting for that official. And after some consideration of details, the old chief summed up what he understood to be the program for the day.

"You will make the talk for the President.

"The band will be there to play music before the talk and after the talk.

"All the soldiers' women will be there with their prettiest dresses on.

"All the soldiers will be there with their new clothes on, and the horse soldiers will ride their horses.

"The ambulances will bring the women, and the wagons will bring plenty of food for everybody.

"And the big guns will be there to shoot a big noise when you put the medal on my neck.

"All my people will be there with their prettiest clothes on, and my men will have eagle feathers in their horses tails.

"And the medicine men will sing to Eyata when the band plays music.

"Then all the head men of the soldiers will shake hands with me, and all the head men of the Mescalero will shake hands with you."

This was considerably more elaborate than he had had in mind, but the commander issued orders accordingly, with a special request that the ladies attend in their brightest costumes.

The ceremony was staged on the open prairie a mile or more from the fort. And there were but a few guards that did not attend. The program was carried out very much as Santana had proposed, and to his great satisfaction. Then the Indians put on a peace dance to the music of the tom-toms and singing, in which big, little, old and young participated, as they alternated between the celebration and the food, while Santana, with his medal on his wampum string beside his medicine, paced back and forth receiving congratulations from everyone.[2]

When the gathering broke up Santana accompanied the commander to his office, and seating himself with great dignity, directed the interpreter to say:

"Now I am the head chief of all the Mescalero, and the President wants me to get Cha, and he killed people on the Tularoso and I must kill him, because I said I would."

Then to that officer's amazement he turned to the commander and continued, "Have all the soldiers come back so Cha will think they will let him alone. Then give my men guns, and have one company of soldiers go to The Mill with four wagons loaded with cartridges and provisions, and take twenty pack mules."

His acquaintance with Santana had never included a gun, and as their eyes met there was no suggestion of levity in the old chief's face. He could not prevent the beginning of a smile, but he made no remark and Santana went on.

"Then I will take one hundred of my best men and go after Cha. And any of his people that we catch without fighting I will send to The Mill for the soldiers to keep. And all his people that fight I will kill. Then we will have our reservation in the mountains and that will be good."

There could be no doubt of the gravity of Santana's proposition, but to the commander his attitude was incomprehensible. But recalling the snappish temper of the day before, he said, "I will have to talk to the other officers first, and that will take some time. Why don't you take your men and help the soldiers get Cha?" he temporized.

"Because," said Santana, "the soldiers fight one way and the Mescalero another way, and Cha's men would be afraid to let the soldiers catch them and would all fight and have to be killed."

The Indian problem at this time was very serious, and little success had been had. The Indians' rights people were gaining strength and influence, and with the avowed purpose of preventing the extermination of the "red man," while exploiters had been able to ignore many of the treaties made with a number of the stronger tribes. And in a number of instances where a large majority of a smaller tribe was peacefully under military control, they had been utterly destroyed by the troops, or enraged settlers, in revenge for atrocities committed by bands of outlaws, similar to Cha's renegades from the Mescalero, while the real culprits, being on their guard, escaped unscathed.

Santana's Mescalero had, in years past, acquired the reputation of being the most blood-thirsty and dreaded of any tribe of its size in the Southwest and now, all but a small minority had been content to remain peaceably on the reservation for the past four years. Santana appeared to have decided to punish his rebellious brother for violating his orders, and was equally firm in his refusal to co-operate with the troops in such punishment for reasons that, to him, were good.[3]

The commander secured his promise to defer his vengeance until orders could be had from the department commander, on condition that Santana should be allowed in the meantime to send scouts into the mountains to learn the exact conditions to be contended with, and passes were issued to ten men the chief had selected as spies.

The commander made the trip to Santa Fe to save time and placed the matter before his superior officer in person, recounting the occurrence at the fort, and convincing headquarters that the main tribe was thoroughly aroused and could not be otherwise controlled, and the necessary orders were issued.

The troops withdrawn from the field, however, were to remain at Fort Stanton in readiness for immediate duty should an emergency arise. Two companies were posted at The Mill, instead of one as Santana had ordered, and a stockade was to be prepared for any prisoners that might be taken.

Santana's program was carried out, in a general way, and on arrival of his warriors at The Mill, he divided them into parties of ten or a dozen each, under the direction of his trusted leaders.

These parties he sent into those localities where he was informed the scattered bands of Cha's followers were to be found. His acquaintance with all concerned made it possible to distribute the personnel of his parties in such manner that the bands they were to approach consisted of their friends and relatives, in most instances, and they were instructed to make no hostile demonstration unless attacked, but to try to communicate with individuals they thought would surrender without resistance.

Santana himself led one of these parties into the Fresnal country where Cha had been reported to have been found, but failed to find him. Peace signs with arrows pointing to a figure recognizable as the house at The Mill were posted on trees and rocks wherever they went, and all the hostiles found were assured of good treatment if they surrendered, and extinction if they did not.

By this means there were several deserters from Cha's followers in the stockade within a week. And although treated as prisoners of war, they were well fed and liberally provided with all possible comforts.

Nearly all the non-combatants, and a number of Cha's fighting men gave up without resistance before he took alarm and gathered his forces to attack Santana's convoy escorting a party of prisoners to the Mill.

He was repulsed, however, and Santana concentrated his forces and several sharp skirmishes followed. Two of Santana's men were killed, and a number of wounded were brought to the Mill for treatment, which had been provided for with both the Indian medicine men and the army surgeons available.

Cha had acquired sufficient good guns for all his men, but of several different makes and lack of ammunition soon put them at a disadvantage, while the aggressors, who under Indian tactics, are usually at great disadvantage, in this instance were provided with the latest military issue and the government pack mules in charge of a detail of scouts, kept a bountiful supply of ammunition and rations constantly available for Santana's men, so their poor marksmanship was effectually minimized, and no time lost in hunting food.

Thus Cha's forces were rapidly reduced by desertions, wounded, and fatalities, until he abandoned his wounded and the few women and children still with them and fell back to the edge of the foothills for a last stand among the rocks, from where, with their better supply of horses, they hoped to escape to their old rendezvous in the Jarillas.

The outlaws were now greatly outnumbered, and Santana had anticipated this move, so the remnant of Cha's band were met by half of Santana's force and with those in pursuit, surrounded. The last engagement was, of course, a massacre, but the insurgents resisted to the last man. In hand to hand combat a half dozen were taken alive, among them Cha, who had been felled by a blow from a war club. These were brought before Santana where he sat on a log with a broken arm to decide the fate of the prisoners. Four proved to be renegades from other tribes whom Santana allowed to choose between being delivered to the military or executed on the spot. Two chose to be made prisoners, and the other two were shot by Santana's orders.

Cha stood braced against a tree between two warriors, blood still trickled down his face and clotted in the hair of one of his loosened queues that partly covered it, and another Mescalero lay dying near by.

"You are my father's son," said Santana, "and your brothers loved you well, but you defied me who am the chief of all the Mescalero, and killed people and took horses when I told you the Mescalero must quit doing these things. Some of the people that were with you want to be given to the soldiers, and some of them are dead, but because you are my father's son I will not take you to the soldiers for they would hang you with a rope and not put you away right, but I will kill you myself and put you away right, for you are my father's son."

Cha straightened himself up against the tree and pushed his captors back. "I care little," he replied; "I think you are like an old woman and afraid to fight the soldiers and the people, and a coward is no brother of mine."

Santana raised his pistol and shot him in the forehead.[4]

COMANCHE AND BUFFALO

Back at Fort Stanton Santana proved more domineering than ever. His medal, which he wore constantly beside his medicine charm, on a necklace of elk tusks, beads, and shells about his neck, gave him an exalted opinion of his importance, while his late success caused him to magnify his already high opinion of his efficiency.

Santana's treatment of the renegades had a salutary effect on his standing with his followers, some of whom had conceived the idea that the old chief had lost his grip.

Santana treated the post commander as an equal but practically ignored the other officers. His business with the agent he made strictly official and considered him an old woman since the affair regarding the gambling. All matters he thought important were discussed with the commander (major), and any matters that the officers could not reconcile with the chief were postponed by mutual agreement to be referred to the colonel. The colonel, the department commander at Santa Fe who had issued the orders allowing him to subdue the renegades, was now only a little less important to Santana than the President, who had raised him to his present dignity. Consequently, this provided a way for appeasing Santana. He had never seen the colonel but accepted his decisions as if they were absolute wisdom, and many trivial matters were disposed of by the major after a few days' delay, without being referred.

Santana had in mind, when he had arrived at the decision to

surrender, that the Mescalero would soon be given a reservation in the mountains, where they might live in peace and in their accustomed environment. This matter had been discussed time and again in the past, and the excuse that Cha must be subdued before the idea could be given consideration was presented. But that, now, was an accomplished feat, and Santana insisted that such an arrangement be taken up with the colonel.

Since Cha had been disposed of, although occasional depredations were reported, some of which were committed by Indians and probably some by Santana's followers, they were comparatively few. Comanche, Kiowa and Apache from the western tribes, were known to have been in the country at times. There were also numbers of outlaw whites and Mexicans robbing and killing throughout the country whose outrages were sometimes laid to the Indians.

The Mescalero were impatient for the move, and Santana declared that they must be allowed to return to the mountains by the following spring or his people would begin to desert him again. And further, he argued, the criminal element could be kept from escaping there, where his people knew all the hiding places.

This contention was urged particularly with reference to marauding Comanche who had stolen some of the Mescalero's horses and a few of their women while a considerable number of Santana's fighters were away after Cha. They had been followed by a band of Mescalero who had been defeated and driven back, but having engaged the marauders, insisted that they were Comanche. However, an investigation had been made, and the report just received that the Comanche had not been out and that there were no Mescalero women nor horses among them.

The Comanche were Plains Indians and lived in the country from which the Mescalero derived their supply of buffalo hides for tipis and a large portion of their robes. These they secured by stealth, rather than force, and their invasion of the plains for this purpose was attended with great danger, often resulting in encounters with superior numbers of the Comanche. This made it necessary that such expeditions include considerable numbers of Mescalero; for, although the Comanche country was an immense territory, the tribe was much more numerous than the Mescalero.

The Mescalero were enraged at their losses and had demanded that Santana lead a large force against the Comanche for revenge and to take horses in reprisal. This he knew would not be authorized and succeeded in delaying the campaign until the time of the buffalo hunt, when he proposed to ask for additional guards who would be able to attack their despoilers without direct opposition to the authorities.[1]

Santana had brought up the subject of the buffalo hunt with the major and asked for passes for sixty additional men on account of the recent raid. When the treaty had been under discussion, the number of Indians to be off the reservation at the same time was forty men and forty women; this number had been strongly opposed as a menace to such military force as was usually available but was finally acceded to. The major refused to give his consent for additional warriors and as usual Santana proposed to refer the matter to the colonel.

A month still intervened before the buffalo hides would be in prime condition, and under ordinary circumstances this was ample time to get orders and adjust the matter. But it so happened that the colonel in command of the department was absent when the communication reached Santa Fe, and the officer in charge, not realizing the importance of the matter, laid it aside for the attention of his superior on his return.

When time for the buffalo hunt was at hand, Santana again brought up the matter of an increased number of guards for the expedition. The major had been anxiously awaiting the instructions he had asked for, but a note just received said his dispatch would have immediate attention on the return of the colonel, within two weeks. He was wholly at a loss as to what he might do without getting himself into serious trouble. To permit a hundred Mescalero warriors to invade the Comanche country in their vindictive mood, without authority or precautions, was a greater responsibility than he was willing to assume. "The colonel has not told me what to do yet," he told the chief, "but I may get a letter any day, and we will have to wait, for I cannot decide this matter."

"The hunt must begin now, insisted Santana, "for soon the very cold winds [northers] will come, and only with good tipis can my people live here on the plains when the very cold winds come."

"The agent will give you more cloth to make tents for this winter so you will not have to hunt buffalo this year," proposed the major.

Santana, however, had not revealed all that was in his mind. His capitulation had not included a cessation of the Mescalero's natural enmity toward their neighbors, and he knew he could not long restrain their tribal hatred of the Comanche. Even his brothers had shown displeasure at the delay.

"No," replied the chief. "The very cold winds tear the cloth tents to pieces, and all our children would die of cold if we had only cloth tents here on the plains. All that were in cloth tents last year would have died if they had not gone into the tipis when the very cold winds came. And now there are not enough tipis for all to go into."

"I will send some soldiers with the hunters for protection," offered the major.

"The Comanche could crawl all around the soldiers," objected Santana, "and kill half my people before anyone woke up, and they wouldn't come in the daytime."

The time allotted for the buffalo hunt was sixty days, and the major expected a further delay of a week or more before he would receive such orders as the colonel might issue for his guidance. Santana was assuming that his appointment as chief gave him authority over all matters pertaining to the Mescalero, and was visibly uneasy in his pressing for an immediate answer.

"I must obey the orders of the colonel," the major told him. "And my orders are to do all that the paper you signed says to do and nothing else without his orders. You can have a pass for forty men and forty women, and if you must have buffalo hides and must have extra men to protect the hunters, I will tell the colonel what you say but will do nothing more until I get orders what to do, unless people are attacked or their stock stolen."

"Now you talk with one tongue," said Santana, "and I will talk to you with one tongue, too, as my friend, not as a soldier. My people will fight the Comanche because they took our horses and our women. And I want them to do it, but if I did not want them to do it they would do that anyway. So if I tell them to fight, they will think we are all together and do as I say, and not fight any people but the Comanche. And you can tell the colonel that you do not know if other Mescalero are gone, because I will come here every day; and you will know that I am here, for I will not go with the hunt.

"The Mescalero will take their own horses if they can find them, and their own women. And if they cannot find them they will take Comanche's women and Comanche's horses, but no other people's things will be taken. And my people of the hunt will not take anything but buffalo."

"I will tell the colonel what you say," agreed the major, "and we will be friends just as we have been. But I do not say yes, and I do not tell you no; so whatever the colonel tells me to do I will do, and what the Mescalero do I will not try to find out."

Santana sat for a time in deep thought and then said, "I will tell you nothing more about this then."

A courier was started at once to Santa Fe with a full report of the conference, and the major's opinion that the Mescalero could not be restrained in the matter except by force, which if resorted to would probably involve the whole tribe, and with his recommendation that their defiance be ignored in so far as possible.

At the camp Santana called his brothers and told them what had passed at the fort, then said, "I think if our people fight the Comanche, the soldiers will be like they know nothing about it; but if our people take any horses or cattle from other people, we will have to fight the soldiers and the people like we did before, and they are many more. It is better to be friends."

Roman reported that some of the Mescalero had already begun a War Dance in anticipation of the arrangements they had expected Santana to make. Roman heard that thirty warriors had joined the War Dance the night before but that no leader had been selected, as they expected Santana to take that position. But now that he had agreed to stay at the reservation, it would be necessary to see that no "hot head" take the lead. So Santana told Cadete to take charge of the war party and Roman to get the hunters off as soon as possible.

The War Dance was held several miles down the river in an open glade surrounded by a heavy growth of cottonwoods and underbrush. Beginning well after dark, it was illuminated by a large fire, quite in contrast to the usual small fires of the Mescalero, and this was concealed by Santana's orders. Several great logs formed the body of the pyre-like pile, with dry branches thrust into the crevices. Flames shot high into the air, not, however, higher than the surrounding treetops, so the illumination would not attract the attention of the sentries at the fort. More than a score of painted warriors leaped and shouted close about the roaring flames, each adorned with his symbolic headpiece. The heat of the fire and their fantastic gyrations caused streams of perspiration to furrow the traditional designs painted on their bodies.

A leather belt about each waist held the ornamented doeskin breechclout in place and supported knife, war club, and such receptacles as held smaller articles required in battle. Their legs were bare, and the low moccasins on their feet, provided with long buckskin fringes pendent from their heels, were beaded at the front in symbolic designs. Bow and arrow quivers were strapped on their backs, and each carried in his hands a gun or a lance, or both.

From time to time the beating of the tom-toms ceased while a member of this nucleus of the recruiting war party proclaimed the cause and object of the proposed expedition. Or, in boastful words and pantomime, they described earlier conquests, shouted their individual songs, and demonstrated their personal prowess in great leaps, bounds, and dodges to illustrate the successful maneuvers by which they had escaped an enemy's onslaught or overcome an opponent.

A semi-visible audience, warriors and a few women, were dancing, shouting, and indulging in improvised fantastic gyrations in the weird shadows at the edge of the timber. Surprising, momentary glimpses of painted torsos, alternating with queer headpieces designed to represent known or imaginary creatures, indicated the presence of other candidates for the enterprise. Experienced and efficient warriors past the prime of life hesitated, not through cowardice, but because existing circumstances had set a limit to the number of men to be recruited for the present undertaking, and only the flowering manhood was to be accepted. Convalescents and untried youths were being turned away, but those pursuing personal grievances and not otherwise barred were already among the accepted volunteers. Pugnacious women among the audience screeched in vain in their efforts to fill the ranks; many candidates came forward to be rejected by Cadete and only a few were accepted. And as the fire gradually faded away, the War Dance was adjourned to be resumed the following night.

Thus were the Mescalero war parties enlisted, when for voluntary service. During the course of enlistment, the warriors adjourned from time to time until the desired strength was secured. Those publicly supporting the cause were definitely held to their obligation until the enterprise was undertaken or finally abandoned by common consent or the one-year limitation for all obligations released them.

The Buffalo Dance was celebrated during daylight— at sunrise, noon, and sunset—then repeated when the darkness of night had fallen so the stars would be propitiated, for, when the kill was successful, the skinning and preparation of the hides and meat continued far into the night. The public participated. The men that were to take part in the hunt wore headdresses surmounted with buffalo horns. Wrapped in buffalo robes, they danced about a firepit, where one or more medicine men fed a fire with buffalo chips and fragrant herbs while chanting prayers appropriate to the occasion.

Santana had selected fifty of his most trustworthy warriors to be included in the war party, who had been quietly consulted and agreed to delay joining the War Dance until the hunters had left with their passes. This way there would be no appreciable lack of occupants at the camp for the agent to observe. These fifty were to join the volunteers the night after the hunters were gone, thus giving the young bloods a few days of exciting anticipation and at the same time limiting the participants to experienced and easily controlled men.

The hunters traveled to the northeast; the country to be visited was an area of low rounded hills where the depressions, in most instances, were traversed by gullies cut by the runoff of the infrequent rains. A few streams, of more or less permanent character, usually provided water, and when not actually flowing, numerous holes excavated by the floods retained an abundant supply for a considerable time after the runoff was past. The Indians depended on such a supply this late in the season, a month or more after the rainy season. Where these wet-weather streams debouched into the more level stretches, in many places water accumulated in ponds of considerable size and for some months provided amply for the immense numbers of buffalo migrating from their summer grazing grounds to the warmer sections at this season. These ponds were dignified by the name of lakes and boasted appellations by which they were identified, but were, in fact, less dependable and more polluted than the water holes in the gullies, after the buffalo reached their vicinity.

At intervals along the draws were clumps of trees, mostly cottonwood, often with thick undergrowth. And about the lakes hardy species of willow and some other shrubs grew profusely where the gradually receding margins of the water furnished moisture for several months of the growing season. The curly buffalo grass carpeted hill and dale to a depth of several inches, with clumps of weeds and brush sparsely distributed. This provided the only chance of concealment except for the rolling hills and the bushes.

This was no man's land. Here the Comanche in roving bands liked to spend the summers. There was abundant grazing for their large herds of horses without depleting the winter supply along the permanent streams further north, the usual home of the tribe. The distances between the lakes prevented mixing of the herds, and a family or a small band of a dozen or so tended a herd of several hundred head.

The Mescalero were normally mountain Indians, and they usually came to this region only at the approach of winter to supply themselves with the great number of hides nature had provided for their comfort. The Comanche claimed no right to the buffalo, but the hunting of the animals with primitive lances and arrows involved a strenuous and dangerous occupation which made the hides their enemies had taken a prize worth fighting for. And the Mescalero, who raised few horses, found the extensive herds of the Comanche rich reward for their prowess. Additionally, when opportunity offered, Comanche women became captives of the Mescalero and were carried off with the captured horses. And war parties of Comanche were organized from time to time to retake the stolen property, and take Mescalero women as captives among the Comanche. As a rule, the recovery of the individual women, previously captured by either tribe was not the object of an expedition, for a woman was a woman; the object was to secure items of the greatest possible value to be had.

The taking of an enemy's wealth enriched the successful individual directly and in no way remunerated a previous loser. But such achievements redounded to the glory of the tribe and its importance as a whole, as well as providing a source of supply for the replacement of losses. Thus, the warfare between the neighboring tribes had made them enemies from time immemorial. However, the enmity between the tribes was of a mortal nature, it did not prevent individual intercourse, and a sort of armistice frequently provided for invited guests from the other tribe to be entertained under guarantee of safe conduct, usually only for a few days while the visitor attended the haheh with the object of securing some noted warrior's daughter for a wife. Consequently, there were a few legitimate wives in either tribe who were full-blooded descendants of the other. A majority of the captives were also married in the usual way by their captors, or to a purchaser for a consideration.

The hunting party proceeded cautiously, with horsemen well in advance to avoid meeting enemies and to find the buffalo. Their object was to find an isolated herd of a few hundred, which, when located, were to be kept in sight from distant eminences while the "kill" was being prepared. This was accomplished by first finding water in a favorable location and establishing camp. The "killers" were then selected and "herders" detailed to bring the game to the vicinity of some place of concealment—a deep depression or a grove of trees—where the mounted killers would be out of sight. Under favorable conditions this required only a few hours, but at times a stampede, or other contingencies, caused radical changes of plans.

Occasionally, too, enemies were found to be in the vicinity, and unless they could be exterminated would bring overwhelming numbers against the Mescalero, making it necessary to defer the kill until they were safely gone or some other locality was found for the continuance of the hunt.

On this occasion such was the case. When the camp site had been decided upon, scouts were sent out in every direction to reconnoiter the country round for half a day's ride, and a camp of Comanche was discovered consisting of ten tipis. The occupants were in charge of a herd of several hundred head of horses and an ideal object for an attack by the war party they knew would be out somewhere to the east and south of them. Precautions were taken to prevent the discovery of themselves, by posting sentinels on elevations from where the Comanche could be watched, with intermediate posts to relay information to the camp. And messengers were sent to find the belligerents, which they did the second day, and guide them to the vicinity of the Comanche camp.

With reenforcements from the hunters, they approached in the night and attacked in the early dawn. The night herders were killed in the first onslaught, and the horse herd stampeded while most of the warriors attacked the camp. All the Comanche men were killed, and six of their women made prisoners without loss to the Mescalero, other than a few wounded.

For three days the horses were driven south as a herd. Then the best were selected, each warrior taking a mount and leading two, and the balance of the captured stock was abandoned. In this manner each warrior controlled three horses and, riding some distance apart, left little sign—and that would soon be obliterated by the migrating buffalo. The horses were taken into the Guadalupe Mountains and turned loose, without any probability of being followed, far from both the Comanche country and the Mescalero camp at the fort.

The captured women were taken to the Fort Stanton area, where they were hardly distinguishable from their Mescalero sisters. Thus, the war party returned victorious after an absence of but fifteen days.

Santana was greatly relieved as nothing had been said of the absence of the warriors. He insisted, however, that the celebration of the victory should be held in the secluded spot where the War Dance had been unnoticed by their guardians.

The fancy trappings of the warriors were taken to them by their women, at a distance from the site of the celebration, and donned with the proper makeup, before their official arrival, which was deferred until night. In the meantime a great fire had been prepared, and most of the tribe was in attendance when the visitors appeared dancing about the burning logs much as on the occasion of the War Dance. In addition to those just returned, all the men who wished joined the procession and displayed their finery, but only a few speeches were made. The women had a feast prepared, and all abandoned the ceremony in a few hours, eating and dispersing at will, so that morning found the camp again tranquil.

More than two hundred horses awaited the Mescalero. The Comanche made their complaint, and the military was convinced that they had been stolen by someone else. The captive women were kept hidden and under guard in the timber several miles away while Comanche with a guard of soldiers searched the camp in vain.

The hunting party had been interrupted by the activities of the warriors, and it was probable that the destruction of the horse camp would not long remain unknown to the Comanche tribe, no doubt resulting in a declaration of war on the Mescalero. This, however, gave them little concern, for their treaty included protection by the military; and several companies of cavalry were available to protect the camp. As for themselves, they had broken camp before the attack began and traveled due east for two days with the same precautions as before but with more care to leave no trail the migrating buffalo would not soon obliterate. Also they were counting somewhat on the obvious trail the concentrated herd of horses would make in a different direction, which would certainly be followed when the theft was discovered.

Then they found another locality with favorable conditions near Round Lake and again made preparations to fulfill their mission. The herd of buffalo they had decided to kill were some three or four hundred in number and were grazing near the lake, where signs indicated they had been watering for some days.

The camp was established some three miles from this watering place, where the wash was unusually deep and provided excellent concealment, with a number of water holes to furnish abundant water for the horses as well as the hunters. A mile or more down the draw was a grove of cottonwoods in which the undergrowth was thick enough to conceal the killers. It was of ample proportions for their purpose and the only place suited to their requirements, but had the objection of being a considerable distance from the lake. Consequently, the buffalo had to be maneuvered in such way as to bring them here from the lake.

The herders followed their quarry to the water late in the afternoon and remained out of sight while the shaggy beasts drank and had their usual wallow in the mud. However, they showed themselves when the herd started to move into the plain, so that the buffalo made their exit in the desired direction. Then following the depressions the Indians kept out of sight, except from time to time when the buffalo showed signs of veering from the desired course. They showed themselves at a distance and thus directed the buffalo toward the grove until, as night came on, they bedded down.

During the night the camp was informed of the progress of the drive, and the killers with their trained horses were hidden in the grove. In the early dawn, when the buffalo resumed their grazing, the herders, still pursuing the tactics of the day before, in a few hours had them near the concealed killers.

Horses were naturally afraid of buffalo and, untrained, could not be made to approach them without great difficulty. But the killers' horses had been trained for this work by being packed with buffalo hides and ridden by their masters clothed in robes. Once accustomed to these tactics, the horses could be induced to race toward the live herd until the riders, with their lances, were within striking distance. By this means many hides were secured. The movements of the horses were directed by pressure of the riders' knees to permit the free use of the hunters' hands. The only encumbrance to the horses were the light primitive saddles of Indian make.

When the herd neared the grove, the herders rode rapidly toward it from a direction that would start the stampede toward the timber and bring the animals nearer the hidden killers. As the herd ran by, these experts abandoned their concealment, and riding beside the galloping beasts, one buffalo after another fell as a result of their well-directed lance thrusts, which were aimed to strike the spinal cord as close to the base of the brain as possible. Those with less well-trained horses kept to the rear of the racing herd to crowd it into a dense mass. And when their mounts could be brought into position they shot arrows into the younger animals there.

The hides of the great bulls leading the herd were especially desired to provide material for shields from the tough, thick hide covering the necks, which, when framed and dried were all but impervious to arrows, even at short range. To secure these, however, required immense courage. To approach within reach of a lance seldom failed to induce a charge from the bull, and an arrow was rarely effective. The misstep of a mount would bring horse and rider beneath the hoofs of the following herd, where little more than a mangled smear would mark the end of the adventurer. Nevertheless, such trophies were secured, to the great honor of the killer, and many a warrior lost his life in such attempts.

In this kill the double row of dead and stunned buffalo extended over a distance of a mile or more and included four great bulls, with no hunter to be mourned. As the escaping remnant of the buffalo herd filed out of sight, the killers turned back, leading their horses, while they finished off the buffalo still living with their knives. Men and women in the meantime were following up the kill for the same purpose. Occasionally a buffalo staggered to its feet and turned upon its persecutors, causing an excitement and requiring the assistance of an archer to prevent a tragedy. But the iron-pointed arrows seldom missed the heart and often passed clear through the body of the beast.

The rest of the day and part of the night was employed in skinning the kill, the women doing most of the work. But some of the men attended to certain carcasses whose hides they desired for special purposes. Others staggered off with loads of tongues and humps to be feasted on in camp during the following days required to prepare the hides and meat for transportation.

Many wolves soon gathered to feast upon the remains, and men on horseback dragged the hides into piles, where a guard protected them from destruction. On these exhausted skinners napped, while others kept the wolves from carcasses of choice meat. Later these would be cut into large strips and flakes to be spread upon the grass and preserved for future use as jerky.

The hides were dragged to camp by ropes attached to horses and there spread on the grass for the sun to partially remove the moisture before being folded into shape for transportation to the reservation. Thus prepared, the hides as well as the dried meat were cached in the cottonwood grove and protected from wild animals with brush and logs while another kill was being made. In the meantime, scouts roamed far and wide in search of another locality in which to continue the gathering of hides.

The second kill was also successful, completing loads for all the horses. And the hunters reached the reservation in due time, to participate in another feast and dance in celebration of a successful hunt.

BACK TO THE MOUNTAINS

The stretching and preparation of the buffalo hides provided an abundance of work for the women during the winter, while the men busied themselves inscribing records of their adventures on those that were to be used in new tipis. New shields were molded over heated clay forms and their buckskin covers decorated with the "heraldry" of their owners. Quivers for bows and arrows, both plain and fancy, were also made of the buffalo hides, as were scabbards for their guns and other arms. Young warriors used the soft tanned skins in the construction of their "fancy dress," which would be decorated in the future with the assistance of their wives or mothers, and added to from time to time until finally adopted as their own.

Santana's worries had been much relieved by the successful return of the two expeditions without any great calamity. His people were all accounted for, and nothing had been said about the absences. The hunters had furnished a guide to lead the investigating party to the place where the two buffalo kills had been made, nearly fifty-miles from the location of the camp that had been destroyed and the horses stolen.

Their usual winter's occupation provided for, Santana's followers were content, but the old chief well knew that the coming of spring would change all this and renewed the demand for a reservation in the Sacramentos. The major failed to dissuade him from the idea.

Santana contended that the bootleggers were continually bringing liquor to his people in such quantities that some of the old women always had some to sell and kept the bootleggers hidden so they were always gone before he learned of their presence. An old woman, whom he had brought to the guardhouse drunk, declared that the whiskey found in her possession was in her water jug when she went to drink, and that she had unwittingly taken a big drink from its contents before she had tasted the liquor. And a number of her friends, whom she called to testify, declared they had gotten water from a certain creek at a certain time and place, described by the prisoner, which tasted strongly of whiskey; but although they liked it and drank a great deal of it, it did not make them drunk.

On another occasion while Santana was with the major, it was reported that an ex-soldier from one of the settlements had been seen receiving a fine robe from an Indian without giving anything in return. This was thought a suspicious circumstance, and the ex-soldier was brought in for questioning. He claimed to have paid money for the robe. Santana followed the Indian and brought him back, but he also said he had received money for the robe, although he could show no cash. Finally, the matter was dropped, but Santana had the Indian watched; and the following day he was caught in the act of recovering a bottle of whiskey from where it had been hidden at the edge of the creek. Such evidence was, of course, insufficient for conviction, but all were convinced that the man was guilty.

Santana insisted that he could control such things himself if the Mescalero lived on a reservation.

At last Santana prevailed, and the Mescalero were given a reservation in 1873, which included the southern slope of White Mountain and the eastern slope of the Sacramentos to the summit. This, to some degree, reconciled the old chief, but it did not satisfy him. The Mescalero wanted their old haunts in the Tularoso country, and the high altitudes of Elk, Silver, and Whitetail

Springs country for their summer residence with its abundant game for hunting. The lower elevations, the Rinconada, Three Rivers, the Tularoso and La Luz watersheds, they wanted for winter when the heavy snows drove the game into the foothills and the plains. For here the high mountains to the east and north were barriers against the northers of the great eastern plains. The reservation given them was well watered but too small, Santana insisted, and his people would go where they wanted to. Many who lived beyond the prescribed limits were not protected by the law and would soon be in trouble with the settlers. As a result, there were clashes and many complaints of cattle being stolen; all laid to the Mescalero. From far away in Texas horses disappeared, and, when followed by their exasperated owners into the mountains, Mescalero hunters were attacked by them, justly in all probability, although they did not find the stolen stock. The whole area was known to be infested with white and Mexican outlaws, who might have been responsible.

The agency, where the Indians had to go for their rations, was located at the fort. The women who attended to the drawing of these were accompanied by few if any men. Infidelity was soon apparent. During the year the agency remained at the fort, children were born to Mescalero mothers with little appearance of Indian parentage. These, together with their mothers, were summarily disposed of, and the Indians refused to permit their women to go near the fort for any purpose.

In addition, the Indian Ring, consisting of a number of unscrupulous traders and suppliers, began a ruthless exploitation of the Indians. Censuses were tripled or quadrupled, and the excess in rations, blankets, and the like sold elsewhere and the money pocketed by the suppliers. The Indian agents were unable to control this problem, but in an effort to gain control moved their headquarters to what was known as Compton's Ranch about ten miles away. Santana demanded a larger reservation.

While the Mescalero were at the Bosque Redondo Reservation (Fort Sumner), some of the most desirable locations in their former habitat had been found by settlers, claiming advance possession under the squatters' right law. A number of these, including The Mill property, were included in the larger tract demanded by Santana.

The settlers' rights of possession would be determined by an official survey of the lands, permitting them to homestead a quarter section each. But until such survey was made and approved, the beneficial use of any amount of land was the only requirement for lawful possession. All the settlers, however, agreed to accept a reasonable compensation for their improvements and abandon their claims. An appraisement was made by a board of military officers and a bill introduced in Congress to appropriate the necessary funds to pay the appraised values.

The reservation was extended by presidential proclamation in 1875, and the agency was established at the north fork of the Tularoso, forty miles from Fort Stanton.[1]

Congress reduced the amount of the appropriation for the settlers' claims, and there was not sufficient funds, after paying off the other claims to pay the appraised value of The Mill property. At Santana's request the doctor and his associates were allowed to remain within the enlarged reservation pending further appropriation for the purchase of their improvements.

Thus, The Mill became the only settlement remaining within the reservation. Their claim was officially recognized, and the doctor was appointed "Indian trader," replacing the loss of the settlers' trade with that of the Indians in the business he had conducted during the several recent years.

The Mill was located about a mile west of the agency, and here Santana often visited his friend the doctor. Neither of them had acquired more than a meager knowledge of the Spanish language, which was the usual means of communicating with the Indians;

Mescalero girls learning to erect tipis and make cradleboards. Blazer Family Collection.

nor had either made any effort to learn the language of the other. However, a perfect confidence and their friendly cooperation provided a conglomeration of English, Spanish, Mescalero, and gestures which permitted them to understand each other.

The Indians' rations were stored in two log cabins, the former residences of dispossessed settlers. And near these a slab shack had been built to provide office room for the agent and sleeping quarters for his clerk, which were the only buildings at the agency. Consequently, the agent's wife and two daughters were quartered in the doctor's house, a part of which had been rented for the purpose.[2]

The Indians now had room to resume their interrupted manner of living. The different bands established themselves in widely separated sections of the reservation, and their ancient disagreements were revived. Old family customs and methods of entertainment, which had been impracticable during the past several years, now became familiar to the new generation.

Tales of the prowess of their ancestors were told to the boys and young men which might have been challenged while other bands were located in such close proximity as to be heard by visiting youngsters of rival families. The women disclosed profound secrets of processes, producing results peculiar to their respective clans; and greater freedom of action soon developed.[3] Santana's daughter, Katsuue, and her husband, Shash, belonged to his immediate following, and their two boys, now five and six years old respectively, were entertained by their father, even at this early age, with fairy stories designed to prepare their minds to receive instruction in the lore of their ancestors.

Shash was the accepted authority of the tribe on all matters dealing with feathers, their emblematic significance, heraldry, and witchery. Shash intended his sons to grow up with the many secrets which had been imparted to him, as well as the discoveries that he himself had made. His science was based on tradition, as most of the Mescalero learning was, and transmitted from generation to generation by word of mouth, supplemented by symbols understood only by the initiated. These tales were public property and always told in the same way to impress certain facts on the youths' growing minds. One of these was how the guiding effect of feathers became known, and Shash's ancestor was the individual first to learn their use.

"Long, long ago," said Shash, "when Lhizhi was the head man of the people, they began to use weapons to kill animals that ate the food which grew on the ground so that the people could eat their flesh, and to fight other peoples who were their enemies. No one knew about feathers.

"But my father's father's father many times was wise, and he used a long thin stick that was very hard—to fix the fire in his tipi when it was cold at night. And the fire made the end of the stick sharp and black and hard where it was burned, so it was good to kill animals to eat when they were close. But when the animals were too far away he had to throw the stick, and sometimes the stick would not go straight and would not kill the animals because the side of the stick was not sharp.

"Then when it was cold and dark one night and dark one of Chete Neh's animals came to my father's tipi and told him, 'Let me come in to get warm,' and my father let him come in to get warm. And my father put down the cover at the door and tied it again so the wind could not take it away. Then my father took the sharp stick that was black to fix the fire and made the tipi warm.

"And when the fire burned and the animal saw the stick that was sharp and black where the fire had burned it the animal made a great cry and was scared but could not untie the cover at the door to get out again. But my father was not afraid for he had the sharp stick that was black where the fire had made it sharp, and he said, 'Are you one of Chete Neh's animals? Do you have some bad spirits in you?' And the animal said, 'Yes, I have four bad spirits in me, and if you kill me with the black stick that is made sharp by fire, they will go into you and you will die.'

"Then my father told the animal, 'If I leave the stick that is black with fire in the hole where I kill you, the bad spirits cannot come out and I will take you far away and leave the stick in the hole.' Then the animal said, 'If you will not kill me with the black stick, I will tell you something that no one knows, and you will be more wise than any of the other people.'

"Then my father said, 'Tell me, and I will let you go when you are warm.' And the animal said, 'Tie eagle feathers to the small end of the pole and it will go straight, and the sharp point will kill things when they are too far away to be killed without throwing the pole.' And when the animal was warm, my father let it go.

"And when the eagle feathers were tied on the pole, like the animal said, the pole would go straight, and the sharp point would kill things when he had to throw the pole."

Katsuue had sat listening to the narration of this legend while darkness was obscuring objects about them. The children had been interested and asked questions until they became sleepy and crawled into the robes on the balsam branches, where they slept.

"Tell me something about feathers," requested Katsuue, as the full moon began to show through the fringe of pines on the mountaintop.

"There are many things about feathers that must not be told to women," responded Shash. "But maybe you do not know why owl feathers must not be used, and why hawk feathers must not be worn by women with child, and why eagle feathers are too strong for women to wear at any time."

Then lifting his eyes toward the rising moon, he sat for a time in silence, until the silvery disk cleared the treetops.

"Owls are the principal birds that Chete Neh made for the spirits of his people who died with bad thoughts, and any part of an owl is very bad medicine that only witches can use."

Then he resumed his silence as a fleecy cloud dimmed the moonlight; it soon passed, and he went on. "But owls can see in the dark, and it is not well to speak of them when there is no clear light in the sky.

"However, I can tell you about hawk feathers that are good medicine, especially for the head, for it is not too strong. All birds can fly and get the good medicine that makes them light and strong. Then the hawks eat the little birds so they can fly very fast and can fly slowly, too. But they get only the medicine that is in the flesh of the little birds they eat, for they spit out the feathers of the little birds and eat only their flesh. So the hawk feather medicine is not too strong and makes the head wise so that women can wear them.

"Eagles eat little birds, too, to get the good medicine in the feathers, but they do not spit out the feathers and they get all the medicine. And the strongest medicine is in the feathers that the hawks spit out and the eagles eat. So the eagles have much stronger medicine in their feathers, and it grows stronger as long as they live and eat more little birds. But a strong man can wear one eagle feather in his hair with a ring and be more wise but not too wise, for the strong medicine stays in the ring until the man uses it."

Paucity of tradition, as well as variety of detail, made it difficult to arrive at what, as a people, the Mescalero believed. There were a number of medicine men, and each had a following; but they varied in influence. Certain basic traditions, however, were common to all and ritualistic differences, to a large extent, were divulged only to candidates for succession to their offices.

Certain clans (sects) specialized in physical ailments, depending principally on incantations, supplemented with secret formulas of their own compounding. There were also those who specialized in certain kinds of ailments, claiming superiority for their concoctions or their personal attributes—witchcraft. And others claimed to be able to produce good or bad effects by absent treatment, which the charms commonly worn were intended to neutralize. They used sedatives and surgery to some extent. Antiseptic herbs and minerals were known and employed as well. But a large part of their ritual had no meaning beyond what might be inferred from observation of their ceremonies and traditions. There was no apparent exchange of information between the several sects. As in the "dance of the adolescent girls," although engaged in the same ceremony, each medicine man, when more than one officiated, contributed consecrated fuel to the sacred fire in the kotulh, prepared by himself, presumably from a different formula than used by the others.

Santana was a loyal supporter of Gorgonio's school of medicine, and to some extent his influence made that sect more popular. Controversies of a religious character were, no doubt, originally the cause of some of the feudal separations of the bands and of the physical clashes often occurring when intoxicated individuals met.

16

ITI'S SECOND WIFE

It was now six years since Katsuue and her friend, Datlih, had been married, and each had borne three children. Katsuue's female child had died in infancy, but her two boys were rapidly developing into sturdy youths. Datlih had not been so fortunate; death had robbed her of all three of the girls she had borne to Iti, and he had of late become unsympathetic with his wife.

Datlih's mother had died more than a year before, her sister had married, and she seldom saw her brother of late. Iti belonged to Nato's band, and their camp was located for the winter in the lower Three Rivers country, some thirty miles from the agency where the friends of her youth resided. Iti had proved a good husband as Mescalero husbands go. Datlih had been abundantly provided for, and, except for the misfortunes with their children, they had lived happily until the last few months.

Iti had lost his horse in a gambling bout and had taken an old, gentle mare that Datlih had been accustomed to using for domestic errands. This forced her to walk while her several duties continued as before. The weekly trips to the agency taxed her most severely. She could walk the thirty miles between daylight and dark very easily without a load, but the return trip with thirty or forty pounds of beef and flour was hard and took two full days. There was soap, and bacon, too, which were issued regularly in abundance, but the bacon was never touched by a Mescalero, for *guuche* (hog-filthy) was one of Chete Neh's animals and harbored the souls of his people who had died bad. They always provided themselves with a sharp stick on which the chunk of bacon, when thrust across the counter, was impaled and traded it to a Mexican, or anyone else, for almost anything; or in default of a customer it was thrown away.

The soap was useless also, for the crushed root of *amole* (soapweed) was better for the infrequent use they had for something more cleansing than mud and water. Beside that, it smelled of grease that might be guuche and she could get something for it, generally. Sugar, coffee, and various articles of clothing were also issued but added little to her load and were worth carrying.

Datlih was a thrifty person, and when riding the mare she took time to bargain for something worthwhile instead of the undesirable rations. And when she had to walk, she continued the practice as a number of her associates, similarly handicapped, had. To do this it was sometimes necessary to make an indirect trip home by way of the settlements along the lower Tularoso. This, with the delay of bargaining, prolonged the journey part of an extra day or she had to travel at night. Iti objected to such delays but liked the acquisition of the few pods of chile or handfuls of beans she gained by such efforts. The use of the mare, however, he denied her, and when she refused to go for the rations as a result, he gave her a beating.

Datlih had made several small baskets that she had intended to exchange at the trader's store for some of the gewgaws she wanted for personal adornment. These Iti took for a gambling stake in an effort to win another horse, with the promise to give her back the mare when he won; but he lost the baskets instead, and their domestic felicity was wrecked.

The horse Iti had lost was an exceptionally fine animal, a trained buffalo horse, and one of the best racers in the tribe. And although Iti, like many others, had refused to gamble with Tatsu on account of his disingenuousness, in the course of events the old gambler had acquired the horse and offered to trade it for Datlih, whom he termed "your barren wife." This proposition did not meet with Iti's approval, and instead of trading he gave Tatsu a severe beating. Iti, because of this, had been brought before a council of the head men for trial. He was convicted, but as Tatsu was recovering Iti was let off with a reprimand because of Tatsu's character and insulting proposition. However, Iti was depressed, aggravated, and despondent.

Santana had reestablished his influence in all matters within his personal observation but had lost some control due to his arbitrary punishment of evildoers, who were, in some measure, protected by the government. And the traditional practices of the tribe were not to be changed by any new ideas.

For the most part, attack on the settlers had stopped. Not that there was any change in their ideas of right and wrong, but the rations provided the Indians made it easier to live in idleness. The young men, enthused by stories of deeds of valor in the past, and a few malcontents among their elders, committed some depredations that were attributed to the Mescalero. Under the old regime Santana would have disposed of a few ringleaders and stopped the disobedience of his orders; but instead the suspects were arrested and released for lack of evidence when brought to trial.

The old chief himself did not worry about occasional brushes with enemy tribes of Indians, although he did not sanction them openly. The Comanche horses that had been left in the Guadalupes before the move which finally brought the Mescalero back to the Tularoso country, had long since been brought to the reservation and divided. Comanche spies had found some of them, and a Comanche war party had made an attack to recover them but was not very successful. The Comanche tried to stampede the horses, a ruse which might have succeeded in the plains. But in the mountains the herd scattered and none was taken except a few that were roped and led away. And although the surprise was successful, the women all escaped but one. Four Mescalero were killed, and six dead Comanche were found. Now, to revenge this fiasco, the recruiting of a party of warriors among the Mescalero had been started. It was originally proposed to raise an unusually large force, but Santana discouraged this with the assertion that such a large number being absent would be noticed by the authorities and confirm their suspicions of Mescalero depredations. With this opposition, the experienced warriors were not keen for the venture and declined the honor of participating. They were living a life of peace and plenty, with occasional drunks and numerous horse races, beside the little games always available that could be participated in daily. Consequently, the young warriors who had already committed themselves lacked the necessary leadership, as well as the courage and numbers to make a start. One of the head men had initiated the enterprise, and a medicine man had joined, but so far only five experienced warriors had been recruited.

Iti had been solicited, and the jibes of the interested women were aggravating his moroseness. He was not counted an experienced warrior, but now some thirty years of age he was known as a man of discretion. His maturity had overtaken him since the main tribe had embarked on the more peaceful mode of life. And although he had engaged in some of the stock raising, rustling, and raids, it had been in a subordinate position.

A half-dozen young warriors, among whom Iti had become a leader, proposed to join the War Dance, but all were without horses, and at least one horse for the group was thought to be necessary. As that was his only excuse the young warriors ganged up on Tatsu in a gambling game and won Iti's horse back. With this they overcame his reluctance and secured his participation. The party was thus increased to thirty men, the number Santana had prescribed as the limit. And although poorly provided with leaders, they decided to make a start.

Before the end of the first day's ride, however, a young owl lay in the trail where it had fallen from its nest and died.[1] This was a hoodoo that might not be neglected. They had been stopped by witchery, and there was something wrong with the ceremony of the War Dance. To remedy this situation it was necessary to repeat certain rites where they had been originally performed, and two days were lost in doing this. Then, two days after the second start, one of the older men's legs was broken when his horse fell with him. This did not cause much delay, for with a night's rest after the injured leg was put in splints, the sufferer was able to ride and, with one attendant, return to the reservation. But this mishap reduced their number to twenty-eight, and the enthusiasm of the party was adversely affected also.

Still misfortune followed them; they found high water in the Pecos, and the medicine man's horse was caught in an eddy so the pouch containing his paraphernalia was soaked before he was able to reach the bank. But fortunately he was one of the liberal-minded doctors and had secured some of the white man's glass bottles to protect the most important articles. These were not harmed by the water, and after the others were spread in the sun and aired for a day he pronounced his kit to be in satisfactory condition.

Nevertheless, it took another day to make supplementary medicine and reassure some faint spirits, for there was a growing suspicion that some witch had placed a hoodoo on the whole expedition. In addition, great caution was necessary on account of the small number in the party. Cattle were found at the edge of the Comanche country, causing the Mescalero to penetrate deeper into the north to avoid meeting white men in charge of them, where the Comanche might be found in great numbers. Two weeks had passed, but no enemies were discovered until they had advanced well into the territory.

The more experienced warriors were again counseling an abandonment of the enterprise when a Comanche camp was discovered.

It was larger than they had intended to attack, but a big herd of horses was being attended by a few men and a considerable number of women. From this they concluded that the warriors who usually protected the horses were away on some errand, and consequently the Mescalero prepared for an attack, in spite of caution recommended by the elders. They had been two weeks in the no man's land full of Comanche, and every day brought the danger of being seen. If a Comanche observer escaped without detection, it would be only a matter of time until they would be ambushed by an overwhelming force. A night and a day had been spent in reconnoitering, and any time the Comanche protecting the horses might return.

The horses were not being herded at night but driven into a deep wash. There a steep bank surrounded them except downstream, where they were fenced in with an obstruction of thorny brush. The tipis were a quarter of a mile away on a rather high ridge, and by driving the stock slowly the noise they would make could not be heard at the camp. The wash, although not wide, was a half-mile long, and some time would be required to drive the animals out. There were no guards set, and all seemed to indicate the Comanche expected no trouble.

Twenty of the young men on foot were stationed between the wash and the tipis, with Iti in charge. Each of these was provided with a rope, and it was intended they should each secure a mount as the horses passed out of the wash and assist in handling the loose stock. The others, mounted, would ride into the enclosure to drive out the herd.

All went well until the horses began to issue from the mouth of the wash. A few had been caught and mounted, and small bunches were being started off in the direction opposite from the camp when the Comanche yell apprised the thieves that they had been outwitted by their enemies.

A greatly superior force had been concealed among the horses in the wash, and all the mounted Mescalero behind the herd were killed. The young men trying to rope the escaping stock were killed or driven off, and Comanche warriors mounted bareback pursued those escaping. A few warriors from the tipi were held back by Iti's men while he assisted others to escape by the head of the wash, clinging to his horse. But this route was soon cut off by mounted Comanche leaving the chase of the fugitives.

Iti and some of his companions were headed off between the warriors from the camp and the wash, while others charged them from above and below. Thus, the footmen might escape by crossing the gully, but the only escape for the horseman was by evading the warriors from the camp on the ridge. This route Iti took. As he passed between the tents, a small female figure ran before him whom he picked up as he raced by.

There was no moon, and the visibility was poor; but he could see that his pursuers were spreading out to prevent him from reaching his companions, while a few fleet horses came directly toward him. To escape, he must ride to the north, where a horde of enemies might be met at any moment. But his horse was fresh and one of the fastest and strongest runners in the country. Instead of dropping his captive, he crowded the horse with her, and when dawn enabled him to see the surrounding country, no enemy was in sight.

His horse was spent, however, and he stopped at the first water he found, hobbled the horse, and bound his captive. Then from a nearby eminence he watched for signs of danger until near night. All night he rode west, and in the early morning he stalked and killed an antelope, which fed him and his captive. She was not the young girl he had thought when he had seen her in the night but a mature woman though quite small. Neither could understand the other, but she seemed to be reconciled to her fate and was only bound when not traveling.

Eleven of the expedition had reached the reservation, two

badly wounded, and news of their defeat soon spread throughout the tribe. One who had been shot through the neck with an arrow belonged to Nato's band, a neighbor of Datlih, and lay in his tent, apparently recovering. He told her that he had escaped by crossing the wash after Iti rode away and that when he reached the other bank her husband was riding through the Comanche camp well in advance of his pursuers. But none had later news.

Another brought word of the death of a comrade by his side, another of Datlih's neighbors. The dead man's tipi and all his belongings had been burned by his relatives and the camp had been moved. Elsewhere those reported "surely dead" were honored in the same manner. Few had had horses, so only a few had been sacrificed. None knew Iti's fate, but Datlih hoped for his return.

Four days elapsed and infection brought death to the sorely wounded neighbor in the camp. The tipis were all taken down, and that of the dead neighbor was burned.

Datlih then gave up all hope of Iti's return and placed all his belongings, including her own clothing and their winter's store of food, on balsam branches and dry grass, and then set fire to the kindling. She stood weeping beside the roaring fire, while a paid mourner screeched nearby where the old mare was tethered, waiting to be killed as a last rite. Datlih had sawed off the hair from one side of her head with a borrowed butcher knife and cast it in the flames; the other half was gathered in her hand for like treatment.

Suddenly, a shout arrested her, and Iti rode into camp to end her mourning, with his captive behind him on the horse. Datlih was stripped to the skin, and aside from herself and the old mare nothing remained of the wealth that Iti had left behind him.

Iti now had two women to provide for and little else. He had his horse, a robe, his arms, the clothing he wore, and his captive and his escape to brag about, when all the rest of the party had failed. Datlih had not even clothing to cover her nakedness; all had been burned in her unnecessary mourning for Iti. And the captive had but the clothing she had worn when taken. All their robes and camp equipment had been destroyed, but this was not the only family in the same condition, nor was it very unusual.

To alleviate their plight, neighbors provided the most essential clothing. And food was no great problem, for they were welcome wherever it could be found. The camp was moved only a short distance, and the impoverished families were permitted to occupy tipis with their friends for protection against the cold nights until the women could set up brush wickiups, which, with borrowed hides, provided some protection.

Iti was not much inconvenienced, and soon provided skins which the women tanned to make clothing for Datlih. Daily additions of skins and furs gradually furnished robes for the women and covered the wickiup with hides, so they soon settled down to their usual mode of life.

Datlih made no objection to the presence of the new woman and patiently taught her the language of the Mescalero while they worked harmoniously for their common good. As they became acquainted, and learned to understand each other, Datlih found that her companion was a Pueblo by birth. She had been stolen by the Navajo while yet a young girl, from a pueblo on the Rio Grande. And after several years residence with them, and having borne a son to her captor, the Comanche had carried her off. She had been a third wife of a Comanche head man, and her third abduction had separated her from her children—a girl three, and a boy four years old.

The Mescalero gave her the name Tu Enne (Pueblo of the Water People). She proved an apt pupil and by spring could make herself understood and had little trouble in following the conversation of her associates. She grieved for her children but philosophically made no effort to escape. Her pueblo home was nearly two hundred miles to the northwest, and the Comanche lived an equal distance to the northeast, while the Navajo were still farther away, beyond the pueblo where she had been born. To reach either of them would be a long hard journey, fraught with many dangers, even on horseback; and to escape with a horse would be almost impossible. Her children she knew would be well cared for by their father's people, as well as she could care for them herself.

Her Navajo boy, if living, would be big enough to look out for himself. The Comanche father was a man of large influence, and his other wives had been fond of her children, the little girl especially. So she knew that to go to them would make little difference in their lot or her own. Consequently, she accepted her situation and was thankful that her present owner and his wife treated her well.

Datlih was an expert basket maker, which Tu Enne was not. But Tu Enne had unusual talent for design and color effects that made her beadwork in demand. However, neither succeeded in communicating her talent to the other.

The approach of spring reduced the demand for tipis, and some buffalo hides were offered in barter for the closely woven baskets that Datlih made for boiling food. They were placed in heated pits, and smooth, heated stones were added to the contained liquid from time to time as required. By this means she had obtained hides for a large tipi and was offered two horses and hides for another small tipi, for making two *etsees* (water-tight basketry jugs) to be used in cooking tulhiba. The making of the drink and utensils for its making had been prohibited by Santana and would be destroyed and the makers punished if his spies found them. But the high price offered was tempting, so Datlih accepted a horse on account and agreed to make them during the summer when she could do the work in some secluded spot at a distance from the camp.

Months were required for making such utensils, for only the choicest materials could be used. Each stitch had to be tightly drawn to hold the liquid, for no filler was used, and none was known that would not flavor the heated contents except the natural juices of the *palmilla* (a species of yucca). The utensils she was to make were to be a *kahne jah* (the length of a forearm from wrist to elbow) in diameter and of equal height; they would hold about four gallons each and were to be provided with built-in loops for handling.

Smaller sizes of such utensils were made with flared tops by which they were easily moved. Various shapes of deep baskets, with or without lids, were used for containers, and their values depended largely on their size and the ornamental designs woven into them. Cold water jugs were woven loosely and smeared with pine gum to make them watertight. No great skill was required for their making, so they were usually made by their users. The pack baskets were still more crudely made of any convenient material and by anyone.

The seed beads used by Tu Enne were bought at the trader's store. Although a bunch of each of the different colors cost a small fortune when a full assortment was purchased at one time, and stained buckskin was used for backgrounds, a large number of bags, awl cases, and various other articles could be ornamented with that quantity of beads. Their making was a pastime rather than labor.

Iti's two women spent a large part of their leisure time exercising their talents, and as that was but little reduced by household duties, it was considerable. The basketry Datlih made was largely from more or less inferior materials, for the perfect pieces of palmilla and the best of the willow wands were laid aside for the contracted etsees. But the better work she did made the common run of shapes and sizes in demand.[2] Tu Enne's beadwork, also, had gained renown and sold at the trader's store for better prices than most, for it helped attract attention to the other items. Consequently, Iti's wives became affluent.

All such articles were used by their associates in the ordinary affairs of life and were also used to wager as stakes at gambling parties. Articles that required hours of patient industry, although a pleasant occupation, when sold at the trader's store brought only a few yards of colored cloth, a few beads, an abalone shell, or some other small adornment. However, when used at parties, they gave hours of exciting entertainment.

With the run of luck, first one and then another of a gathering of friendly contestants would win a large proportion of the accumulated trinkets, and a party would be arranged to take the lot to market. A day would be set for the expedition, and the early dawn would find them on their way with babies and dogs in profusion. At the store the lucky winner would dispose of her booty piece by piece by bartering with the clerk. Then she usually made presents of her purchases to the original makers of the articles, keeping for herself only the satisfaction of the bartering and deciding what the neighbors ought to have. The long ride home on horseback, amid laughter, gossip, and shouts of glee, prepared the way for another round of entertaining games.

Although both Datlih and Tu Enne were popular, there were some individuals who for various reasons were not included in the social clique—for example, because they had bad husbands who worked them too hard and opposed their absence from their duties; or because of sickness; or because they were so ill natured that they became estranged.

Tradition had decreed that women should not make any two ornamentations identically the same, so that the invention of new designs was an exacting science. Occasionally, accidental duplications were discovered which subjected the makers to grave consideration by a council of their peers, presided over by a person versed in the tradition affecting the case. These, after deliberation and the advice of the one informed, decided if the tradition had been violated, and if so whether any of the articles should be destroyed or might be changed, and how to conform to traditional requirements. This was one of the secret traditions, and the penalty for willful violation was known only to the elect. The tradition was recognized as important with grave but unknown consequences for violation.

Designs on weapons were also unique. Each man adopted a device for his shield by which he was recognized and which no other was allowed to use, and certain bands of color were used under the feathers of a warrior's arrows by which they could be recognized when expended and recovered. Thus, game killed by a group of several hunters was known to their women, and cared for accordingly, while the hunters pursued the chase.

Mescalero woman with her baby in a cradleboard. Blazer Family Collection.

GOLD

When the sun grew hot in the late spring, Nato's band moved its camp some ten or fifteen miles up the Rinconada toward the summit of the mountains. The vegetation had begun to grow around the camping place they had left, and Iti's two women had provided themselves with a supply of such materials of their crafts as the willow thickets, the hillsides, and the swampy land of that vicinity offered.

At the new camp, with Iti's consent the large tipi that Datlih had traded for was erected well up on a ridge, where a few hundred yards away a small spring flowed from the hillside into a dense thicket covering the bank of a deep gorge. A path led directly from the tipi to the spring for bringing water to the camp, but from this path to the bottom of the gorge the thicket remained in its natural state, almost impassable. In this thicket, well down the slope but above where the summer freshets could reach, Datlih established herself for the fulfillment of her contract.

Opposite Datlih's secret location the bank of the gorge was precipitous, making entrance from the west impracticable from its mouth, a short distance below the tipi, for nearly a mile where an abrupt drop in the water-worn channel barred further progress. Here where the runoff from the summer rains had left an excavation, there was a pool of water that never fully dried up, and wild animals came there to drink. For a hundred yards below the pool, the moisture from the retained water sustained a luxurious growth of grass and weeds which in turn attracted bears. Because of their almost constant presence there the place was called Bear Gulch and was avoided by the Indians, although the luscious roots and sprouts of the water plants were prized for food.

The low hills and ridges of the adjacent country were sparsely vegetated with great sugar pines, and many of the yellow boles had been mutilated, stripped of their bark in great patches to secure the inner bark for a laxative tonic, spring medicine. To the north-ward the steep slope of White Mountain rose abruptly two thousand feet above the camp to timberline with its bald apex still glisten-ing, in spots, with the winter snow. From here the runoff from Old Baldy was diverted by summits to the north and east. Spring had arrived. The deciduous growths were nearing full leaf while the conifers on the northern slope beyond the valley, to the south, rose in tiers of mottled green.

Along the foot of the cliffs bounding Bear Gulch on the west was a faint trail, and the waning runoff from the winter snows was now but a trickling stream in its gravel bed. Datlih could by this route reach her retreat without leaving sign that would be notice-able and clandestinely ply her trade. Tu Enne alone shared her secret, and while Datlih did her work she remained about the tipi, prepared to start for the spring with her water jug at any moment. From along the path above the thicket, by some irrelevant phrases she was to repeat, Datlih would be apprised of any threatened dan-ger of being discovered.

The perfect pieces of willow wands Datlih had saved from the material gathered for several months had been stripped of their bark and laid aside for the etsees contract; and likewise an abundant supply of the choice centers of palmilla leaves had been provided. These materials were securely bound in bundles and tossed into the thicket below from the trail to the spring. So there was no oc-casion for carrying the materials that might betray her.

Only the longest even-sized willows were suited to such perfect work, and these must be of equal diameter throughout their length, free from knots or buds, and not more than a quarter of an inch in thickness. These were to form the base of the fabric. The palmilla leaves were fibrous and, when stripped, made three strands of which the center one was suited to this work, being of quadrangular section, while those strands taken from the edges were triangular and suited only for the construction of baskets not impervious to water. For these etsees the fibers had to be the strongest possible to withstand the necessary strain and make a perfect closure at every stitch. These were recognizable by the maturity and seasoning of the leaf, which in turn was disclosed by the age and thrift of the plant and the color of the leaf, as well as its position on the plant.

Palmilla plants were of great value to the Indians. Their growth was slow; a handful of the long, slim, thorn-pointed leaves grew from the apex of a head and matured each year, retaining their green color during the winter. From the center of these the flower stalk developed, not unlike an over-grown asparagus shoot in appearance, an inch and a half in diameter. Until these were some two feet high, they were crisp and juicy, forming a nutritious food when roasted, although the sweetish taste was somewhat spoiled by a soapy flavor. Their large roots stored a viscid juice, that, when crushed, served as soap. Although particularly suited to cleansing the hair, it could be adapted to any purpose requiring suds. The wirelike feeding roots, dark crimson in color, lent themselves to the decorations woven into baskets for common use but not those used for the watertight etsees.[1] The mature flower stalks reached a height of as much as ten feet and provided light, strong poles for many purposes. In season they bore a large number of white, pink-tipped, lily-like blooms, which were followed by cucumber-shaped fruits, insipid and containing a great number of seeds, which also served as food for man and beast. The yearly growth of leaves drooped when succeeded by a new growth but retained their attachment to the parent plant. Thus, year after year the maturing leaves covered the previous crop with a layer of fresher green added to the skirt-like sheath protecting the stalks and roots.

In the foothills of the Sacramentos, at altitudes of from four to six thousand feet, these plants grew in abundance, and from these Datlih selected her materials. Last year's leaves still retained their vivid green, while the crop of the year before, faded by the weathering of a year's exposure, was assuming a yellowish tint. Previous crops, longer exposed, provided a range of colors through the greens, yellows, and browns, to greys and whites of the fully bleached leaves near the ground.

Their color alone was considered for her ornamented baskets, but for the more exacting requirements of the contracted jugs the material must be fully matured yet unaffected by decay. These leaves were in the light brown range. In the smaller plants this shade had reached the ground and was deteriorated by moisture, while in the largest plants the proper color was too high up, and the year's exposure to the sun and wind had affected the thornlike points. This made them too brittle to penetrate the stitches without making too large a hole to be well filled by the strand. So judgment as to color and the age of the plant was essential, and in this lay Datlih's superior talent.

All material for the basket work was kept thoroughly saturated with water so that the pulp between the fibers of the palmilla strands would be pressed out in order to completely fill the openings made for their passage through the willow strands forming the base of the etsee. This helped to ensure the pliability of the materials.

The end of a willow was split for a short distance, and the resulting halves were split again to form four thin slices. The sliced portion was then wrapped tightly with a strand of palmilla and the wrapped end bent into a close *carrate* (coil) by stitches passed through the wrapping to make a solid disk. The process continued, enclosing round on round of the width in the tightly drawn stitches by opening a small hole with an awl at the edge of the disk and pass-ing the strand from the inside so that the surplus pulp remained to be later scraped to a smooth surface, while the stitches on the out-side were only the fibers of the strand. During this process the wand was held to produce the desired curve for the body of the vessel, and extra stitches were added as the circumference increased or omitted to reduce the size. Thus, hour by hour the vessel assumed a jug-like shape to be completed in a day, a week, a month, or more according to its size and the diligence of the maker.

Datlih finished the first jug in about two months after the camp was moved and received a horse, thus providing separate mounts for each of the two women. The second jug was well under-way, for which she was to have another horse and the buffalo hides for a small tipi.

In the meantime Iti had joined another raiding party; this time, however, the objective was not the Comanche, for the last raid on them had proved so disastrous that none cared to under-take another. Instead, Iti had joined four kindred spirits to make a trip of several weeks, far down into Texas, not with the expecta-tion of bringing back a herd of horses but to secure a few saddlers;[2] one each was the limit of their ambitions. They had gone on foot, and the "fight medicine" had been made in secret and only as a precaution, for they did not intend to fight but to take the horses by stealth.

Had Santana known of this expedition, he would certainly have prevented it, for he now took counsel with the doctor on all his problems involving matters in which others than Indians were concerned. And such an expedition, several months previous to this time, had resulted in the horse thieves being followed and nar-rowly escaping with their lives by abandoning the stolen stock. The Texas Rangers had recovered the horses only a day's ride from the agency and came in to report the matter and demand the arrest of four Indians they had seen clearly through their glasses and could identify. The agent had asked the doctor to use his influence with Santana in an attempt to apprehend these, and the old chief admitted that he knew what had happened and brought the offenders in. One of them, their leader, was an important man among the Mescalero whom Santana wished to protect; but the others he was willing to have taken. This the doctor had pointed out was not according to the white man's idea of justice, for they considered the leader of such an enterprise to be the worst offender.

There were but six of the Rangers, and the nearest troops that might assist in making the arrest by force were at Fort Stanton forty miles away, so that Santana was in a position to dictate terms. He proposed to guarantee that there would be no more such raids by the Mescalero and called attention to the fact that no one had been killed or other harm done, that the pursuit was all the loss sustained. The doctor told the Rangers of Santana's trustworthiness since the capitulation of the Mescalero and suggested that his influence in preventing a recurrence of the offense might well be of greater value than the punishment of the offenders. And the ringleader would no doubt be out of reach before assistance could be had.

Santana's proposition was accepted with the understanding that should there be any more depredations committed by the Mescalero, Santana personally would be held responsible for the arrest of these men, including their leader. As an inducement to their vigilance, Santana appointed the paroled men as observers especially charged with reporting to him any indication of their promise being violated.

Two weeks had passed, however, before Santana discovered the absence of Iti and his companions. His observers had been outwitted and knew nothing of the absentees, but when the matter was called to their attention they found Iti's horse and discovered the identity of his comrades. However, their destination and the proposed length of their absence could not be determined.

Santana's suspicions were aroused, and he took the matter up personally. Any information he could get went to the doctor, and Santana had him write it to the captain of the Rangers and hire a Tularosa man to take it to the post office at Mesilla, the nearest at the time, from where it would be delivered by stage.

Neither Iti nor any of his companions ever returned to the reservation nor were heard of by the Mescalero. Nor was what the old chief had done about it ever told. But the idea prevailed that such information given to the Tejanos (Texans) amounted to a death warrant for violators.

Datlih was at work on the second etsee when Santana came to Nato's camp investigating the absence of Iti and the others. Tu Enne, alarmed, signaled from the spring. The unfinished work was concealed, and Datlih left her hiding place to return to the camp. However, some of her neighbors had told Santana of having seen her enter Bear Gulch not long before, and she was the one he wished particularly to question. She had started down the trail but heard the men entering the gorge before they saw her, and she turned back. They followed her up the trail to where the obstructing drop in the bed of the channel stopped her further progress, and she was hard-pressed to find something to do that would be a reasonable excuse for her presence there. Her only thought was that her clandestine basketry had been reported, and they had come to punish her.

There were no bears from which she might be running, so after removing her moccasins, she went into the marsh, and when the men arrived was industriously digging for roots in the soggy ground near the pond.

"Where is Iti?" asked Santana.

"He may be in some of the other camps, but I do not know," replied the woman. "He went away on foot a half moon ago and told us to care for the horse; but he did not say where he was going."

"When will he be back?" demanded the inquisitor.

"When will he be back? He did not tell us. He may be drunk or gambling, he said nothing about that."

Several more questions about Iti elicited no information, but not a word about the etsees for tulhiba, and they left her in a quandary. To follow them immediately might look suspicious so she lingered. There were small pieces of flint among the gravel near the edge of the pool, and to occupy her time while waiting she selected a few that she thought suited for striking fire with the piece of broken file she carried in a pouch at her belt. In gathering these she noticed some small metallic particles in the sand, and further search discovered some as large as grains of wheat although most were smaller. Some were flakes large enough to wrap around the point of her awl but were too soft to make a noise as jingles.

This discovery suggested that if the awl would penetrate the globular pieces a hole would be all that was needed to make beads of them, and she found by experiment that they could be pierced and that by rubbing them on her buckskin skirt they took a high polish. These she thought would make a beautiful contrast in the beadwork Tu Enne was doing. She gathered a handful, all the fire pouch would hold. One was large as a bean and had a wirelike projection from one side that she bent around one of her brass wire earrings to serve as a bangle.[3]

Thus interested, she forgot the passage of time while the treasures accumulated, until a scratching and grunting noise behind her made her aware that she was in Bear Gulch, and turning her head as she knelt by the pond she saw an old bear and two cubs descending by way of a fallen tree from the top of the cliff. The gulch was only some twenty feet wide, and the perpendicular rocks on either side were twice as high as her head. She might have climbed out at several places had there been time to choose her footing, but the bear was only a few jumps away. Before her the drop in the channel was an incline, steep and worn into the solid rock, but it was away from the bear so she made her retreat in that direction.

A leap took her halfway up the sloping trough, where, with her bare toes and knees with hands braced against the rock on either side, she held herself but could not advance further. When she eased the pressure ever so little, she began to slip. Only a few feet further and she could have reached a depression and been safe, for the incline was too steep for any bear to climb; but here she was straining every nerve to keep from sliding back.

The bear had not seen Datlih until she made a leap but now was growling and snarling at the cubs to drive them back up the log to the top of the cliff. However, they were thirsty and resisted her efforts, finally escaping and running to the pond beneath the frightened woman. The old bear followed and directed her growls at the trapped fugitive while the cubs drank their fill; then, having discovered nothing menacing in the unusual sight clinging to the rock above, the old bear also drank deliberately, raising her head from time to time to emit her growling snort. The bears seemed satisfied with their drink and, with deliberation, left by the way they came. As soon as Datlih was certain they were gone, she loosened all holds and rolled into the pond at the foot of the slope, so exhausted that she nearly drowned, although the water was only six or eight inches deep.

The doctor had been forage agent for several years, and all military movements through the Sacramentos passed this point as it was on the only practical road through the mountains. His friendly relations with the Indians had also brought him a commission as licensed Indian trader when the reservation was extended over the Tularoso country in 1874. The general public also made The Mill a common stopping place, and thus it had become a landmark and known throughout the country. Few weeks passed without detachments of soldiers stopping overnight and often remaining for several days. These, of course, were accompanied by officers of various ranks and numbers, and the district commander had accepted the doctor's hospitality on several occasions. Consequently, Santana had become acquainted with the division to the old chief's great satisfaction, while colonels, majors, and lesser officers were frequent visitors.

The trader's store was an interesting place for these men to pass the time, and the common soldiers and noncommissioned officers gathered here when off-duty to buy trinkets of the Indians or watch their peculiar customs. It became a popular entertainment, in which all joined, to hire Indians, especially half-grown boys, to display their skill in long-distance target shooting with arrows, throwing stones with slings, foot-racing, endurance running, concealment, and many other Indian specialties. Considerable amounts of money were sometimes wagered in backing up the rival exhibitors, and the Indians themselves were glad to join the sport. Their best professional dancer was Agustin, a Hot Springs Apache, who had been adopted by the Mescalero after having been driven from his own tribe for some offense. He had the reputation of being their best long-distance runner.

There had been considerable stock rustling among the settlements to the west, supposedly by an organized band of outlaws, and the military had been called on to assist the civilian authorities in their apprehension.

Three detachments of cavalry had been detailed for this purpose and were stationed at La Luz, Tularosa, and The Mill in readiness to take the field. Tularosa was nearly twenty miles west of The Mill and La Luz some ten miles southeast of Tularosa. But the actual distance between The Mill and La Luz was but some sixteen miles. Yet, as there were two high mountain summits intervening, direct communication between these points was not attempted; instead, couriers went by way of Tularosa.

A dispatch was being sent to La Luz, and Santana asserted that Agustin could go on foot and return an answer before the courier, with relays of fresh horses at Tularosa. The captain doubted this and said so, on which the old chief offered to bet his fine robe against fifty dollars that he could. Other officers also joined in the controversy with the result that a purse of twenty dollars was raised, ten to be paid Agustin for the trip and a bonus of ten more if he brought an answer to a note confided to his charge before the courier returned.

The direct route required a climb of more than two thousand feet within the first two miles then down into a deep valley and another climb to the second summit from which the descent to La Luz was near four thousand feet. The Indians bet their limit on their man, and their confidence led some of the officers to take a chance at two to one with their fellow officers. So there were several hundred dollars in cash in the trader's safe awaiting the result, beside ponies, robes, and a host of other bets in the doctor's hands as stakeholder. The result was that Agustin beat the courier by more than an hour.[4]

The following week the district judge and other court officials passed the night at The Mill on their way to Lincoln, to hold court in the newly organized county of that name the following week. Thus, it occurred that a dozen or more of the prominent men of the territory were present when Datlih and Tu Enne arrived at the trader's store with baskets and beadwork for barter the following morning. While Datlih was trading with the clerk, Tu Enne offered a small purse to a lieutenant, asking a dollar for it. It was a beautiful piece of work, but small, and he objected to the price. She called his attention to several shining metal beads she had incorporated in the design as making it of special value.

He had not noticed these before but now examined them carefully, believing them to be gold. He then asked her if the trader had that kind of beads. "No" she replied, "no one but me has that kind of beads, and they were very good medicine to make women like men." He then bought all of the trinkets that were decorated with the metal beads.

The clerk was glad to have the visitors buy the trinkets from the Indians, for they often accumulated in stock to the value of several hundred dollars and were in little demand. However, many of the women had good stock to sell, such as buckskins and pelts, so he bought trinkets in order to retain their good will more than for the profit in the transactions.

Two of the attorneys with the judge's party were Colonel William Logan Rynerson and Colonel Albert Jennings Fountain, both of whom had earned their titles with the California Column during the Civil War. Both men had spent several years in the gold fields of the Pacific coast, and to these the lieutenant took his purchases after securing all that were to be had. They had no way of testing the beads but believed them to be gold and worth all he had paid for the trinkets, or more. At their request Tu Enne was pointed out but she would not tell where she had found the beads. Though she finally said that another woman had given them to her, she refused to identify the woman.

News of the gold find was soon made public, and the excitement ran high all day. Tu Enne was watched, and when she and Datlih started off together, they were detained by half a dozen men who offered them considerable sums of money to show where the gold had been found.

The Indians, also, had been watching and when the big nugget on Datlih's earring was noticed and its purchase proposed, Santana took a hand. He dragged Datlih from her horse, tore the ring from her ear, and threw it into the creek. Then he informed the crowd that had gathered that if any Mescalero told where the gold had been found or should dare to show the place, they would be killed at once, and that anyone found near the place would not be allowed to leave.

This settled the matter for the time being, but the fact that there was gold somewhere in the country was not forgotten. There was no place where gold was known to exist within hundreds of miles of The Mill at that time, and when they were again alone together, the doctor asked Santana if he would tell him where the gold could be found, but the old chief refused.

"I will not tell you," he said, "for I have told my people that none must tell any other if they know, and that if any white man shall look for it near where it is, he, too, shall be killed, even if the Mescalero must again fight the white people and the soldiers until all are dead. If I told you, I might think you had told your people. If some of your people found where it is, then I would have to kill you, my friend. For the gold is on the reservation, and if the white men find it, they will take the reservation from my people."

Several years after Santana's death Datlih and Tu Enne were recognized at one of the pueblos on the Rio Grande by an officer —then retired—who had been present when the gold was found in their possession. He bribed them and secured the story in detail of how, when, and where it had been found, including the names of those present when Datlih gave the beads to Tu Enne and told her where she might find more.

With this information the officer, accompanied by six others of those present when the gold had been seen, went to The Mill and inquired of the Indians for the persons said to know where it had been located. Of these, however, only two young men, who had been described as "little boys," were found. They were given a mule and provided with a small buckskin bag, which they were to fill with nuggets to prove they knew where the gold was. This they did, being absent two days. They then agreed to lead the party to the find and receive a horse and one hundred Mexican pesos in compensation. These guides, however, were waylaid on their way to camp and shot to death with arrows.

The following day the mules were returned to the gold hunters

by one of the head men of the Mescalero with a warning that if they
were found in Mescalero country after one more day they would not
be permitted to leave alive.

Within a distance of forty or fifty miles, both north and east
of that location, several paying gold mines have been developed,
but the Mescalero still preserve their secret, if, in fact, it has not
been lost with the death of the older generations.

Mescalero basket weavers. Courtesy Rio Grande Historical Collections, New
Mexico State University Library.

LOSS AND CHANGE

It was several months before Iti's return was finally given up, and the widows went into mourning for him. They burned all the possessions he had left behind and killed his fine horse, the horse Datlih had received on account of the first etsees, as well as the old mare. They had, however, anticipated this by providing new clothing for themselves, which they now considered to be their own; and Datlih had recently finished the second jug and received a horse and the small tipi in payment. These she also claimed were hers, and refused to destroy since they had not been in her possession while she was Iti's wife.

This was a matter affecting the whole community, however, and was made the subject of a council meeting in which the widows were accused of not complying with the ancient law of Eyata made in the long ago. No one knew how, when, or where Iti had died, although all conceded that he was dead, and after due deliberation the council held that the widows were alone responsible should it be found that he had been alive when these articles had been acquired, and consequently his. They refused to pass judgment without further knowledge of the facts. The neighbors, nevertheless, declared that if the things they refused to destroy were actually the property of the deceased, his spirit might return to them, with no telling what dire results to the community.

Consequently, the widows were driven out of camp, and all

avoided them. They set up their tipi several miles from any other habitation. This and Datlih's horse, beside the clothing they wore, was the sum of their possessions. Their robes and even the awls, knives, and other equipment worn at their belts had been sacrificed to the memory of their husband. No one permitted them to come near or lent the least assistance. They had made ample store of nuts, dried fruits, jerky, and other winter supplies, but these also had been included in the sacrifice. They had had Iti's ticket, good for three rations at the agency, but when he was reported dead it was canceled, and they had no friend or advisor and thus no way of being reinstated in their own names.

Nuts, wild fruits, grass seeds, and the tubers of wild sweet potatoes, mesquite beans, and a deer they trapped kept them alive until Datlih was able to make a basket with a knife and an awl improvised from bones, which she shaped by whetting them on a stone. This she traded for beads, and an old boot they found gave Tu Enne a start at making beaded trinkets. The trader's store was the only place they were received as before, and here their contact was business only. They asked no friendly advice, and none was offered.

An old woman, ostracized as a witch with bad medicine, wanted to live with them, but they were afraid of her. She had a ration ticket and a horse but little else and was often unable to attend to the horse. She was glad to trade the horse for Datlih's tipi, which she set up near the agency, where the grass was too scant to keep the horse. With this horse and the one they already had, they made their way to Tu Enne's people at one of the pueblos on the Rio Grande.

U'ah, Santana's old wife, accidentally met her son-in-law face-to-face in the early spring of 1875 and a few weeks later became ill with pulmonary trouble. A medicine man pronounced it due to the bewitching effect of the encounter and incurable. This was, according to the ancient tradition, said to have been ordained by Eyata in the long ago to prevent mothers-in-law from making trouble between their daughters and their husbands. And it was also ordained that a man meeting his mother-in-law must hide his face or conceal himself on pain of some great misfortune. Consequently, it was the custom for everyone to warn both parties of the approach of the other, and such meetings seldom occurred. U'ah's sickness proved fatal, probably on account of her belief that the meeting had doomed her to certain death.

Santana mourned her sincerely and lost much of his arrogance. His two young wives were little consolation and had never held his affection to any considerable extent. Now he all but despised them and seldom went near their camp; instead, he had a tipi set up near the doctor's house and spent much of his time with his old friend. The large flat stone that served as a doorstep to the doctor's residence became his favorite resting place in pleasant weather, and the doctor's room, with the bright piñon fire, always welcomed him at other times.

Long, halting conversations between Santana and the doctor lasted late into the nights, for neither of them could understand the other well. The great silver-tip bearhide that had served the doctor as a rug for many years was spread before his bed, and sheepskins about the hearth took its place to make a comfortable seat for the old chief without violating his superstitions. Here he often passed the night. A homemade willow rocker was the doctor's favorite seat, and with the old chief half reclining by the hearth and the doctor in his chair, each told the other of his bygone days.

Santana's father had been the principal head man of the Mescalero, but he would not pronounce his name on account of some tribal superstition. When Santana was but a young man and his marriage had completed his status as a warrior, he was included in an expedition against the Navajo in retaliation for a recent raid.

They had been traveling for twenty days and had reached the Navajo country, they supposed, without having been observed.

The Navajo, he explained, were very many more than the Mescalero, but like Shishi Ind'h (my people—the Apache) comprised many different bands that lived far apart and did not usually fight together but were friends. The band they had gone to punish consisted of as large a number of warriors, and they had expected to surprise them; but in some way the enemy had learned of their approach and secured the assistance of another band.

There were about a hundred of the Mescalero, who were marching through a defile, some distance from the camp they had intended to attack the following morning. The combined forces of their enemies were concealed in the thick brush on higher ground on both sides for a long distance, and they waited until the head of the Mescalero was nearing the end of the hidden lines. The bed of the defile was timbered to some extent with scattering trees but insufficiently to provide much protection from an attack from both directions. The adjacent ridge had no timber, but the thick brush was about waist high. The Mescalero were strung out in single file with the horsemen alternated with those on foot, and it was Santana's opinion that their opponents were double their number.

The Navajo yelled, and a flight of arrows from both sides apprised them of their danger. Most of the riders and some of the horses fell at the first onslaught, and those not disabled began to retreat down the draw as no doubt their enemies had expected, for the Navajo in their rear now showed themselves and began shooting arrows at the retreating Mescalero as they came in range.

Santana had been walking between the horses of his father and his uncle, near the head of the column but was not injured. The first attack had been directed at the leaders who were riding, nearly all of whom were killed or wounded.

"*Tuhota, tuhota,*" ("Don't run, don't run") shouted the youth (Santana) as he dodged the continued flights of arrows, protected to some extent by the trees and his shield. The Mescalero's bows were in the quivers at their backs, the bows unstrung to preserve their resiliency, while the slings about their waists could be brought into use almost instantly with the bountiful supply of stones underfoot.

His shout was taken up by his comrades and the rout checked. *"Kleteh, kleteh"* ("Pop rocks, pop rocks"), he shouted again. This ammunition was inexhaustible in the wash where the Mescalero were, but among the brush on the hillsides few stones of the proper size could be found, and the Navajo's arrows were rapidly exhausted. To shoot accurately, they must expose themselves above the brush to free their bows from the interference, and the Apaches, closing up their ranks, soon met every attempt to shoot an arrow with a shower of stones.

The extended lines of the Navajo replaced the warriors whose arrows became exhausted, and they, falling back, also used their slings. These, with the advantage of their higher elevation, had a longer range than those of the Mescalero in the depression; but the treetops largely offset this advantage, and the battle continued until dark, although many Mescalero fell that day.

Neither of these tribes fight in the dark, except in emergencies, and the Navajo, thinking the remnant of the Mescalero would not be able to escape them on the morrow, fell back for the night.

More than half the Mescalero had been killed or fatally wounded. Although half of those able to travel were sorely hurt, Santana's presence of mind had saved these few. Those mortally wounded were put out of their misery, and those able to travel started home during the night in groups of four or five. These groups separated and were well concealed by morning, and the pursuing Navajo met warm receptions from the few they found.

About thirty of the defeated Mescalero reached their people alive, and thus began Santana's leadership, which he held until his death.

ANTELOPE HUNT

Katsuue, Santana's daughter, and her husband, Shash, with their two boys, Sitlis and Tlu, accompanied an expedition to the plains west of the Sacramentos to hunt antelope for hides. For this purpose antelope were taken during the summer when the flesh was, with the exception of barren does and a few of the young bucks, lean and stringy so that only a small portion of the kill was preserved for food.

Such expeditions were usually made up of members of the different bands, for the hides were required by the hundreds and provided the material for all their lighter clothing. Accustomed as the Indians were to the cool climate of the mountains, the dry, hot plains were not conducive to pleasure but broke the monotony, and the antelope hunt took on the nature of a picnic.

A few experts did the actual killing, but the heat made prompt treatment of the hides necessary. Consequently many women were required for the work. The women encouraged their older children to go for the assistance they could give, and the younger ones had to be taken so they could be cared for by their mothers.

At this time of year the fawns were nearly grown and their hides much prized for the fine texture and delicate finish of the buckskin they produced. The herds ranged in thousands like sheep, nibbling the new growth from the tall matured grass. They did not have a need for much water, as they found sufficient moisture in several kinds of cacti and other water-conserving vegetation that grew abundantly in their feeding grounds.

The herds, when undisturbed, moved in comparatively compact bodies in unison as they grazed, the bucks on the outer edge surrounding the does, and most of the younger fawns gathered toward the center. One of their controlling traits was curiosity, which was only exceeded by their timidity. The herds bedded down at twilight wherever they might be, and unless disturbed, made no move until dawn when they began to graze. This behavior made it possible for the Indians to secure the great number of hides they needed, and the prolific herds showed no diminution from year to year.

The Indians camped in some depression in the country frequented by the antelope, where they would not attract attention. They set up light stocks of palmilla or other poles to support tanned hides for shade so the breezes made existence tolerable. The party was then divided, some to take the extra horses to the nearest water, while others, usually women, remained in camp to keep the children out of mischief. The remainder, including the killers, rode from one eminence to another until a herd of antelope was sighted. Those discovering a suitable herd would bring the other searchers to them with a smoke signal, and the herd would be watched from a distance until they bedded down. Then the killers would decide on the best method of approach, while the others returned to camp.

The killers usually included a representative from each band participating. During the night they approached as near as possible to the sleeping herd, without causing alarm, and awaited the dawn. By taking advantage of the wind, their approach might be within a few steps of the nearest animals if conditions were favorable. But a slight eminence was desirable for their location, and the high grass was usually sufficient concealment. Each killer was armed with a lance, a war club, and his bow and arrows; he was also provided with a slim stick four or five feet long, to the end of which a small flag or streamer of some bright-colored material was attached.

When the antelope began to move in the early light, one or more of the flags would be raised above the concealing grass and moved about until noticed by members of the herd, which would immediately give the alarm by a loud snort, arousing the herd and causing them to bunch in a mild stampede. In the meantime the flag would be lowered, and the herd at a little distance would follow the gaze of the antelope that had first seen the flags. The reappearance of the flags caused renewed excitement and sometimes a fresh stampede, but usually their curiosity proved sufficient to start the older bucks on a tour of investigation.

This would take the form of a large circle about the unfamiliar objects, and when the does began to join the investigation the flags would be held stationary or the sticks driven into the ground. From time to time additional flags would be raised to increase the excitement and encourage laggards to join the circle. Round and round the bucks would lead, drawing nearer and nearer, the does running outside the bucks as the ring grew smaller with the younger animals outside.

In the growing light the fluttering pennants moved in unison with the grass in the morning breeze, but the curiosity of the herd, now fully aroused, crowded the leaders into a smaller circle about their hidden enemies until the Indians sprang to their feet and began the slaughter with their spears. This was not accomplished without danger, however, for the bucks, prevented from escape by their crowding mates, would in their frenzy charge the hunters with their sharp horns and hoofs to gore and trample the killers, occasionally succeeding. However, a half-dozen expert hunters back-to-back would often bring down a hundred or more of the animals before the extremities of the herd would take alarm and relieve the pressure permitting them to escape. The bows and arrows then came into play, as the retreat developed, and usually left dozens trampled and added to the massacre.

The camp would be abandoned in the early morning of the

day of the kill. And while a few watered the horses that had not drunk the day before, all the rest of the expedition went to the place of the slaughter to begin the skinning and the preparation of the flesh of such carcasses as were suitable for food. This often occupied most of the day.

Shash was one of the killers and Katsuue one of the scouts on this occasion. Sitlis and Tlu, their sons, remained in camp under the special care of their aunt, an older sister of Shash, while their parents helped to locate the herd of antelope. Noon had passed, and the women in camp had been amusing themselves at their gambling game of *tsitse* (stick and stone) for several hours when the westering sun shifted the shade of the hide awning under which the boys had been sleeping, and the heat of its direct rays awoke them.

The ladies' game in progress, which might be compared to bridge among modern ladies, was a very common means of passing leisure hours. There were no cards required, and the necessary paraphernalia was available almost anywhere. Any hard substance, preferably a good-sized stone, could serve as a table. It was then surrounded by any number of players provided with six half-round sticks cut to a length of about six inches. These might be played for odd or even, counting the flat sides or the round falling up. Or they might be notched in any manner agreed upon and the score counted by the way the notches fell at each throw.

Each thrower in turn grasped the sticks in a bundle and threw them endwise against the stone, and the winner was determined by how the counters fell. Bracelets and earrings of copper and brass wire and other small articles of adornment were usually the stakes played for, but as the game went on, articles of more value were often wagered or traded to a winner to redistribute the wealth.

The guardians were so preoccupied in their game that the boys were not noticed as they slipped away. They found food and filled themselves. However, there was but a small amount of water left in the jugs and having been joined by a friend, Eijalhika (fat boy), among them they finished it. The women who had gone to water the horses would bring more water when they returned, but that would be late in the evening, and it appeared to the boys' best interest to be absent when the women discovered the water to be all gone.

Where to go and how were matters to be considered. To hide in the tall grass would leave them exposed to the hot sun and shut off the little breeze that helped to keep them cool. An old gentle mare had been left at camp to be ridden in case of emergency, but no other horse. She was hobbled and grazing at a little distance from the awnings, and they removed the hobble and put the thong of which it was made around her neck to lead her over a nearby ridge out of sight of the camp. But they were all too small to mount un-aided, and there was no gully that she could be led into, and no rock, log, or anything else to serve the purpose. They tried a palmilla, but the sharp-pointed leaves pricked their naked legs.

Sitlis, however, could reach the mare's mane, and with a frantic effort he mounted like "skinning a cat," then reaching down gave a hand to Tlu, who also clambered on. But Eijalhika was entirely too short, and those on the horse would be dragged off with his weight if they reached low enough to give him a hand. However, by leaning far over in the opposite direction Sitlis supported Tlu on his foot, and by holding to his brother's belt Tlu could reach the short one and all were soon aboard. In coming to camp the party had passed an alkali pond where the water was so bad that the horses wouldn't drink it. But the children had waded in it and the boys remembered the wet, cool, muddy pond as providing an agreeable sensation. They didn't think it was very far away, and thus they decided that to visit for a cool bath would be something worthwhile.

They found the incoming trail not far from camp and followed it back. But the mare didn't care to go fast and in spite of all the kicking the boys could do, the mare stopped frequently for choice bits of grass. The distance also was greater than they had thought, and when they reached the pond the mare wouldn't stop but smelled the water and waded in to the deepest place and lay down.

Although the boys were in the water where they had intended to be, the mud in the bottom was so deep that the fat boy was caught in it with the mare on one of his legs and nearly drowned before the older boys could get him on his feet. However, the mud and water only reached his waist, and when he got his mouth clear he let out a yell that gave the mare an excuse to escape, and curl-ing her tail over her back, she started for camp at a lively trot.

Even though it was well toward evening when they found themselves afoot, the boys enjoyed the mud for a while before start-ing home. The sun was sinking behind the mountains, and the evening breeze had driven the heat from the plain when they started. However, the trail of the Indians through the high grass was quite plain, so there was no danger of missing it. They were not afraid of the dark but were tired and thirsty, so started at a trot; but the fat boy couldn't keep up, so they had to slow down.

Darkness soon overtook them, and the coyotes were howling all about; but they paid no attention to them, for they knew the coyotes would not attack them so long as they kept moving. How-ever, when a wolf howled in the distance behind them, the coyotes stopped their clamor and the deep silence was startling. The bay of another wolf somewhere to the right and ahead, not far from the direction the trail led, gave the boys some concern, for they had been told that if a pack of wolves gathered they were likely to at-tack anything.

The wolves howled again and again and were joined by a cho-rus of others, not nearby; but in the intervals of silence the boys could hear a pattering of padded feet on the trampled grass on the trail behind them. They had unconsciously quickened their pace, and the fat boy was panting; although they could see no sign of camp, they had to let him rest. Their father had shown them how to wrap a robe around their left arm if attacked by a dog and let it be bitten while they defended themselves with a club or a knife. Wolves were like dogs, but the boys had no rocks, knife, club, nor a substitute for any of these. Here in the hot country they wore nothing but what nature provided and a breechclout, a wild cat skin tanned with the hair on and held in place between their legs by a narrow belt around their waists.

There was no moon, but the bright stars in the sky made it light enough to see quite a distance ahead along the trail, and there was nothing in their path. The pattering on the trail behind them stopped when they did, and they could not see what made the noise. While they rested they took off their breechclouts and wrapped them around their arms, hoping to find some weapon along the trail. Although they were now badly frightened, they were by no means ready to give up without a fight.

As they again walked quickly, the pattering feet behind started once more, and now they could see something on the trail but not what it was; it came no nearer when they stopped. Sitlis felt something under the grass that proved to be a clod, and he took the fat boy's breechclout from him and folded the clod in this. Then Tlu took the lead and with the fat boy between them Sitlis brought up the rear and they moved on, for the menace following them could be seen and scared them more than the howling wolves still out of sight.

But from far down the trail ahead a new sound soon reached them, "Kloop, kloop, kloop, kloop;" it was not like the pattering sound behind which was little more than a rustling of the grass beaten down on the trail but heavier. The boys stopped and fairly held their breaths until they could see that a bulky object on the trail before them was Katsuue, their mother, riding in search of them, followed by half a dozen men.

The mare had trotted into camp where everyone was in a frenzy, searching for the missing boys. This had been a clue to the riddle of their disappearance, and the searching party had backtracked the mare. Now the boys were safe and wiser.

LAW AND TRADITION

At this time Santana was making every effort to reduce the drunkenness of his followers. He liked liquor himself, and this fact reduced the effect of his efforts, for he had, in times past, indulged much too freely, and temperance was the object of his present exertions.

He wanted a law so contrived that certain individuals, to be publicly known, would be allowed to make a limited amount of tulhiba for sale while anyone could make it in small quantities for his own use.

Santana had tried total abstinence by his own decree, but public sentiment had made that a failure, and the frequent debauches, assisted by the bootleggers, were taking an awful toll on the Mescalero. His idea was to make the *tubisno* (abstaining guards) responsible for the drinkers being limited to an amount within their capacity, so they retained their senses. But, as much better informed reformers have discovered, the details necessary to accomplish this objective are very hard to define.

The Indians had no written law, and the traditions on which their rules of government were founded were to some extent conflicting. However, a certain mode of construing their application was recognized as the law, or constitution, of the tribe. The head men—accepted leaders of the several factions—met as a court to decide to what extent ameliorating or aggravating circumstances should affect the application of the law in any given case. Thus they reconciled their own differences of opinion and arrived at a judgment, not a sentence or a vindication of the accused. Such judgment was proclaimed by the council, not to an officer for execution, but to the tribe as a whole, which were thereby made a court of last resort.

Public opinion was the power behind the judgment and decided whether it should be enforced or not. If there was any great difference of opinion, the culprit was often permitted to escape and seek sanctuary with some other tribe. But an aggrieved person might execute the judgment, with such assistance as he might secure, with immunity from the law. An aggrieved person not demanding satisfaction was held to be a coward and unworthy of respect, for the culprit was denied any assistance or protection. He was an enemy of the tribe or an exile for a year.

These laws were basically traditional, but subject to amendment, to some extent, by approval of the tribe. Such approval was not by plebiscite but by what was called *lha asti* (much talk), and when occasion arose new laws were made, or old ones amended or abolished by the same method.

The better minds were naturally those to assume the leadership among their associates, and they developed into what might be compared to a legislature, which usually took the lead in proposing changes in the law. However, no members of the tribe were denied the privilege of expressing their opinion, and young men were sometimes the authors of accepted laws. By this method no law was recognized until approved by so large a majority of the influential—not the number of individuals—that public sentiment alone made it effective.

Santana had proposed that there be such a law as he had in mind but had outlined his ideas so vaguely—for he was undecided on several points himself—that only a multitude of conflicting ideas had resulted. All conceded the necessity for such a law, but the lha asti had been going on for months without perfecting the details. Meetings were impromptu in both time and place. Any gathering was likely to take up the matter for discussion, and accidental meetings often became large gatherings suggesting and debating details.

There was no opposition to the basic idea of the new law, but the medicine men would have liked to recover their former control of the whole matter. The tradition was that Eyata had disclosed the method of making tulhiba to the medicine men and prescribed the manner of its use, but they had allowed the secret to become public property and lost control.

Santana had talked to the doctor about what he wanted to do but in this matter got little satisfaction, for he was told that the white men had been trying to find a solution to the same question for a great many years and that all the laws they had made about it had only made trouble.

"But Mescalero laws are different," argued the old chief. "When we have a law, it is the law of everybody, and if somebody does not do as the law says, they are no longer Mescalero but enemies, even of their mothers. So when this law is, it will be a good law. But all want to get a little drunk sometimes, and when they are a little drunk they do not know how drunk they are, so some get crazy and some go to sleep."

"Why don't you have all the liquor at one place so no one can drink too much and make everyone go there when they want to get a little drunk, so the men that don't drink can make them quit when they have enough?" suggested the doctor.

"We do not have one man to punish people that do not do what the laws says as the white men do, and when they are enemies they are enemies to all the people and are treated like enemies by all the people. If there is a law to make all that get drunk enemies, none will get drunk. But if the law says people may get a little drunk, some good people will be very drunk and be enemies when they do not know they are very drunk. And to have all the liquor at one place would be just the same."

This brought on the question of how other laws could be enforced without injuring the good people.

"The old laws," said Santana, "are like Eyata made them, and everything he made is good. But Chete Neh wanted to make all the people and all the animals and everything think bad thoughts, and Nant'a said that the good people who did not think bad thoughts must make more laws for the people, so that Chete Neh's people who did not like the old laws and the laws the people made would be enemies. The laws the people made were for the people, for they could think, and not for the animals and other things that could not think. The people, when they grew up, could think good thoughts like Nant'a wanted them to think or they could think bad thoughts like Chete Neh wanted them to think. And all the laws were for all the good people and against the bad people. Thus, all the people could know when the bad people were enemies, and the enemies would be killed."

"How about good people who do bad things that are not very bad? It seems to me that everybody does bad things, and if they were all made enemies and killed there would soon be no people left, either good or bad," suggested the doctor.

"That" replied Santana, "is why the good people had to make more laws, so all the people would not be enemies for doing things that were not 'like killing'; for when people steal, the law of the people says they can pay and not be enemies, and when they hurt someone, they can be beaten and not be enemies, and the head men can say what can be done to them so they will not be enemies."

"And what is 'like killing'?" asked the doctor.

"Killing is 'like killing,'" was the reply, "unless it is an enemy. And some other things are 'like killing,' and all the people know the law and know whoever does those things will be an enemy and be killed."

"Tell me some of the things that are 'like killing' but are not killing," requested the doctor.

"When anyone is far away and has only one horse, it is 'like killing' to steal his horse, because he might die and not get home. And if a man is far away and has more than one horse, it is 'like killing' for him if he will not let another man ride his other horse because he might die and not get home. And it is 'like killing' if a tipi is shut and the door tied down when there is no one there, so someone cannot go in to keep himself from dying. And when food is put away to keep it, it is 'like killing' to take it all. But if someone is very hungry, he may take a little so he will not die.

"Other things are also 'like killing' sometimes. And all of the laws the people have made the head men can think about. And what the head men think is the law for one year about that thing. The one who has done the bad thing is *tan ju,* or an enemy, for one year if he does not let the one he did the bad thing to do what the head men think."

"I have been told that it is 'like killing' for a man to take another man's woman," said the doctor.

"That is the law, too," replied the chief. "But a woman is like a horse. If a man is there he must protect his woman or his horse; and if he cannot protect his woman, his horse, or any other thing he has, and the other man uses the woman or the other thing and gives it back, it is not 'like killing' but like other bad things that the head men consider law. But any man may kill another to protect any of his things, and it is not 'like killing.' And if a man takes anything of another when he is not there, it is 'like killing' if the head men think that is the law."

"Then if a man is sick or hurt and cannot defend his things, anyone can take whatever he wants?" was suggested.

"No," objected Santana, "for when anyone is sick or hurt, everyone must help him, and all the people would defend his things until he is well. Or if he dies they would destroy his things, and his women could defend themselves when they have no man."

"Why is it different if a man is there or not?" asked the doctor. "That is the old law and cannot be changed, and the head men cannot think about that," was the answer. "When a man or an animal or anything is stronger or better in any way than another, he may destroy the other and take whatever he wants. And that is the good law of Eyata so the best things and the best animals and the best men will live, and the others will die. Thus, there will be only the best, and not too many people or animals or other things in the world when there is little rain to make food grow on the ground."

"Is that the reason you quit fighting the people and the soldiers?" asked the doctor.

"I cannot tell you that for sure," Santana admitted, "for many things are the reason; I do not know all the reasons, and I do not want my people to know what I think about that. But you are my friend, and I will tell you what I think, and you can tell me what you think; then maybe we can both know why. All the Indians are not so many as they used to be, and the white people in our country are more than they used to be. We killed some, and other tribes killed some of the white people and some of the soldiers. But still there are more, and the Indians are less, and I think their old law is different. And I think the Indians must learn the law of the white men and do like the white men do, for they fought among their different tribes for many years and still there are more white men and less Indians.

"And when there was little rain and the wild animals were all gone from the white man's country because there was not enough food growing on the ground, they made more food grow on the ground. And they ate cows and other animals that they had and were not hungry.

"Now their number is greater in our country, and they do not know how to fight Indians, but there are less Indians. I think all the Indians that do not learn the law of the white man and his ways will soon be dead. And I think the only way we can learn the white man's ways is from the white man, and we must be friends to the white man to learn his ways and his law."

"I think you are right, " agreed the doctor, "but while you or I live the Indians cannot learn the white man's law, for the white men think many good thoughts that the Indians do not know are good thoughts, and that is what makes the difference in the law. But our children's children's children will begin to see the Indians and the white men as all one tribe, and all will know the same law."

"Yes," conceded Santana, "the white man's law has some things that the Indians cannot know, and they must forget those things they know before they can know the white man's law. The white man's law says that people must not be killed just because they are not the best people. But Eyata's law says that only the best people and the best animals and the best things should live. And that is what the Indians know because when only the best live their young will be the best. And Eyata's law says it is right to kill enemies, for the best enemies can kill the most enemies. But the white man's law says kill only a few enemies and make the others slaves. The Indians know that will make too many people in the world when there is little rain to make food grow on the ground."

"Then the law of Eyata is the reason the Indians wanted to kill the Mexicans and the white people and keep them from coming into their country?" asked the doctor. "Why did you change that law and quit fighting the white people and the soldiers?"

"That law cannot be changed," said Santana adamantly, "for it is the old law, and that is the reason my brother was an enemy and had to be killed. But when the head men knew that the white men had been fighting for many years among their different tribes and killed a great many, and then were friends together, we knew those people were not like our people and that their *Ta incha* (big father) had made a different law for them. So they could kill enough of their own people to have plenty of food on the ground, in their own country and the country where they go, when there is little rain.

"Then I knew that the reason those people were coming more and more when the Indians killed a few was because they were a different people and had a different kind of law; and by their law they were not enemies but friends to the Mescalero.

"And I knew we must be friends; we must be friends to them or all be killed. Then some of my people said, 'That is what the padres told us,' but we did not know that the different law they knew was for a different kind of people, for they said their law was for all kinds of people.

"But I knew that the padres' law could not prevent there being too many people in the world when there was little rain; and I knew their law was for a different kind of people and that they had a different way to keep from having too many people. And I wanted a law that the Mescalero would not kill other kinds of people and would not take their women or their horses or other things, and the lha asti about that was for many years.

"Then the soldiers said they would give my people food and other things they needed so they would not have to kill enemies and other kinds of people; and my people said that was better and that was the law. But my brother and some of the other men said that law was because we were afraid like women and would not fight because the other kind of people were too many. Then they went away and fought other kinds of people and were enemies to the Mescalero."

"So you do not want to kill other kinds of people now? But you did want to kill them until you found they were too many and would soon take the country?" asked the doctor.

"Yes," he admitted, "that is what I wanted, for they had many things that we wanted, and to kill them was the way we knew to get those things; and I thought they were enemies like other Indians.

But I do not know if they can take the country, for Eyata made it and it is his and no one can take it. If the Mescalero live here and other people are stronger they can kill the Mescalero or make them go far away to some other place. But if we got stronger we could come back and kill them or make them go some other place and live here again, for the country is part of Eyata's world and cannot be taken."

"But don't you know that it is not right to kill people and take what they have worked for?" asked the doctor.

"You are not a Mescalero," was the reply, "and you know the law of the white man and think like their law; but you are my friend and know no better, and I will tell you.

"When Eyata made the world it was his, and the people he made were his, and the animals he made were his, and everything he made was his. And everything he made was good, and nothing he made wanted what any other thing had, for all had all they wanted. And there was plenty of food growing on the ground, for there was plenty of rain.

"Then Chete Neh was, but it was not good, for Eyata did not make Chete Neh. And when Eyata was far away to make a new world, Chete Neh made little rain come. And there was not enough food growing on the ground for all the people and all the animals and all the other things that Eyata had made. And Chete Neh made the people have bad thoughts when they were hungry. And the new world that Eyata made was for the good spirits of people who died, and some of the people who died had the bad thoughts of Chete Neh, and their spirits were not good and could not go to the new world that Eyata had made. They were the spirits of the people of Chete Neh.

"And the spirits of the people of Chete Neh must stay in this world, and Chete Neh could not make people, for it had no spirits that were good. And Chete Neh put the spirits of its people into crazy people and witches and animals and birds and other things that Chete Neh had made, for they had to stay in this world and be Chete Neh's people.

"Now I think maybe the new world is full of good spirits of people who have died. And all the other kinds of people in this world are the people of Chete Neh with bad spirits in them, who will live in this world and be more and more. And the Indians will be less and less until they are all dead and be the people of Chete Neh, or their spirits will be in the new world that Eyata made. So I do not know if it is right or wrong to kill people and take their things, but I do not do that anymore, for it may be wrong and I am not hungry."

The psychology of Santana, as expressed in the foregoing conversation, was probably an outline of the accepted beliefs of the Mescalero. It should be noted, however, that the meeting of the head men was the basis of the law, although nominally based on tradition. Representing as they did the sentiment of the several divisions of the tribe, their harmonized judgments were a fair cross section of public opinion and were carried out without considerable opposition.

The law stressed assistance for a comrade. Ownership was conditional in emergency. A stick or other weight was the usual method of securing a tipi door, but if tied down it indicated some special reason of the owner that his possessions within should not be interfered with. It usually meant that provision had been made for an expected crisis, some fetish, medicine, food, and so forth; and all else was made available without untying the door.

Food, in an emergency, was public property but not subject to distribution during the absence of the owner. Cached food might be resorted to in emergency but in the least quantity to serve the requirement. All property of a deceased person had to be destroyed—a law probably originating in attempts to control contagious disease.

One year was the effective limit of law, and reprisals after that time were subject to consideration of the head men and legal penalties. A year of exile was equivalent to capital punishment, in most cases, as hundreds of miles of hostile country intervened between the culprit and any sanctuary. Within those many miles he was subject to thirst, starvation, heat, cold, wild animals, and the enmity of other tribes, besides the uncertainty of his reception by a foreign tribe.

Chete Neh was a sexless, invisible something often indicated by the neuter pronoun *it* and Lhizhin (black), too, was in common use to indicate the malignant spirit. *Dih* (was) also conveyed the idea of "came," "existed at some period." The equivalent of hell was to exist in this world in spirit, a subject of Chete Neh. One of the controversies that divided the bands was whether a bad spirit, a subject of Chete Neh, might be made good during a subsequent existence and go to the new world.

Drought appeared to be the calamity most feared, and the very old recalled that in their youth there occurred a period of three consecutive years of little rain when no children lived and all old people died.

The term "enemies" included everyone but Mescalero in good standing.

It was a custom approaching the dignity of a law that when a general debauch was contemplated, one or more individuals were appointed to remain sober, according to the number of persons expected to participate and the amount of intoxicant available. These appointees were supposed to maintain order and prevent controversies likely to result in serious trouble. They were called *tubisno deh neh* (not drinking anything strong) and were endowed with unlimited authority, including the right to use any necessary force without incurring lawful penalties; they were commonly known as tubisno.

This rule was based on the belief that the Deity had taught the medicine men the art of making tulhiba. This they were instructed to furnish to individuals suspected of treasonable intentions, or conspiracies, in such quantities that they would become drunk and divulge their secrets while the medicine men remained sober, with the object of frustrating such designs. In time the formula, however, became public property and the beverage so popular that the medicine men lost control of the rite; and these guardians of the peace were substituted for them when a supply of liquor became available.

Although Gorgonio's sect still adhered to the principle that getting drunk was a divinely appointed privilege subject to the control of the medicine men, many of his followers, who in other matters adhered to his teachings, patronized the brewers of tulhiba whenever a supply was ready.

Santana was of Gorgonio's followers, but observing the bad effects of the drunkenness among his people, had the strength of character to reform. At this time he practiced temperance and made every effort to stop the drunkenness of his people. When he learned of a hidden brewery, he promptly destroyed the equipment and the beverage in process of manufacture and punished the brewers as severely as he dared. But public sentiment was against him. The habit of drinking liquor was so strongly ingrained in so great a number of his people that he believed a general uprising against his authority would result from an absolute ban on the manufacture and sale of intoxicants.

In late October 1874, the usual light snowfall was followed, a couple of weeks later by a heavier storm; and the accumulated fall lay in drifts a foot deep or more in many places that were shaded on the north exposures of the hills. But on the south slopes and level areas, where the sun and wind were effective, it had all melted off; and in many places the ground was dry by the middle of December.

Santana's band was camped in the vicinity of the agency, with their tipis scattered for several miles up the main canyon of the Tularoso, and in the south fork to above the headspring, with a few down the canyon to the west. Nato had taken up his winter abode in the lower Three Rivers country; Caballero's people were in the Nogal Canyon; and several of the smaller bands had established themselves in the Rinconada and vicinity. Only Natsile and his followers still remained in the higher and colder portions of the reservation usually occupied only during the summer, around Elk, Silver, and Whitetail Springs.

Thus, the tribe was scattered over most of the nine hundred square miles included in their reservation. Immediately about the camp their locations were comfortable. But many intervening stretches were deep in snow, and the icy trails between the camps and the agency merged where practicable so that the Indians could get their weekly ration supply. Thus, Santana's strategical location enabled him to learn much of the news of the different camps from the people's gossip when they came for rations, although he had little chance for personal observation.

A group of old women from several of the scattered camps had established themselves well down in the foothills of the north watershed of the Tularoso, at a spring several miles from any of the other camps. Here they were brewing tulhiba which they furnished in small quantities to Indians from different parts of the reservation; but the source of supply was kept secret for some time.

Santana had suspected their occupation, but his spies had failed to discover their hidden brewery. Although their immediate neighborhood was devoid of timber, dead brush sufficed for the small amount of fuel required for their operations, and the barren, gravelly nature of the ground made trailing difficult.

The liquor was unusually potent, and it was observed that the few drinks sold at exorbitant prices made the purchasers much more intoxicated than the usual run of tulhiba. The agents

Mescalero woman in front of her tipi. Courtesy Rio Grande Historical Collections, New Mexico State University Library.

delivering the stuff told their customers that in a short time there would be an abundant supply available to provide a grand debauch for all that cared to indulge. This information reached Santana, and he redoubled his efforts to thwart the project but failed.

The time and place were finally announced for the rendezvous. And a large number of Indians had already gathered and named four of their number as tubisno before Santana arrived with a force of men to stop the carousal. His interference had been anticipated and the liquor made available at several places. Due to its potency, a goodly number of the assembly were already quite under its influence. These people were around the supply points and threatened resistance, while others were at hand intent on drinking, so that Santana's posse was unable to control the situation without starting a disorder which might involve the whole tribe; consequently, he withdrew.

The drunken orgy developed rapidly, and several of the drinkers became crazed. Two of the tubisno were killed while attempting to separate antagonists, and the other two were compelled to drink. A free-for-all fight followed that left a dozen dead and twice as many seriously injured. It was later found that the brew had been mixed with whiskey of the "rot gut" character commonly furnished by the bootleggers, and several of the Indians died directly from the effect of drinking it.

Santana lost much of his influence as a result of this occurrence but still retained a sufficient following to punish the authors of the scheme. There was no public trial, but by some means the old women were induced to drink a sufficient quantity of the beverage, or something else, so they all died within a few days of the conclusion of the debauch. The assembly had been made up of members of the different bands, and the resulting feuds widened the breaches that had previously separated them.

The old chief, however, proved equal to the occasion and secured the cooperation of the military. And when a company of cavalry arrived at The Mill, he had the murderers arrested by his own people and delivered to the troops. These were convicted in the Federal Court and given prison terms. One of them, however, escaped from the military prison at Leavenworth and found his way back to the reservation, more than a thousand miles; there he was killed by a brother of the man he had murdered.

The success of this stratagem, although its accomplishment required nearly a year, allowed Santana to regain lost influence to a large extent; and the tragedy itself strengthened his position with relation to the problem of drunkenness. Because a group of influential members of the tribe had taken advantage of public sentiment in an effort to depose him, Santana dared not apply his former methods of control to a half-dozen of these well-known individuals. However, the sentiment against mass drunkenness was gaining ground so that all but occasional limited carousals were prevented.

SMALLPOX

During the winter and early spring of 1876, smallpox raged among the Mescalero, and a large majority of those infected died. Their medicine men knew nothing of the proper treatment of the disease, and some contended that the survivors were cured by Chete Neh. This contributed to the number of suspected witches, and the survivors would not be convinced of their immunity.

Those falling ill with a fever were immediately removed from the camps so that their deaths would not make it necessary to move the whole community. Their fevered condition usually led to their tipis being pitched on some eminence where they were exposed to the wind. Here they were provided with a supply of provisions and water and abandoned to their own resources. The doctor advised Gorgonio against such practices and told him they should be kept warm and avoid drafts, but that did little good. However, the doctor, being immune, moved several so disposed of near The Mill, and one of these recovered. The Indians' fear of the dread disease was so great that a number of women and children were known to have been killed when suspected of having the "rotten sickness" to prevent its spread.

All employees at The Mill were supposed to be immune from having been previously infected. However, a number of them contracted the disease, or varioloid, and one man died. Santana left The Mill when the disease was first discovered in the settlement. He established himself several miles away and escaped contagion.

Roman's family was exterminated by the disease. He alone survived and was fed and clothed by the doctor when he applied for aid. In mourning his wife and children, he had reserved nothing whatever and appeared with a breechclout of grass secured with a willow withe about his waist as his only clothing. The other Indians had threatened him when he tried to reach the agency for help. The stock in the trader's store was low, so he was given two cheap blankets, thick and warm but coarse, also a denim blouse for a shirt and a pair of heavy shoes. From one blanket he contrived a pair of leggings, then returned the shoes, saying they were too heavy and he was used to the snow on his feet. He brought the shoes to the doctor's room and was invited to sit by the fire, but the doctor was busy and made no effort to engage him in conversation. There he sat for some time in deep thought. The doctor thought he had fallen asleep when Roman said to him, "You are my friend, a good friend to me; and I am a good friend to you. I want to give you back this blanket that is not pretty, and I want you to give me one of the pretty red blankets you have because we are friends. This one is warm and good, but I have nothing pretty."

"Those red blankets cost more than a horse," objected the doctor, "and I can't afford to give them away when the others are just as warm."

Roman sat with his eyes cast down as though he had not heard. Then looking up he fixed his gaze intently on the doctor's face and said, "You do not know how good a friend I am to you. Do you remember about ten summers gone when you went to Mesilla and rode a mule that was blind? You went to Tularosa in the afternoon, and when it was dark you went on along the road until the moon came up. Then you put the mule in the brush on one side of the road and took your saddle and other things to sleep in the shadow of a bush on the other side; then you went to sleep this way." Roman lay on his back on the floor with this arms crossed on his breast. "The blanket was on the ground, and your head was on the saddle and you had two pistols with white handles in your hands while you slept."

"I remember that time," admitted the doctor. "I was going to Mesilla to court and had to be there the next day, and some people had been killed on that road two days before, and I was afraid."

"Then you know about that," resumed the Indian. "Santana wanted to know where you were going, for he thought you might know the Mescalero were in the Sacramentos and would tell the soldiers at the fort. So he sent six men with me to see and told us not to let you go to the fort and not to let the bad Indians kill you along the road; for he wanted you for our friend. So we sat there, sometimes one and sometimes another all night, for we thought when you slept you would let the pistols fall and we could get them. But you kept them in your hands, and when it was a little light I took hold of one pistol, but you held it tighter when I pulled a little and began to wake up. Then you went on, and we saw you go to Mesilla and not to the fort."

The trip described had been a memorable one and undertaken under great necessity. Several massacres had occurred in the country traversed by the road within the month, and it was considered a dangerous trip. The mule the doctor had ridden was easy riding and being blind, seldom brayed, which the doctor had considered an advantage should he desire to conceal himself.

A red blanket was added to Roman's wardrobe, and the doctor heated water and had him bathe with a disinfectant, while he fumigated the clothing the Indian had handled and explained that this action would keep him from making other people sick.

Roman was very weak and had not been able to perform the last rites for his wife and children, all of whom had died during a day and night. But in the belief that Chete Neh would not go where there was "black from fire," he had burned their tipi over them where they lay and added brush to the flames until they were buried in ashes. No Indian had permitted him to approach them, much less give him assistance, and he told the doctor that he was afraid the wind and rain would uncover them and some of the animals of Chete Neh would eat them. Consequently, he led a party from The Mill that dug a grave and buried the charred corpses.

Roman told other Indians of the treatment he had received, and a number who had recovered were convinced of their immunity. These were provided with disinfectants by the agent, who also attended some of the afflicted. The more humane treatment no doubt saved lives in many cases. The epidemic was checked, but isolated cases developed from time to time all summer.

An itinerant photographer visited the agency that summer and was much disappointed when the Indians refused to be photographed. The doctor asked Santana why they objected and was told that photography was witchcraft, and if it was practiced on Indians they would die. In order to convince the old chief that such was not the case, he had pictures taken of himself, and a number of his employees, and also the house with several of his people.

When the pictures were developed, they were shown to the Indians, but only Santana had sufficient confidence in the doctor's assurance that there was no witchery about it to agree to being photographed. At that time the exposure of the plate required some time, and the subject was posed in such manner as would prevent movement with an adjustable support to the head. When Santana had been posed and the support adjusted to his head, he leaped to his feet and refused.

An incredulous, suspicious group of his followers had gathered to watch the ordeal, and when he lost his nerve they laughed and cheered with both derision and relief. Then Santana declared, "My wives left me alone when they thought I had the 'rotten sickness.' I do not care if they die, and I will make them have their picture taken."

This was accomplished after several days of arguments and threats and finally a beating; and this was the only photograph of a Mescalero for many years. In fact, until snapshots were available, and even in the 1880s, they would not willingly be photographed but hid their faces when a camera was seen, for these two women died a few months later and confirmed the Indians' belief that there was death-dealing witchery in photography.[1]

In the fall of 1876, Santana was taken ill with the smallpox, and his tipi moved out of camp. He insisted that his wives remain with him and enforced his order for a time with a six-shooter, making one of them stay nearby during the necessary absences of the other. They were devoted to each other, and neither deserted until the old chief succumbed to fatigue and fell asleep. Then both escaped. The doctor was told of Santana's condition, and he had him brought to a room in the house, where careful nursing brought him through the crisis. When the doctor was called away for a few days, the convalescent went back to his tipi where he took cold and developed pneumonia, so that when the doctor returned he found him dead. Santana's remains were buried by the doctor within the grounds now occupied by the Mescalero agency and his effects were destroyed by the Indians.

During his earlier life, Santana had been notorious as one of the Indian leaders responsible for some of their most atrocious crimes. He was a contemporary of Mangas Coloradas (Red Sleeves) and was also known as Big Foot by the military scouts on account of his notably large tracks. His change of attitude toward the settlers and transients, as described by himself, may or may not have been a central reason for his efforts toward making peace with white people. However, the Mescalero's point of view is well described in his statements, and no doubt his change of heart saved a remnant of his people many years of painful experience.

"Preservation of the species" was no doubt his fundamental reason for change. His ability to control the tribe as he did demonstrates his strength of character. From his point of view, he made a noble sacrifice, in that he set aside the great honor he might have gained by encouraging a continuance of hostilities. Many of his followers resented his attitude and to an extent held him in contempt. But they did not have the courage to oppose him openly, awaiting only some unexpected circumstance to weaken his influence and advance a leader. However, his personality commanded the fear, or loyalty, of the mass of his people.

Santana's death was a great misfortune to the Mescalero, for, although probably not less than sixty years of age at the time of his death, he was a strong man physically, possessed a keen intelligence, and had extraordinary qualities of leadership. By example he had won considerable sentiment against the course of drunkenness, and a few more years of his leadership might well have prevented the Mescalero's relapse into their former habits. Had his decision to maintain a friendly attitude prevailed, the considerable number of Mescalero who did so would not have joined Victorio in his outbreak in the early 1880s and would not have been annihilated with that leader by the Mexican troops.[2]

Indian police force, 1895. Blazer Family Collection.

CONCLUSION
by Almer N. Blazer

About 1873, the Congress of the United States created the Mescalero Reservation, which embraced the original reservation and about an equal amount of land just north of it. The northern half of the reservation was soon opened for settlement when rich mines were found on the northern line of the reservation.[1] Between the time of leaving the Bosque Redondo and their settling down on the reservation there was little restraint over the Mescalero, and they raided in Texas and along the Rio Grande, often going into Old Mexico. In 1862, the first agent, Lorenzo Labadie (1862–1869), was named and was stationed at the Anton Chico agency, a military post which had been established well before the Civil War. The Mescalero did not like the military and would seldom come in for their rations. In 1855, Fort Stanton was established and except for a short period during the Civil War was the Mescalero agency until late 1874. The agency at that time was moved to Blazer's Mill on the Rio Tularoso near the present site of the Mescalero agency. The post office was called South Fork.[2]

The government rented one-half of Dr. Blazer's residence for the agent to live in. Dr. Blazer had located there in the sixties and built a two-story adobe building with a fort on top as a defense from the Indians. As he had a number of Mexican and American employees it was also a protection for them and for the agent's family. The rental for the house, or the half of it, was seven hundred-dollars a year. The commissary was maintained at the present site of the agency, which is about one-half mile above Blazer's Mill.

The first agent was W. D. Crothers (1874–1876) from Springfield, Missouri. He was succeeded by Major F. C. Godfroy (1876–1879), who in turn was replaced by Major S. A. Russell (1879–1881). The title of major was conferred on all Indian agents. Major Llewellyn took charge (1881–1884) and built a residence for the agent at the present agency.[3]

The Indians came in a few at a time, and after once getting the rations they usually continued to call for them. The theory of Uncle Sam was that it was cheaper to feed than to fight the Apache, so they made a treaty with them to give them the reservation to be theirs and their children's forever unless they themselves violated the treaty by leaving without permission. In addition to the land allotted them, each Indian, large or small, was to receive a weekly ration of a stated amount of beef, flour, coffee, sugar, baking powder, soap, and other articles of food, as well as clothing and cooking utensils, axes, and blankets.

To the credit of the Mescalero, they did not violate their part of the treaty. Did the government do as well? The first violation on the part of Uncle Sam was when they cut off the northern half of the reservation.

Next, they brought the Jicarilla Apache from Rio Arriba County and placed them on the land with the rightful owners. The two tribes, however, did not affiliate. During the two years the Jicarilla remained on the reservation they practically exterminated the game, which had always before proved adequate for the Mescalero because of their more conservative hunting practices. It was believed that not a single elk remained, and of the thousands of deer but a very few were to be found on the reservation. When this occurred, the Jicarilla became restless and were permitted to return to their old haunts. After two hundred deserted the reservation in late 1866, the remaining five hundred or so were removed to a new reservation on the western slope of the Jemez Mountains, where they remain today.

The surrounding country, too, was rapidly filling up with settlers, who also contributed to the death of the principal food supply of the Mescalero.

Lastly, the government long ago ceased to give the Indians the promised rations. This later action is justified by the condition of the men today, as had the practice been continued they would still be "blanket Indians" being fed by the "Father" in Washington. Further, the beef issued to them by the government was not sufficient to maintain their accustomed diet, which had been mostly meat, and recourse to farinaceous foods, which they had not learned to prepare, caused alimentary troubles and discontent that required a generation to overcome.

In order to make the Mescalero move self-sufficient, the agent tried to teach them to work, giving them small farms, seed, farming implements, and a farmer to instruct them. They also received wagons, harness, oxen and some cows. They always had plenty of horses or ponies, as they were pleased to call them.

The first wagons sent them were purchased by the Indian Department in Washington. Wagons were sent to a number of reservations at the same time and were all bought by someone connected with the Indian office. The party handling the matter may have been a good office man, but he knew nothing about selecting wagons for the mountain districts. He did not know that the mountain roads are six inches wider than the plains country roads. So when the wagons came they were six inches too narrow for the roads and were not satisfactory. The Indians did not take to the use of wagons and insisted on riding a pony while driving the oxen, as they did not believe in walking as the bull-whacker had to do. They abandoned the wagons whenever possible; or they sold some to those who were willing to take a chance on buying government property.

One Indian built a road up a steep mountainside between the

agency and Blazer's Mill. The road was so steep that the oxen could not pull the wagon over halfway up, so he unyoked them from the wagon and left it to stand there for several months. One day about a dozen Apache, all grown men, went to the wagon and pushed it off down the steep mountainside, and when it landed at the bottom there was nothing unbroken that it was possible to break. They spent several hours laughing about the matter.

Another bright idea of someone in the Washington office was to send out some horsepower corn crushers to be used in crushing corn to feed to stock, as the farmers did in farming localities. The Apache raised only a small amount of corn, just enough for roasting ears and enough to make tulhiba, the Apache name for a home brew, the manufacture and use of which the government forbade. After the corn crushers had lain around the agency for several years, they were condemned and sold. This writer bought one at the sale for fifty cents. Many such experiments were tried in the early days in an effort to induce Indians to adopt the white man's ways.

After the death of Geronimo at Fort Sill, in 1913, many of the band exiled with him were allowed to move to the Mescalero Reservation and are now at the subagency at Whitetail Springs. In the early days all of the Mescalero were "bronco," and many of them would not come in for rations. But the agent offered every inducement at his command to encourage them to do so. From the time when the reservation was first organized there had been a boarding school, where the children were housed and fed. As an inducement to parents to allow their children to go to school, the child's rations were given to the family while the child was fed at the school, so the family got extra rations.

With the first agent a police force was created, consisting of a captain, lieutenants, and some twenty privates, all of whom were Indians. They were under a white man, who was chief of police, and were paid a salary and each issued a pistol, saddle, bridle, and a police uniform. The uniforms were used by only a few at first,

Lieutenant V. E. Stottler, "civilized" the Mescalero children by force. Here the girls are dressed alike in Mother Hubbard dresses, the boys in Civil War type uniforms with caps, military blouses, and stripes down the trousers, 1895–1898. Blazer Family Collection.

Children marching to the Mescalero School, 1918. Blazer Family Collection.

except the vests, which were popular on account of the convenient pockets. In the course of time all the Mescalero clamored for the rations, and then the government began tightening its grip on them. The surrounding country became filled with white settlers, causing the Apache to realize that they were overpowered and outnumbered. Consequently, little by little they submitted to the agent's policies.

The first thing was an attempt to get them to wear the white man's clothes. The first policeman to wear citizen's clothing was Old Boneski, a Tonkawa, who lived with the Apache and had a Mescalero wife. The agent, Colonel Cowart, had a suit of clothes which was too small for him, so he gave it to Boneski and paid him five dollars to wear it. Boneski came to the agency several times with the suit on and then discarded the coat, explaining to the agent that it was too hot to wear a coat. The agent accepted the excuse. On his next appearance at the agency he had on the vest and the pants, which appeared to be all right. However, the agent soon noticed that Boneski watched his every move and wondered why Boneski never allowed his back to be toward the agent. Finally, the agent's curiosity overcame his politeness. He seized Boneski, turned him around, and saw that the seat of the trousers had been entirely cut away. Boneski explained that he was not accustomed to wearing trousers but only a gee-string, so he had cut away that part of the pants which seemed to him useless. From then on only the vest was in evidence.

When the grip of civilization tightened still more, the agent forbade the contracting of plural marriages by policemen. The Mescalero were nearly all polygamists. The agent did not disturb any of the matrimonial arrangements then in existence but allowed no new plural marriages. If a policeman made a new plural marriage, he was discharged. If a new man was added to the force, he must have only one wife. Next, all were required to wear their uniforms at all times. Lastly, the policemen were required to have and keep their hair cut short. So little by little control over the Mescalero was extended, and finally all of the tribe adopted the white man's customs.

The Indian Department wished to teach its wards something of the white man's laws and how they were administered, so three Indians were appointed by the Great Father at Washington to be judges for the tribe. These judges were to adjudicate all small offenses such as are termed misdemeanors in our courts. The judges were paid the salary of five dollars each per month. Their deliberations were held in the agent's office and under his direction to a great extent.

The first three judges were Natzili, meaning "Cow Belly" on account of his enormous girth; Noto-go-lindo, meaning "Have You Got Any Tobacco?"; and José Torres, a Tonkawa who had married a Mescalero woman. One of the first important cases to be handled by the court was a damage case. Natzili, who was said to have been a noted athlete in his younger days, attended a tulhiba *tiswin* (party) and became boastful of his prowess as a footracer. Attending the party was a young athlete named Horse Thief. Natzili wagered three dollars that he could outrun Horse Thief and posted the money with a stakeholder. Horse Thief was easily winning when Natzili refused to go on and took his three dollars from the stakeholder. Horse Thief took a shinny club that some of the schoolboys had dropped there and struck his adversary on the head, knocking him down; then he tore the buckskin shirt off him and recovered the three dollars which he claimed he had won. Natzili complained to the agent and had the case brought before the judges for adjudication. Natzili was the prosecuting witness, Horse Thief the defendant. The other witnesses declined to testify, as Natzili was the head war chief. When the testimony was all in, Natzili insisted on giving his judgment, which was about as follows: Horse Thief was to return the three dollars, buy Natzili a new buckskin shirt, and allow him to strike Horse Thief on the head three times with

Mescalero War Chief San Juan, wearing presidential medal, 1884. Blazer Family Collection.

Natzili, Mescalero war chief after San Juan, 1886. Blazer Family Collection.

Left: *Agustin (1910), a Warm Springs Apache. Banished by his tribe for some "criminal act," Agustin was taken in by Mescalero. He was a noted runner and lived to a very old age—about 115 years.*

Right: *Agustin's wife Mary. She was Dr. Thompson's first patient at Mescalero. Photographs courtesy Rio Grande Historical Collections, New Mexico University Library.*

the same club. The other judges concurred in the first part, to return the three dollars, but refused to award a new shirt as they said that they knew personally that Natzili had worn the shirt for fifteen or twenty years. They also refused to allow Natzili to strike Horse Thief with the club, saying that as Natzili was still very angry he might strike him too hard and kill him.

Sixty years of neighborly acquaintance with the Mescalero have enabled me, in some measure, to understand their point of view. Personal friendships, real and valued, have resulted, and have shown me that their humanity was not of a different species from other peoples. Good, bad, and indifferent characters existed among them, and their environment had much to do with their mode of life. From their standpoint the violent acts of which they were guilty were justifiable and were in many cases in reprisal for equal or worse treatment of themselves. In other instances, however, their vengeance fell on innocent parties through ignorance of the real offenders. All too often blame was laid on people innocent of the crime.

Santana died a year before my arrival here as a boy, and the exploits related are based on my father's recollections as well as on those of the old timers. Added to this are my personal observations of the uses the Mescalero made of natural resources and of their dances and ceremonials, which I occasionally attended.

Many of their functions were of such a character that an outsider would not care to attend them, and probably would not have been permitted to do so. However, I have recorded a few customs which in earlier times were secret, with a death penalty provided for divulgence. These were described in later years when they were no longer practiced, by an old woman grateful for assistance I had been able to give her.

The stoicism, patience, ingenuity, and endurance of the older

Indians was notable; a number of instances were known of individuals who amputated their own limb in an emergency. Chronic sores were cauterized with live coals without assistance. And it was common practice for the men to extract their beard with tweezers, which everyone carried for the purpose. On occasion when hunting was difficult, game would be followed for days before being taken. Clothing was improvised from all sorts of material. On long rapid marches good horses were frequently exhausted and abandoned while footmen continued on.

Isolated as they have been, and few in number, the Mescalero have been overlooked, probably to their advantage, and have not been as greatly affected as other tribes by close contact with many of the so-called "civilizing influences" of non-Indian society. However, while within the past fifty years, since the establishment of the reservation in 1877, they have faithfully adhered to their traditions; at the present time a large majority of them, including all the younger generations, live in neat, well-appointed cottages, clean and well kept. They speak the English language fluently, while many of the children use English among themselves, and the old Mescalero language is being forgotten.

Many have embraced Christianity and attend regular services. A neat, substantial Protestant church, with a community center, is served by a resident pastor and assistants to provide for their spiritual needs. And a stone church of cathedral proportions is nearing completion by the Catholics, while their congregation is being regularly served by a resident priest and assistants, in temporary quarters.[4]

APPENDIX I
Joseph H. Blazer

Joseph Hoy Blazer, Almer N. Blazer's father, was born in Washington County, Pennsylvania, southwest of Pittsburgh, on August 20, 1828, the eleventh of twelve children and a descendant of Scotch-Irish immigrants and early Dutch pioneers. Most of the information we have comes from what others have said about him.

He grew up on a farm in McDonough County, Illinois, where his family raised hogs, cattle, hay, and grain.[1] According to family records, Blazer's formal education was limited to frontier schools. In spite of his limited schooling, he began the study of dentistry at age nineteen in St. Louis, Missouri, and completed his studies four years later in 1852. He began his practice in Mount Pleasant, Iowa, in that same year. On September 26, 1853, he married Lucy Jobes of Mount Pleasant.[2]

Within a few years after Dr. Blazer began practice, he developed a crippling form of arthritis which in a very short time disabled his hands to such a degree that he was unable to continue his profession. Concerning this, Almer N. Blazer commented tersely; "We were reduced to poverty because of it."[3]

In July 1861, he enlisted in the Union Army with the rank of corporal. A year later, in October 1862, he was seriously injured in a skirmish when his horse fell on him, fracturing some ribs, one or more of which punctured a lung. He was given a discharge "due to disability" in December 1862.[4] He did not rejoin the Union Army after recovery but secured a commission as sutler to his old regiment. The regiment was disbanded in Shreveport, Louisiana, in 1865.

As sutler he had acquired four six-mule teams and wagons. At a quartermaster sale he purchased six more teams and wagons and started a trading and freighting business. It was on a trip in 1866 to Franklin (now El Paso) that Blazer contracted smallpox. He remained in the town over the winter to recuperate and in the spring contracted with the government for a shipment of corn to be delivered to the Bosque Redondo Reservation. During this trip he passed by La Maquina, where he would subsequently make his home.

Before Joseph H. Blazer's arrival at La Maquina, the landowners in the canyon and at Tularosa had met and agreed on a joint effort to dig a new channel for the river by first clearing a passage through the tules covering the floor of the canyon. With the growing population, the water rights and water usage for irrigation had become an acute problem. Blazer became the leader and spokesman for the canyon group. The most pressing water problems were brought to his attention, and he worked out an extended plan which all factions quickly adopted. There was still some ill will, however, brought about in part by the greed and dishonesty of a few landowners. Out of this latter group a serious altercation took place which almost cost Blazer his life.[5] In general, though, Blazer was looked upon by all factions as a generous friend, a fair and honest competitor, and a man who knew how to get things done.

Around 1873, with the help of the local priest, Blazer organized the first school in Tularosa. The first teacher he hired was the elderly lady who had nursed him through smallpox a few years earlier.

The Tularosa community paid three bits per day (37½ cents) for common labor, four bits (50 cents) if the laborers boarded themselves. Blazer increased the wage to a minimum of one dollar per day. This produced a more efficient workforce that would work harder and stay longer.[6]

Because he was considered fair, just, and impartial, Blazer was in great demand for jury duty, usually as foreman, in a land where most citizens were illiterate and too easily swayed by the "high-falutin" rhetoric of unscrupulous lawyers.[7]

While he was away on a trip in 1869, the mill burned. The fire was apparently of "incendiary origin," according to Almer N. Blazer. It was set either by "Anglos"* or Mexicans or both, dressed as Indians, or by Comanche. There was no money to rebuild. Undaunted, Dr. Blazer, whose range of acquaintances had expanded rapidly, found a partner. George C. Abbot, a wealthy merchant who lived in Presidio, Texas, made a deal with Blazer. He bought out the other owners, Nesmith, Dixon, and Ryan and, in return for Blazer's wagons and other related properties, plus his one-third interest and his managerial abilities, made Blazer an equal partner in the new venture. Blazer was also given one-half interest in an El Paso lumberyard.[8]

During the entire Lincoln County War, Dr. Blazer steadfastly remained neutral, a fact perhaps best illustrated by his role in the first battle of that war, the battle at Blazer's Mill, on April 4, 1878.

The McSween faction had formed a posse of twelve men led by Dick Brewer, with Billy the Kid as a posse member. They were riding about in search, they said, of any members of the Dolan faction, whom they intended to arrest. They stopped at Blazer's near noon and demanded lunch. Almer N. Blazer, age thirteen, and two friends were playing near the creek when they saw the influx of riders. They started toward the house when Buckshot Roberts rode up on his mule. Just as he greeted the boys, whom he knew, one of the posse spied him and shouted, "Here is Roberts!" Roberts grabbed his gun from its scabbard on his mule, yelled at the boys, "Get out of the way!" and ran to a house adjacent to the big house, where the Indian agent, Fred C. Godfroy, lived and whose cook was

---

* Southwestern term for Caucasian (non-Indian, non-Hispanic) Americans.

preparing the requested meal. Then the shooting began. Of what happened next Almer N. Blazer wrote:

> *Father had found Brewer dead at the mill when we arrived there. He told us that he was shot through the head and that nothing could be done for him until it was safe to go and carry him out. It was only a little while after this that three of the ["posse"], including Billy the Kid, came to us having made a circuit to the south of the mill where they were out of sight of Roberts' position. They were looking for Brewer and became excited when father told them what had happened to him. The Kid told father that he would have to go and put Roberts out of the house, to which father replied that he would not. Then the Kid said that he would kill him if he didn't, to which father answered that he thought Roberts would do the same thing if he tried to put him out, and he didn't see much difference so far as he was concerned. The Kid then called father a damned old fool and said they would burn the house, to which father replied that he knew no way to prevent that either.[9]*

Joseph H. Blazer never carried a gun at a time when practically all grown men sported a pistol or rifle. Paul A. Blazer, Sr., his grandson, considered the reasons for this unusual behavior:

> *The bane of grandfather's life was his violent temper. I think that was the reason he never carried a gun. He was so tall and strong and his arms so long that he seldom had a chance to hit a man twice. . . . It seems that Jabez Hedges [his daughter Ellie's husband] while not a louse exactly was not a very good provider and maybe lived it up some too. Grandfather had given Ellie a team of very good mares. Hedges found himself without money one spring and without saying anything, mortgaged the team to the post trader at Fort Stanton for money to make a crop. Harvest time came and passed. Dr. Blazer happened to be at Fort Stanton one day, and the trader inquired about Hedges. That is how grandfather found out about the business. When he got home, Hedges was there*

. . . . Grandfather gave Hedges a thrashing right there on the chip pile. Hedges left and, as far as I know, no one ever saw him again.[10]

Given the hard necessities of life, most frontier people took a firm stand in crucial matters. Blazer's fury and the consequent thrashing it provoked would have been considered perfectly appropriate and exactly what Hedges deserved. Blazer assumed responsibility for Ellie (who was ill at the time and died in 1888) and her five children.

Joseph H. Blazer's fiery temperament influenced Almer N. Blazer's relation to his father. It is clear from Almer N. Blazer's references to the doctor that he never crossed or defied him. Instead, he waited until another day before broaching the same subject, knowing that time and his father's sound common sense would take care of the problem.

While he was on a business trip to the Midwest in 1882, Blazer hired twenty-five-year-old Miss Julia McWade to serve as a tutor for the Hedges children. Miss McWade brought with her a sister, Mrs. Hattie Allen, and Mrs. Allen's son, Frank. Gramma Jule, as she was called by the Blazer children, was a very intelligent, strong-willed, outspoken lady. She married Dr. Blazer in 1884.

By 1899, the year after Joseph H. Blazer's death, the Allens and Gramma Jule were claiming the entire farm and business and were attempting to force Almer N. Blazer to stay entirely away. This brought about two or three years of legal battles, with a final settlement made of cash to Gramma Jule. The entire property was awarded to Almer N. Blazer.[11]

More than most men of his time, Joseph H. Blazer symbolized those early Americans who created the culture which Max Weber called in his great study of cultures *The Protestant Ethic and the Spirit of Capitalism*.[12] He was among those who brought order and civility, the kind of people who stood tall, walked free, and created a milieu which made "gun-toting" an anachronism. One is compelled to add, ruefully, that today Billy the Kid is better known and more widely emulated.

When he met Santana for the first time, as Almer N. Blazer recounts that meeting, he observed Santana and listened to what he had to say, judging him to be a man of character. Santana was looking for a man who "talked with one tongue." In Dr. Blazer, he found the integrity, the honesty, and the courage he was seeking. For the entire tribe, he was a rarity—an Anglo who was their friend and advisor. Even today, courtesy is extended to the many members of the Blazer family living on or near the reservation.

The only land on the Mescalero Reservation which remains a Blazer property is a narrow strip of hillside rising precipitously above the new highway. Like a sentinel, it overlooks with serene indifference the scene where Blazer's Mill was once the hub of a small, troubled, and now perished world. Today, it is a quiet spot, looking much as it appeared before La Maquina came to the canyon years upon years ago, a sunbathed place sparsely wooded with piñon and cedar trees. Traces of algerita shrubs planted long ago remind one to walk prudently lest he disturb the old-timers buried there who lived, labored, and died within earshot of this wind-washed hill.

Here a member of this goodly company, Joseph H. Blazer, takes his rest.

APPENDIX II
Almer N. Blazer

Almer Newton Blazer was born in Mount Pleasant, Iowa, on June 19, 1865. He attended a primary school three years before moving to New Mexico Territory in 1877 with his two sisters, Ellie Hedges and Emma Blazer.

Because Almer N. Blazer's mother, Lucy Jobes Blazer, developed tuberculosis during the Civil War, the family had been advised to seek a more salubrious climate. This was, of course, the principal reason his father, Dr. Joseph H. Blazer, took his wagon train to the Southwest after the regiment, which he served as sutler, was disbanded in Shreveport, Louisiana. Lucy Blazer's health declined rapidly, and she died on November 1, 1869. The children remained in Mount Pleasant in the care of an aunt and uncle until the fall of 1877, at which time Dr. Blazer felt that it was finally safe for them to move to the still unsettled and unpredictable frontier.

Almer N. Blazer, always in delicate health, contracted pneumonia during the winter of 1876–1877, following which he continued to lose weight and developed a chronic cough with intermittent fever. He was diagnosed as having "galloping consumption," an especially virulent form of tuberculosis. The family was told that his chances of living more than a year were almost nil.

The trip to New Mexico took a full month. The railroad ended at Pueblo, Colorado, but, as Almer N. Blazer wrote:

We got on a little car, [narrow gauge?] and it brought us to a place called Cucharas. There we changed again and came to El Moro, a short distance from Trinidad, Colorado, and [this was] the nearest to home (Mescalero) we could get by rail at that time [roughly 300 miles distant].[1] We finally arrived at Anton Chico. Here, father came to us sometime in the night. I had been asleep, but he had me dress and go with him to a hotel, where he had put up in town. The doctors in Iowa had given me up to die within a year with T.B., and I guess he was considerably worried about my cough, for the others stayed in camp that night.[2]

Almer N. Blazer's health improved, however, and he soon mastered both the Spanish and Apache languages. He became a proficient hunter, a skilled tracker, a good marksman with a gun, and was well liked by the Indians.[3] He also learned from the Indians about the flora and fauna of the region and their uses, an interest that grew and developed all of his life. Later, he would write stories concerning incidents that occurred while hunting with both Indians and with some noted Anglo-American hunters and trappers, who were among the more colorful personalities of the time.

He went to school briefly, in Las Cruces, New Mexico, and studied for a year at St. Michael's School in Santa Fe. That was the extent of his formal education. He wrote: "When I got back home, the grist mill was being installed, so I began learning the milling business and had no more schooling."[4]

There were always books, magazines, and ideas in the Blazer household. Young Blazer, who was an avid reader with wide-ranging interests, became well informed about everything which involved his world.

He became an apprentice to his father, and, like him, a man who wore many hats. During that apprenticeship, he served as a miller, lumberjack, farmer, overseer, bookkeeper, and accountant. Working with machinery stimulated and brought to the fore an innate talent for the science of mechanics. He became interested in developing a pump which would deliver water from underground. He was invited to work at New Mexico A & M (now New Mexico State University) at Las Cruces. There, he spent 12 years developing his projects. Blazer's spiral pump proved mechanically successful after years of experimentation and was marketed by the Humphrys Company of Mansfield, Ohio. Unfortunately, the centrifugal pump was perfected at the same time and proved more popular than the Blazer pump, which finally had to be abandoned. Dame Fortune never seemed to smile on Almer N. Blazer.

Almer N. Blazer was married on January 25, 1888, to Belle B. Blackford in Monroe, Wisconsin. Four children were born to them: Vida, May 22, 1889; Paul Almer, July 31, 1890; Noel Edison, October 28, 1894; and Howard Thompson, October 13, 1897. Howard died in 1908 of a protracted fever, probably typhoid.[5]

Almer N. Blazer continued to work with his father and live near him at Mescalero or Tularosa for the next fourteen years until Joseph H. Blazer's death in 1898.

Belle Blackford Blazer died in January 1917. Almer N. Blazer married Clara Smith on February 20, 1918, but she died in the influenza epidemic of that year in December 1918. On August 29, 1920 he married Miss Fanny Dennis, a school teacher from Wichita, Kansas, who had been teaching Pueblo Indian children at San Felipe Pueblo near Bernalillo, New Mexico. Aunt Fanny, as she was fondly called, ran a boardinghouse for students at the College of Agriculture and Mining in order to help defray expenses.

The coming of the railroads and generally improved transportation caused business at the Mescalero grist mill to diminish to such a degree that it was no longer economically feasible to operate. The mill was finally closed in 1922. By the time Almer N. Blazer returned to Mescalero in 1931 at the age of sixty-six, the Great Depression was in full swing. There was little or no income, although the farm did furnish a bare subsistence.

Over the years Almer N. Blazer developed a reputation in

academic and historical circles all across the Southwest as a prime and dependable source of information, not only in matters pertaining to the Mescalero Apache but on the history and development of the territory in general. Writers and scholars frequently wrote or visited him to obtain information on questions of local historical interest.

While at New Mexico A & M, he received an inquiry from William R. Leigh, a New York artist. In the 1920s Leigh had become interested in writing as an adjunct to painting and wrote to Blazer concerning his interest in the Southwest and the Mescalero Reservation in particular. A long correspondence between the two men was begun which lasted until Blazer's death in 1949. Leigh, in his quest for information, encouraged Blazer to write about his own stories, the tales told by the Indians as well as those told by the many early frontier characters he knew.

Blazer began his writing career in August 1932 with a brief serialized history of the territory for the *Alamogordo News*. Several articles were written for *New Mexico Magazine,* including "Blazer's Mill," (January 1939); "The Beginning of an Indian War," and "Loaded for Bear" (November 1939); and others. In August 1939 he wrote for the *Frontier Times* an account of the opening battle of the Lincoln County War, entitled "The Fight at Blazer's Mill in New Mexico."

His two most ambitious works were the present account of Santana's life, and "Los Jirones,"[6] a seventy-thousand-word work of historical fiction. In both of these works Blazer is at his best, giving scope to his skill in handling detail, whether in depicting the customs and traditions of the people, or in giving descriptions of the equipment they used in their daily lives, the food they ate, religious attitudes they held, and so forth. Both works provide a wealth of information that would otherwise have been lost.

In 1943, Almer N. Blazer sold all that was left of the original Blazer property to the Mescalero Apache people. He reserved the right for his family and for his son, Paul A. Blazer, and his family to live on the property as long as they wished during their lifetimes. During the 1940s he continued his efforts to record the past as he knew it until his death on March 13, 1949.

He is buried in the Blazer family cemetery on the hillside above his old home, where many of the participants in the events he chronicled have, like him, found surcease from all their sorrows.

Mescalero girls dressed for haheh, *Mescalero puberty rites. Blazer Family Collection.*

NOTES

ABBREVIATIONS

Blazer Family Papers	BFP
Court Records	CR
Rio Grande Historical Collection Blazer Papers	RGH-BP
Katherine D. Stoes	RGH-Stoes
National Archives, Washington	NAW
National Archives, Fort Worth	AFW
Gilcrease Museum Archives	GMA
New Mexico State Library, Sante Fe	NMSL
U.S. Grant Presidential Papers	USGPP
Weissbrodt Papers	WBP

FOREWORD

1. C. L. Sonnichsen, *The Mescalero Apaches* (Norman: University of Oklahoma Press, 1982), 141.

PREFACE

1. William R. Leigh to Paul A. Blazer, 8 June 1953, GMA, Tulsa, Oklahoma.

2. Duane D. Cummins, *William Robinson Leigh: Western Artist* (Norman: University of Oklahoma Press, 1980).

3. Almer N. Blazer to William R. Leigh, 4 March 1931, GMA.

4. Harry Hoijer, with ethnological notes by Morris Edward Opler, *Chiricahua and Mescalero Apache Texts* (Chicago: University of Chicago Press, 1938).

EDITOR'S INTRODUCTION

1. An obvious contraction of Santa Ana, the name of the notorious Mexican politician, who was in his heyday at that time. There were four other contemporary chiefs with the same or similar names: Santana, a Comanche, friend when convenient of Englebert Krauskopf, a scout and gunsmith from the German community of Fredericksburg, Texas (Pioneer Museum, Fredericksburg, Texas); the Kiowa Apache chiefs Satanka and Satank, both of whom died while in the hands of their American captors (Robert M. Utley, *The Indian Frontier of the American West 1846–1890* [Albuquerque: University of New Mexico Press, 1984], 146); and Santos, head of a Mescalero band.

2. Morris Edward Opler and Catherine H. Opler, "Mescalero Apache History in the Southwest," *New Mexico Historical Review* 25 (January 1950): 1.

3. C. L. Sonnichsen, *The Mescalero Apaches* (Norman: University of Oklahoma Press, 1982), 142.

4. Both of these chairs are in the possession of Arthur D. Blazer, Capitan, New Mexico. [Photographed July 2000 by Don Begley; see back cover.]

5. Averam Burton Bender, *A Study of the Mescalero Apache 1846–1880*, (New York: Garland Publishing Co., 1960), 41.

6. Report by Captain A. W. Bowman of a meeting with Apache chiefs, April 21, 1850. Sonnichsen, *Mescalero Apaches*, 69.

7. James A. Haley, *Apaches: A History and Culture Portrait* (Garden City: Doubleday and Co., 1981), 186.

8. Sonnichsen, *Mescalero Apaches*, 70.

9. William A. Keleher, *Turmoil in New Mexico 1846–1868* (Santa Fe, New Mexico: Rydal Press, 1952), 15.

10. Bender, *Study of the Mescalero Apache*, 42–43.

11. In times of severe stress when dire calamity, whether natural or imposed by military force, reduced them to a strategy for survival, the Mescalero, as they expressed it, "threw away" the very young and the very old; i.e., they abandoned them. Survival of the group was the prime consideration.

12. Bender, *Study of the Mescalero Apache*, 35.

13. Bender, *Study of the Mescalero Apache*, 33–43.

14. Bender, *Study of the Mescalero Apache*, 43.

15. Captain Richard S. Ewell to Major W. A. Nichols, 10 February 1855, WBP.

16. Lieutenant General Garland to War Department, Washington, D.C., 28 February 1855, WBP.

17. Dr. Michael Steck to D. Meriwether, 6 March 1855, WBP.

18. Dixon S. Miles to Dr. Michael Steck, 9 September 1855, WBP.

19. Major Jefferson Van Horne to W. A. Nichols, 16 June 1856, WBP.

20. The renegade Cha, whom Almer N. Blazer considers a son of Barranquito and a "brother" [half brother? cousin?] to Santana, Cadete, and Roman, is identified by Jefferson Van Horne, August 13, 1856, as Shawano, a brother of Santana and the head of a band that had stolen some horses from some Mexicans near Manzano.

The rift between Santana and Cha came about because Santana knew that it was useless to continue fighting the Anglos and sought a peaceful solution while Cha believed that Santana had become a "woman." Cha thought that the only way was to fight until death. This split in the tribe was noted by many reporters of Indian affairs. Shawano gains much credence here in Van Horne's and Bender's reports as the man "Cha" in Almer N. Blazer's account. Jefferson Van Horne to Dr. Michael Steck, 13 August 1856, WBP; Bender, *Study of the Mescalero Apache*, 64.

21. Lawrence Baker to W. A. Nichols, 10 March 1857. In Bender, *Study of the Mescalero Apache*, 69.

22. Bender, *Study of the Mescalero Apache*, 71–73.

23. Keleher, *Turmoil*, 324–25.

24. Haley, *Apaches*, 233.

25. Bender, *Study of the Mescalero Apache*, 100–103.

26. Haley, *Apaches*, 235.

27. Bender, *Study of the Mescalero Apache*, 103.

28. At no time is there any indication that either Almer N. Blazer or Joseph H. Blazer knew of Santana's prolonged absence from local, state, and federal records. This entire episode in the lives of the Mescalero was already past history when Dr. Blazer arrived at La Maquina in 1868. There was, therefore, no reason for the cautious and reticent Santana to relate such a story to his friend the doctor. His concern was with the present and the immediate future. This fact may have substantially influenced the way Almer N. Blazer wrote the manuscript "Santana." Without knowledge of Santana's immediate past, he, as well as his father, had to assume Santana's presence at the Bosque Redondo with all the other Mescalero. The resultant errors have been clarified and corrected as explained in the preface.

29. Bender, *Study of the Mescalero Apache*, 107.

30. Congress appropriated farming implements and seeds for about 400 Mescalero and 6,000 Navajo, only one-half the total number at the Bosque Redondo. Bender, *Study of the Mescalero Apache*, 125.

31. General Carleton to John P. Usher, Secretary of Interior, 18 August 1864. In Bender, *Study of the Mescalero Apache*, 125–26.

32. Of the 9,000 Indians in custody at the Bosque Redondo, 455 were Mescalero, 20 Gila Apache, and 8,550 Navajo. See Bender, *Study of the Mescalero Apache*, 129.

33. Bender, *Study of the Mescalero Apache*, 129–30.

34. Bender, *Study of the Mescalero Apache*, 130.

35. Keleher, *Turmoil*, 457.

36. Bender, *Study of the Mescalero Apache*, 186.

37. Sonnichsen: *Mescalero Apaches*, 157.

38. A. J. Curtis, Indian agent at Fort Stanton, writes to Superintendent of Indian Affairs Nathaniel Pope in Santa Fe on November 21, 1872 (NMSL):

> *I am pained to inform you that I have just received information that Cadete was killed in La Luz Canyon near Tularosa on his way home from court. He was accompanied by Juan Cojo, the interpreter, and was in advance of me. There has been some jealousy on his account and I fear he has been killed by Indians or Indian of this Agency.*
>
> *I would respectfully say that several bands of Indians have come in recently. The names of some of the principal men are as follows: José Pino, Plato, Agapito, Alouso, Alausan, Payi-wha-ja, Chitah-Roman, José Pita, all Mescalero Apaches, and the following Lipans—Pettsaway, Aubrais, Coloras, Espene, Bescocha, and Santana. I would further say that it is a very necessary part at this time to supply and to have this supply to issue and help to reconcile them to the killing of Cadete which they consider an outrage. . . .*

39. In another report, dated November 30, 1872 (NMSL), Curtis wrote Pope concerning the discovery of Cadete's body:

> *As you are already informed, while Cadete was returning from court in company of Juan Cojo, the interpreter, he was shot in Canyon La Luz. I went out with a detachment of cavalry as soon as I learned the facts (to investigate the matter) accompanied by several of Cadete's band and Santana the Indian who found the body of Cadete.*

We proceeded to Plaza La Luz and could learn nothing of the citizens which could throw any light on the subject of our inquiry.

We then proceeded up the canyon and took the trail of Cadete's horse to where he was first found, and then visited his grave a short distance off. Santana first discovered blood which he trailed up until he found his body. He had been riding alone for over six miles and bleeding, and when found, his blanket and pistol were undisturbed, which seemed to fix the crime upon the citizens of La Luz, and great apprehension was felt lest the tribe should hold the citizens responsible and seek revenge....

The most reasonable conclusion is that the interpreter got into a quarrel with Cadete—snatched his pistol (as he had none of his own) and shot him, the ball entered the right shoulder. Then Cadete must have drawn a knife and killed the interpreter. In accordance with their custom he killed the horse also (which belonged to the Indian Department) then started on taking a trail up La Luz Canyon and must have rode 24 miles after he was wounded before he fell from loss of blood. I immediately called for a council of Indians and exhibited the bloody clothes of Juan Cojo which they all recognized and expressed themselves satisfied that they had killed each other, and I have the pleasure now to report that all is quiet as before and there is no reason to fear any outbreak or disturbance. . . .

40. L. Edwin Dudley to John Philip Clum, 18 February 1873, Microfilm Roll 564, NAFW.

CHAPTER 1

1. On the origin of the name "Tularosa" Almer N. Blazer wrote:

The name of the stream [Tularoso Creek] has been confused with the name of the village they began at this time [1862]. This has led to a misinterpretation of the word which is a descriptive name and no doubt originated by the early Spanish explorers. The [Tularoso] canyon or narrow valley was originally quite level from hillside to hillside . . . and was covered with swamp grass known as tule interspersed with thickets of willow and cottonwood groves. . . . The singular name of tule is tular. The ending oso affixed to any noun indicates a multiplicity of the object referred to. Rio Tularoso means river of a large number of tules or tulares. The masculine ending "o" is proper for el rio or el cañon [masculine nouns], but when the [feminine noun] "plaza" is referred to the feminine ending, "a" is proper [e.g., La Plaza Tularosa].

Almer N. Blazer, Early Otero Co. History, BFP.

We have elected to retain the proper Spanish usage as Almer N. Blazer did, despite the fact that the "a" ending is common usage for all nouns with "Tularosa."

2. The first real campaigns and reconnoitering of Mescalero territory began in 1853. They became more and more frequent until the pincers movement carried out by Christopher "Kit" Carson under orders from General Carleton and two companies under Colonel Joseph West in 1862 decisively defeated them and forced them onto the Bosque Redondo. They escaped from the Bosque Redondo in 1865 and returned to their homeland. This post-Civil War episode probably was the first serious threat to the entire tribe after they vanished from the Bosque Redondo. Averam Burton Bender, *Study of the Mescalero Apache 1846–1883* (New York: Garland Publishing Co., 1974), 101.

3. This estimate of the Mescalero population at that time (1867) is probably far too high. The largest number in the Bosque Redondo was 455 men, women, and children. A more accurate estimate would be 500 to 750 men, women, and children.

4. *On March 24, 1863, Major Arthur Morrison with Captain A. H. Pfeiffer's Company of New Mexico Volunteers en route from Fort Stanton to Fort McRae, came upon a wounded Mexican at San Nicolas Spring, who stated that he belonged to a train [that]...had been attacked by Indians and nearly all the party killed, he being wounded in three places and left for dead. Major Morrison with Lieutenant Bargie and eighteen men of the company went in pursuit, and when they reached the salt marshes [Carrizo Springs] at daybreak of the 25th, found ten wagons stripped of everything portable, and within a circuit of three miles, seven dead bodies of Mexicans, which they buried. They then followed the trail of the Indians toward the Sacramento Mountains, then toward the Sierra Blanca until noon, when they met a party of Mexicans from Tularosa, in pursuit of the same Indians; they had been informed of the massacre by another wounded Mexican who had escaped. The Indians had at this time twenty hours start and were hidden in the recesses of the Sierra Blanca. Major Morrison returned to San Nicolas Spring. . . . Estimated number of Indians, forty-five in all, twenty of whom were warriors; arrows indicate they were Apaches; seven Mexicans killed and seventy head of cattle stolen.*

[Apache side of the incident, very likely true, is the Almer N. Blazer account]. Estelle Bennett Burton, "Volunteer Soldiers of New Mexico and Their Conflicts With the Indians in, 1862–1863," *Old Santa Fe* 1 (April 1914).

5. The renegade Apache Shawano is identified by Captain Jefferson Van Horne as a brother of the late Santana. This is undoubtedly the "Cha" referred to here. Jefferson Van Horne to Department Headquarters, 16 June 1856, WBP.

6. This restriction on Cha's movements, though a breach of Apache custom to allow dissent without any stipulation, was obviously necessary to Santana's plan to obtain a negotiated peace.

7. There were nine, including the Agua Nueva band, as Barranquito and Santos told Lieutenant Colonel Dixon S. Miles in 1854. In addition to their two bands, there were seven others, those of Santana, the most hostile, Barela, Francisco Hanero, El Marco Dinero, Captain Bigotes, Mateo, and Chino Guero. Dixon S. Miles to W. A. Nichols, 18 September 1854. In Bender, *Study of the Mescalero Apache*, 41.

8. Fort Stanton was established a few miles west of what is now the town of Lincoln in the autumn of the same year Captain Henry Whiting Stanton was killed—1855. See Bender *Study of the Mescalero Apache*, 37.

9. Originally a sawmill known as La Maquina, it was maintained prior to 1846 by a Mexican garrison in order to furnish lumber to Paso del Norte (present-day Juarez) and villages along the Rio Grande. Almer N. Blazer, "Early Notes on Otero County," BFP.

CHAPTER 2

1. The forage agent-merchant was Pat Coghlan, a power-hungry Irishman with an easy conscience. See C. L. Sonnichsen, *Tularosa: The Last of the Frontier West* (New York: Davin-Adair Co., 1961), 245–61.

2. The numbers of veterans involved, as well as the number of Indians, were less than half those given here. The use of the number one thousand is reminiscent of the bluff Santana used on Major Enoch Steen and could possibly be related to Almer N. Blazer's use of that number. The discrepancy in time between that described in the Major Morrison report and in Almer N. Blazer's log of some weeks or months after the incident is probably related to the way he heard this story from the Indians.

CHAPTER 3

1. See "Pinos Altos New Mexico," *New Mexico Historical Review* 23 (1948), a reprint of an article that appeared in the Silver City Enterprise Print in 1880 by R. S. Allen. It mentions (307, 316) a William Skillicorn as a successful operator of the Pacific No. 2 gold mine and part owner and operator of the Mud Turtle Mill using a rather primitive way of extracting gold from the ore by the arrastre method, i.e., separation by grinding the ore. If Almer N. Blazer's dates are correct, it is quite possible that this is the same man who was the first operator of La Maquina. The unusual name in a sparsely populated area; the arrival after General Kearny and Doniphan passed through the area, who likely mustered out such a person when his enlistment was fulfilled; the interest in milling and the machinery; the known trading of lumber and grain to the military at Fort Fillmore; and the stories heard around the camp of gold strikes in the Mimbres area, all make this man a very probable candidate. However, no proof has been found.

2. Captain Stanton was killed in the Sacramento Mountains on January 18, 1855, and at the same time Santana was reported as dead. The Mill was destroyed by Comanche about 1856, and Skilicon disappeared from the scene. Almer N. Blazer's chronology has been readjusted here. WBP, 1855.

3. John C. Cremony *Life Among the Apaches* (Lincoln: University of Nebraska Press, 1990), 198, mentions a Whitlock (no first name or initials) as an illustrious member of the California Column. Dan L. Thrapp, in *Encyclopedia of Frontier Biography*, Vol. 3 (Glendale, Calif.: Arthur H. Clark Company, 1988), 1557, names a James H. Whitlock, army officer, member of the California Column, mustered out at Las Cruces on November 30, 1864. He joined the First Battalion, Veteran Infantry, California Volunteers, and served under Kit Carson until his discharge on December 12, 1866. By April 1867 he was back in La Pluma, California. Ownership or operation of La Maquina is not mentioned. If Blazer's date of assumption of ownership by Whitlock (1860) is correct, then James Whitlock could not have been at La Maquina in 1860. The California Column reached New Mexico Territory in 1862. Whitlock served as commanding officer at Tucson and did not reach the Mimbres area until 1863. It must be assumed that his military career precluded operation of The Mill at the same time. It is, therefore, unlikely that this James Whitlock was the proprietor. Jerry D. Thompson, *Desert Tiger: Captain Paddy Graydon and The Civil War in the Far Southwest*, (El Paso: Texas Western Press, 1992) introduces a Dr. John Marmaduke Whitlock, who killed Paddy Graydon at Fort Stanton in an impromptu duel, and was killed in turn

by Paddy Graydon's men. Dr. Whitlock's home was in Santa Fe and Sapello (near Las Vegas). Since this event occurred in 1862, Dr. Whitlock could not have been involved with La Maquina.

4. The last Mescalero left the Bosque Redondo in November 1865. Santana, as explained in the introduction, did not go there. At that time only nine Mescalero Apache remained at the Bosque Redondo. See Averam Burton Bender, *Study of the Mescalero Apache 1846–1883* (New York: Garland Publishing Co., 1974), 129.

5. Often referred to as Dr. Blazer, he had been a dentist in Iowa before the Civil War. Arthritis had crippled his hands to such a degree that dentistry had become impracticable. Family biography by Almer N. Blazer, BFP.

6. This was Cavino Dorame, whom he had hired in El Paso in 1866 as his wagon boss. He became a trusted friend and longtime employee. BFP.

7. The story of the reward for Santana and the finding of big footprints at the scene of the massacre may well have been factual, though no record of this had been found. The massacre and the events preceding and following it were certainly true, and Santana's version of what had happened there is probably accurate. Such unobjective reporting was characteristic of Anglo reports of that time.

CHAPTER 4

1. U'ah's alarm was undoubtedly real and came from a fear of "bear sickness," which Opler describes as "a malady marked by deformity and occurring when an individual is frightened or attacked by a bear, or has unknowingly crossed a bear's tracks, touched bear fur, or invaded a bear's den. Morris E. Opler, "The Concept of Supernatural Power among the Chiricahua and Mescalero Indians," *American Anthropologist* 38 (January-March 1937).

2. No official records of this meeting have been found. Most such efforts, especially when initiated by the Indians, seemed to reach a figurative Anglo-American wastebasket. The historical evidence, however, tends to corroborate the basic story.

There were at least two dissident groups of Apache, the Agua Nueva band with Mateo and Venancia as its leaders, and that led by Shawano (Cha), the renegade brother of Santana and Cadete. In a letter to James Collins, superintendent of Indian affairs, 15 February 1858, Dr. Michael Steck noted that Venancio was said to be the son of the fiery old Gomez, chief of a Lipan band ranging in the Davis and Chisos Mountains. It was thought, according to Dr. Steck, that his hatred of the Anglos probably stemmed from the fact that his father had been killed by one John Glanton (Glendon). Shawano (Cha), according to Almer N. Blazer, broke with Santana because Santana sought to make peace with the Anglos. Cha called Santana "a woman" and went his own way, attracting a heterogeneous group of renegades from various tribes, who terrorized the Mesilla and El Paso area as well as the area from Dog Canyon south. See Bender 13; Dr. Michael Steck to James L. Collins, Superintendent of Indian Affairs, 15 February 1858, WBP.

Almer N. Blazer's story relating to Cha is no doubt an amalgam of stories involving both these dissident groups, all true but fused into a single tale. Whether or not Cha's death at the hand of Santana is literally true does not matter except as an illustration of Indian justice. It is certainly true figuratively, because Santana and the majority of the tribe literally "threw him away" when they banished him from the tribe; and thus, Santana's edict was his death warrant whether Santana shot him or someone else did. Dr. Michael Steck to James L. Collins regarding both Venancio and Shawano, WBP, 1856.

CHAPTER 5

1. The nearest water was close to the mouth of the Alamo Canyon, ten to fifteen miles to the north near the site of present-day Alamogordo.

2. Dog Canyon (Cañon del Perro) was, for the Indians, a favorite access to the Sacramentos from the floor of the Tularoso Valley. It was a steep precipitous climb from the valley floor (3,500 feet) to the crest of the Sacramentos (9,000 feet), about twelve miles as the crow flies. The canyon is very narrow at its juncture with the valley floor, with high, sheer cliffs especially on its north side. Although it is essentially a box canyon, there is a steep, narrow trail, which the Indians used to climb up and over the cliffs. Such terrain afforded the Indians an easily defended escape route, as well as use of their favorite methods of fighting—heavy rocks rolled over the cliffs on the enemy below or large stones hurled with sling shots.

CHAPTER 6

1. *Tulhiba* is the proper Apache spelling for a liquor brewed from corn, although it is more commonly known as *tulipai* and *tiswin*.

2. At the junction of Nogal Canyon and Tularoso Canyon there is today a farm known as the Walters Place. This was originally Blazer property which was traded to Jim Walters. Nothing more is known about Fred Scott, the sawyer.

3. This account of the arrangements for the treaty—the cautious approach by the colonel, the continuous evaluation by Santana, and the details of the preparation—all have the ring of truth, but as previously stated no record of this treaty has been found even though it was written in triplicate.

4. Not a single copy of this extraordinary agreement has been found, nor has the colonel in charge ever been identified. Although common knowledge today, early frontier people probably did not know that in all early societies before the development of writing the cultivation and use of memory was of paramount importance. To maintain continuity and reliability and to be able to speak with "one tongue," messages had to be conveyed to the outposts with the exact meaning intact. The veracity of this story seems to be verified by Blazer's obvious amazement as related in his graphic account of Santana's prodigious feats of memory, in which he praises Santana's memory as most unusual.

Ace Daklugie, the Chiricahua Apache, in his later days on the Mescalero Reservation had this to say about memory:

Next to our religion, I learned of my people and their brave men and deeds. . . .

We had no written language and were forced to remember what we heard or were told. Our lives depended on accurate recall of such information, and particularly upon the reliability of messages sent by a chief to his people by runners. They had to accurately record his orders in their heads.

CHAPTER 7

1. Old Baldy, also called White Mountain or Sierra Blanca, is a 12,000-foot peak in the White Mountains, part of the Rocky Mountains. This range blends imperceptibly to the south into the Sacramento Mountains. A vague dividing line might be Tularoso Canyon on the western slope and the Rio Ruidoso on the eastern. To the southeast the Sacramentos become the Guadalupes.

2. Mr. Blazer may have meant universal in the sense of being a means of communication common to all Indians. However, as Benjamin Capps wrote: "Though communication by gesture is probably older than speech itself, no system has ever proved more versatile and expressive than that developed by the Plains Indians." Benjamin Capps, *The Old West. The Indians* (New York: Time Life Books, 1973) 31.

3. The literal translation of Rinconada is "corner." A remote area on the southwest slopes of the White Mountains, part of its watershed empties into the Three River Ranch holdings, which once belonged to A. B. Fall.

CHAPTER 8

1. For further discussion of this ceremony described by a Mescalero Apache, see Dan Nicholas, "Mescalero Apache Girls' Puberty Rites," *El Palacio* 46 (September 1939). See also Hoijer, *Chiricahua and Mescalero Apache Texts*, (Chicago: University of Chicago Press, 1938) 148–53.

2. Today, *chuchupate* (wild angelica root), found in the higher elevations on Sierra Blanca and similar areas, is today one of the favorite herbal medicines of the area. It is an herb that was used in many ancient and modern cultures. In pre-Christian Latvia peasants carried the stems in an annual summer procession. In China it is a tea. In Norway bread is made of the roots. In the Southwest it is popular as a cure for any intestinal problems. William H. Hylton, ed. *The Rodale Herb Book* (Emmaus, Pa.: Rodale Press, 1974), 340.

3. The Chiricahuas, with whom Eve Ball's book *Indeh: An Apache Odyssey* is mainly concerned, called this Deity "Something above the sky," Ussen. As both Harry Hoijer and Morris E. Opler point out (see bibliography), the two tribes have very similar beliefs, religious rites, and languages. "Something above the sky" was considered the Creator but one which played no active role in their religious ceremonies. Their myth has it that "Something above the sky"; White Painted Woman who was impregnated by the Water and bore a child known as Child of the Water (Eyata for the Mescalero); and Killer of Enemies (Chete Neh for the Mescalero), who put evil thoughts in the people all existed at the beginning. Harry Hoijer, *Chiricahua and Mescalero Apache Texts* (Chicago: University of Chicago Press, 1938) 5, 215–17.

4. *It is said that this ceremony and the directions for conducting it were given to the Apache by White Painted Woman, the mother of the culture hero. Child of the Water was her son, and Killer of Enemies one of the evil people. All four existed from the beginning. An evil giant ate all the new children that were born but Child of the Water killed the evil giant with his arrows and then became the savior of his people, the culture hero.*

While the tipi is being erected the Medicine Man chants a song which refers to the bringing together of the ceremonial poles for the tipi, thus it is believed that both the poles and the girls bodies are blessed.

It is their tradition that White Painted Woman gave directions for the performance of this ceremony to the Apache. If these directions in regard to the building of the ceremonial tipi and the performance of all the other elements are carried out, she promised to confer long life and good fortune upon the girl who had come to womanhood. Hoijer, Chiricahua and Mescalero, 6, 151.

CHAPTER 10

1. The attempts to teach the Apache to farm without first trying to understand their culture and the roles played by the women and men always failed (and still does one hundred years later). This was first attempted at the mouth of Alamo Canyon in 1855, with some success, although a skirmish with the army caused the nomadic Indians to flee before the few crops had ripened. It was tried again at the Bosque Redondo using essentially forced labor, but the crop was eaten by cut worms. At Fort Stanton it again failed and has continued to fail despite repeated attempts at Mescalero, although the women did maintain small plots to grow squash, pumpkins, and sometimes enough corn to produce *tulhiba.*

2. According to Stewart Culin, the game of hoop and pole was played throughout North America north of Mexico with endless variations. Culin maintains the game is always played by men though women did watch and bet. The principal gambling game of the Apache, it is played on a specially leveled field, and has religious connotations which forbid interruption or disruption of the field. The hoop and poles used by the Mescalero Apache are ably described by Almer N. Blazer. Stewart Culin, *Games of the North American Indians* (Washington, D.C.: Government Printing Office, 1907), 442–50.

3. Fort Stanton was reoccupied by Kit Carson under orders from General James H. Carleton when Carleton replaced General E. R. S. Canby as head of the military for the Territory of New Mexico, which still included Arizona at that time (1867).

CHAPTER 11

1. No record of such a journey by Santana has been found, although there are many records of chiefs being taken to Washington in order to impress them with the world the "Great White Father" occupied. Natzili, one of the Mescalero chiefs who succeeded Roman, was taken there by agent W. H. H. Llewellen. Although Santana's absence from the Bosque Redondo and the

isolationism he practiced for so many years made such a journey unlikely, it is possible that Santana did make such a trip. If so, the journey would have occurred in 1868 or later since, in Almer N. Blazer's account, he is introduced to President Ulysses S. Grant. Such a trip could not have originated from the Bosque Redondo; it is possible, therefore, that it could have originated from Fort Stanton. In his letters, Curtis, describing the death of Cadete, does mention Santana in a way that makes him sound like someone he knows and trusts.

Almer N. Blazer reminds us in one of his letters to Leigh: "Most of the incidents I have heard recounted by the participants. Although certain characters [which] appear to have been involved in these incidents were in reality enacted by others." GMA.

Whether Santana made such a journey or not, Blazer's account remains a true and moving portrayal of the childlike wonder which is always displayed when an intelligent human is suddenly introduced to the gewgaws, the gadgets, the gigantic machines, and all the artifacts of a complex industrialized world that are totally foreign to anything he ever imagined: the joy and wonder of examining a worthless bauble; the fearful awe which a river of unimaginable immensity induces; the panic roused by the sudden start of the "iron horse;" and all that galaxy of impedimenta with which the Anglo burdens himself in search of happiness, but which seem to decrease happiness in a direct ratio with the increase of externals amassed.

CHAPTER 13

1. Known locally as the Battle of Round Mountain (El Cerro). A report from Lieutenant Peter Vroom to Captain Frank Stanwood dated March 1868 reads: "A small band of Apache, well armed and mounted, about halfway between Nesmith's Mill (La Maquina and later Blazer's Mill) and Tularosa killed ten Mexicans and drove off some 2200 sheep. On the same spot Apaches murdered an American and two women. Lieutenants Vroom and E. E. Whitman with a detachment of more than thirty cavalry from Fort Stanton set out in pursuit but were unable to overtake the marauders." Averam Burton Bender, *A Study of the Mescalero Apache 1846–1880*, (New York: Garland Publishing Co., 1960), 148.

2. No record has been found to verify this episode of the medal presentation.

3. According to Almer N. Blazer's manuscript "Santana: War Chief of the Mescalero Apaches," the renegades who had dared to raid north of Dog

Canyon and in the neighborhood of Blazer's Mill had broken Santana's orders. He had given his word that if they did depredate north of Dog Canyon he would kill Cha and his band. This he would do but in his own way.

4. Dr. Michael Steck, in a letter to James L. Collins, superintendent of Indian affairs, reports that three renegades had come to an Indian encampment about an hour before the Mexicans attacked it. All three were killed, among them their chief, the celebrated Shawano (Cha), who had been the terror of the country for the last three years. Although the identity of individual Indians was often mistaken, if Dr. Steck's report is correct then it was Venancia and the Agua Nueva band that crossed the forbidden line. Blazer's story may or may not be literally true, but it is most certainly true figuratively. It seems properly a part of the Apache epic. Dr. Michael Steck to James L. Collins, 15 February 1858, WBP.

CHAPTER 14

1. Passes for the Indians to leave a given area were a problem for all. The Indians needed to leave an area to gather fruits, seeds, roots, and mescal, or to hunt buffalo and other animals for their hides or their meat during appropriate seasons. Often the army refused to allow these activities, partly because of a standing order that no passes could be given but also because although the Indians often promised to only hunt or gather, they often broke their promise and depredated.

CHAPTER 15

1. The extension of the reservation boundary in 1875 to include the western slope of the Sacramentos encompassed all of the Blazer properties. Surveys were made, and an evaluation of the properties was done, but the lands were not purchased. It would be another thirty years before the title in the Blazer name was secure. Agent Crothers succeeded in moving the agency to what is now Mescalero but resigned almost immediately. BFP.

2. This agent was Frederick C. Godfroy, who later became involved with Pat Coghlan's nefarious enterprises. Godfroy reported that he had rented one-half of the Blazer building at South Spring (one mile below the new Mescalero headquarters) for $125.00 per month. Frederick C. Godfroy to Commander J. Q. Smith, 27 October 1876, NAFW M234, Roll 569.

3. The term clan is rather loosely used here by Almer N. Blazer to signify a family or families led by one chief and commonly called a band. According to Grenville Goodwin, the Chiricahua, Warm Springs, Mescalero, Lipan, and Jicarilla Apache do not have clans. See Grenville Goodwin, "The Characteristics and Functions of Clan in a Southern Athapascan Culture," *American Anthropologist*, 39 (1937), 394.

CHAPTER 16

1. Every Apache knows that owls are bad luck and that their hooting is a warning of danger or death. That does not mean that the owl itself is bad—just that he foretells something that is. Daklugie conversation with Eve Ball, *Indeh: An Apache Odyssey* (Provo, Utah: Brigham Young University Press, 1982) 92.

2. It has been said that "Baskets are the Indian woman's poems: the shaping of them her sculpture. They wove into them the story of their life and love." Mescalero basketry has been recognized as being among the best in quality and design. The *etsees* (large watertight jugs) which Datlih created were made from choice palmilla leaves. Palmilla (yucca torreyi) is a narrow-leaf yucca which is especially adapted to the development of watertight jugs in the hands of a skilled artisan. BFP.

CHAPTER 17

1. The plant whose roots were most commonly used for cleansing was amole, also known as Spanish bayonet or Spanish dagger. The botanical name is *Yucca aloifolia*.

2. A colloquialism; a one word description of a horse broken to ride and accustomed to saddle and bridle.

3. Daklugie explained the Apache attitude toward gold: "An Apache may pick up nuggets from the dry bed of a stream, but he is forbidden to 'grub in Mother Earth' for it. It is the symbol of the sun and hence sacred to Ussen [Eyata]." Eve Ball, *Indeh: An Apache Odyssey* (Provo, Utah: Brigham Young University Press, 1982), 61.

The strange madness which seems to take control of Anglos when gold is discovered, and which causes them to steal, cheat, even murder, no doubt gives added impetus to the Apache taboo.

4. Of historical interest in relationship to this story are pictures of old Augustine and his wife, Mary, taken when he was believed to be about one hundred fifteen years of age.

CHAPTER 21

1. According to Almer N. Blazer these two wives of Santana were twin sisters. This is a rarity in itself because the Mescalero usually killed one of the pair when twins were born. This photograph has the distinction of being the first picture of Indians ever taken on the Mescalero Reservation. BFP.

2. Colonel Joaquin Terrazas was the commander of the Mexican force which finally tracked down and cornered Victorio in the Tres Castillos Mountains. The ensuing battle resulted in the death of Victorio. Terrazas had slain and scalped (for the bounty) seventy-eight Indians, sixty-two of whom were warriors and the remainder women and children; he also took sixty-eight prisoners and recovered two captives. Dan L. Thrapp, *Victorio and the Mimbres Apaches* (Norman: University of Oklahoma Press, 1980), 303. For a sketch of the life of Colonel Terrazas, see Ibid., 373.

CONCLUSION

1. At present-day White Oaks and vicinity. According to Frank D. Reeve, the *auri sacra fames* had its way, and the reservation was reduced in size by about half to accommodate the "accursed craving." Frank D. Reeve, "The Federal Indian Policy in New Mexico 1858–1880, IV," *New Mexico Historical Review* 13 (January, April, July 1938): 267–69. See also Henry F. Dobyns, *The Mescalero Apache People* (Phoenix, Ariz.: Indian Tribal Series, 1972), 57.

2. The South Fork post office, with Joseph H. Blazer as postmaster, was established in 1875 after the agency headquarters had been moved to its present location. The original post office cabinet, a single small cabinet approximately five feet wide and two and one-half feet high with a dozen or more letter slots, two locking doors, and a few larger magazine slots seems to have been adequate to accommodate the population in the area at the time. This cabinet is still in the possession of the Blazer family. BFP.

3. The change to civilian agents was a part of the new peace policy organized before the inauguration of President Grant but not put into operation until he took office. Its major effects were: A more humane treatment of the Indians (gradually), the establishment of reservations; and peace. Av-

eram Burton Bender, *A Study of the Mescalero Apache 1846–1883* (New York: Garland Publishing Co., 1974), 189–93.

4. Father Braun, a chaplain at Ypres and Verdun in World War I, brought his admiration of French and English cathedrals home with him, influencing the architecture on the Mescalero Apache Reservation. In the interim between wars Father Braun was a priest but also a fund-raiser, a stone mason, a common laborer, and architect—a man possessed by a dream.

Dorothy Emerson, *Among The Mescalero Apaches: The Story of Father Albert Braun,* OFM (Tucson: University of Arizona Press, 1980).

APPENDIX I

1. Biography of Blazer Family by Almer N. Blazer. BFP. See also Paul O'Neil, *The Old West: The Rivermen* (New York: Time Life Books 1975), 76–81.

2. The June 18, 1860 census report showed Joseph H. Blazer, a dentist, born in Pennsylvania, with $1,100 in real estate. Jobes, born in Ohio, was then 24, and they had one child, Ella, two years old. A son, David, was born in 1854 and died October 31, 1855.

3. Almer N. Blazer, "Early Life," BFP.

4. Letter from Mrs. Margaret Campbell, Bloomfield, Iowa, 9 July 1991, BFP.

5. Almer N. Blazer wrote:

> One day in 1872 Dr. Blazer was attacked on the street in Tularosa by one of the dissatisfied parties, and being unarmed, would no doubt have been murdered had he been other than an unusually strong man. He defended himself by kicking his opponent in the stomach three different times as he charged him with a knife, each time receiving a deep cut across the calf of the leg. The doctor succeeded in reaching his buggy, getting out of town and into the canyon, where he received first aid and gained a companion. [By using] relays of horses, they reached Fort Stanton before Dr. Blazer bled to death. There he received surgical aid and in time recovered. BFP.

6. Almer N. Blazer, "Early Notes on Otero County," BFP.

7. Almer N. Blazer, "Early Notes," BFB.

8. Almer N. Blazer, "Early Notes," BFB.

9. Unpublished paper on the battle at Blazer's Mill by Almer N. Blazer, BFP.

10. Paul A. Blazer to his brother Noel Blazer, 14 March 1962, BFP.

11. Almer N. Blazer, in an affidavit to help clear title to the Blazer land, wrote:

> My father told me that he went home to Iowa when my sister Emma was born 31 March 1868 (Emma Blazer Thompson) and found that my mother was suffering from [advanced] consumption and decided the move to the Southwest would have to be made on that account. About a year later in 1869 he was able to arrange for the purchase of an undivided one-third interest [in La Maquina] for $3,000.00 and again went to Iowa to raise what money he could. He found my mother's health much worse. She gave him several hundred dollars her father had given her and told him that if she died, he should divide it equally between the three children.
>
> I know of no available proof of the money my mother furnished for the purchase of the mill property except the above statement of my father and the corroborating fact that in 1877 a deed was given to Mrs. Ella Hedges, my oldest sister for the lower ranch; the upper ranch was offered to my sister, Mrs. Emma Thompson.
>
> All of which my father told me was to comply with my mother's request that the money be divided equally among us.

RGH-BFP. Legal papers. Property affidavit, one of five affidavits enclosed with a letter to the Commissioner General Land Office, Washington, D.C., dated May 18, 1912.

12. Max Weber, with Talcott Parsons, trans. *The Protestant Ethic and the Spirit of Capitalism* (New York: Charles Scribner's Sons, 1958).

APPENDIX II

1. Katherine D. Stoes in a short biographical note on Joseph H. Blazer confirms the supposition that it was a narrow-gauge railway track on which the Blazer children traveled from Pueblo to Cucharas and then by another similar narrow-gauge to El Moro. Dr. Blazer had been detained by jury duty in Mesilla but had arranged for them to travel with an ox train from El Moro. Dr. Blazer met them with an ambulance south of Las Vegas, New Mexico. Mrs. Stoes's recollections came from stories Dr. Blazer told when he was a guest of her grandfather, Samuel Herron, in Mesilla. Katherine D. Stoes Papers, Ms 208, New Mexico State University, Las Cruces, New Mexico.

2. Almer N. Blazer believed that piñon smoke cured his tuberculosis. During the later part of the trip, an early winter snowstorm had forced them to make camp. Blazer had already endured a harrowing day with almost constant coughing, and during the night the wind filled his tent with the acrid smoke of green piñon logs and branches. The next day his "cough was gone," as he said, "and never returned." His "galloping consumption" was probably a lung abscess, a residual from the bout of pneumonia, which the smoke-induced episodes of violent coughing had ruptured and expectorated. The piñon was probably a factor, albeit a hazardous one, in the cure. Almer N. Blazer, "Early Notes on Otero County," BFP.

3. Paul A. Blazer to Noel Blazer, 1962, BFP.

4. Almer N. Blazer on educational facilities, BFP.

5. Almer N. Blazer's family was living in Tularosa at this time. Sanitation was practically nonexistent. Typhoid fever was a common problem.

6. "Los Jirones" is the story of a wealthy Mexican family victimized by the persecutions of Antonio Lopez de Santa Anna, whose enmity they had incurred. After many harrowing trials they migrated to America where they settled in Mesilla, New Mexico Territory. There, the younger son, Venturito José, was captured by the Apaches. The narrative thus includes a description of life among the Apache. Reunion of father and son finally takes place, and they start a new life in Tularosa, where they become landowners and respected citizens. The story was never published. BFP.

BIBLIOGRAPHY

UNPUBLISHED MATERIALS

Blazer Family Private Papers, Paul A. Blazer, Jr., and Arthur D. Blazer, Tularosa, New Mexico.

Biographies of Joseph H. and Almer N. Blazer written by family members. One four-page unsigned biography of Joseph H. Blazer.

Correspondence: Personal letters between family members.

Letters from many prominent authors and would-be authors requesting and exchanging information.

Genealogy charts. Letters referring to Blazer family genealogy.

Legal papers: Sales of properties. Partnership agreements. Affidavits on acquirement, possession, and occupancy by Joseph H. Blazer of certain real estate embraced within the limits of the Mescalero Apache Indian Reservation, Otero County, New Mexico.

Newspaper articles from the *Alamogordo Times*, C. W. Morgan, editor. All the articles written by Almer N. Blazer for the newspaper on early Otero County history and related stories in continuous undated sheets 1932–1940. Miscellaneous clippings. Obituary. Unpublished articles and stories by Almer N. Blazer: "The Mescaleros and Their Home," "Marachin," "Haheh," "Indian Courts," "Elk and Bear," "Bear Hunting," "Old Mescalero Customs," "Al Howe," "Cherokee Bill."

Court Records: New Mexico, Dona Ana County, Las Cruces. Gillespie County, Fredericksburg, Texas: census, bills of sale, deeds, marriage records. Mason County, Mason, Texas-: census, deeds, marriage and divorce records. Menard County, Menard, Texas: census, deeds, power of attorney, partnership agreements.

ARCHIVES

Gilcrease Museum, Tulsa, Oklahoma. Letters, Almer N. Blazer to William R. Leigh 1923–1937. Letters, William R. Leigh to Almer N. Blazer 1922–1930. "Littlefoot," unpublished novel by William R. Leigh.

National Archives, Washington, D.C. Department of the Interior. R. G. 75 documents relating to the negotiation of unratified treaties with various tribes of Indians 1801–1869, Microfilms T-494 (three rolls).

National Archives, Southwestern Branch, Ft. Worth, Texas. Department of the Interior. Letters received by the office of Indian Affairs 1824–1881. R. G. 65, microfilm rolls, M234 series, 1824–1881. State Department. Territorial papers, New Mexico, R. G. 59, 1851–1872. Microfilms T-17 (four rolls).

New Mexico State Library, Santa Fe, New Mexico. Indian Agencies, New Mexico superintendency of Indian Affairs. R. G. 75. Microfilm roll #750, 1869–1880.

Rio Grande Historical Collection, New Mexico State University Library, Las Cruces. Blazer Family Papers (MS 110). Joseph H. Blazer—correspondence, financial documents, legal documents, notes on Mescalero Indian Agency 1888–1895. Almer N. Blazer—correspondence, financial documents 1883–1907, legal documents 1896–1949 and 1966, literary file notes on manuscripts "Santana: Last War Chief of the Mescalero Apaches" and "Los Jirones," patents and inventions 1897–1949, miscellaneous. Emma Blazer Thompson and Dr. J. Howard Thompson—letters, financial documents, speeches by Dr. Thompson, and a brief history of El Paso printed after his death by C. L. Sonnichsen. Blazer Family—Paul A. Blazer correspondence 1937–1965, Water commissioners' reports 1936–1939, miscellaneous. Noel E. Blazer—Correspondence 1924–1947, legal documents 1964, educational trust, literary production thesis, New Mexico College of Agriculture and Mechanic Arts, patents and inventions, miscellaneous 1906, 1917, 1922.

Miscellany: Verbatim reports of a public meeting held at Mescalero, New Mexico, Sunday afternoon June 12, 1932 under the auspices of the Alamogordo Chamber of Commerce: Tom Charles of the Chamber of Commerce presiding; George Coe (a participant in the fight at Blazer's Mill) and Almer N. Blazer (fifteen pages). Letter Almer N. Blazer wrote to Colonel Maurice F. Fulton on who really killed Shotgun Roberts. Letters from A. A. Anderson on various interviews with acquaintances of Billy the Kid. Rynerson report of the District Court, Lincoln, April 1878 on the murderer of Charlie Bowdry.

Items on other family members. Transcripts of letters written by Mescalero Indian agents. A Mescalero Apache vocabulary supplied by Percy Bigmouth, a Mescalero. Oil painting. Newspaper clippings. Maps of the Mescalero Apache Indian Reservation.

Photographs: daguerreotypes, ambrotypes, tintypes, albumen prints, stereo views, panoramic views, and copy prints. Also includes mounted prints cabinet cards, and *cartes de visite*. New Mexico Territorial photographers represented include E. A. Bass, A. J. Buck, D. B. Chase, C. W. Marks, Almeron Newman, A. F. Randall, and Ben Wittick.

Katherine D. Stoes Papers: Ms. 208, short biography of Joseph H. Blazer.

Ulysses S. Grant Presidential Papers series 2, 1862—April 1871; series 3, 1871–1876; series 4, 1884–1885, microfilm. Southern Illinois University Libraries, Carbondale, Illinois.

Weissbrodt and Weissbrodt, attorneys, Washington, D.C., records (R. G. 88–73). These are documents acquired and created by the Weissbrodt firm on behalf of the Mescalero Apache Indians for their case before the Indian Claims Commission and before the Court of Claims. They represent a thorough, painstakingly collected set of records pertaining to the Mescalero from all federal government departments and all New Mexico territorial and state governmental agencies, as well as letters from agents to these agencies pertaining to the Mescalero.

BOOKS

American Heritage Editors. *Book of the Pioneer Spirit*. Narrative by Alvin M. Joseph, Jr.; Peter Lyon; Francis Russell. New York: American Heritage Publishing Co., 1959.

American Heritage Editors. Narrative by David Lavender. *History of the Great West*. New York: American Heritage Company, 1965.

Armitage, Susan and Elizabeth Jameson, eds., *The Women's West*. Norman: University of Oklahoma Press, 1987.

Ball, Eve. *Indeh: An Apache Odyssey*. Provo, Utah: Brigham Young University Press, 1982.

_____. *Ma'am Jones of the Pecos*. Tucson: University of Arizona Press, 1969.

Bartlett, Richard A. *The New Country: A Social History of the American Frontier, 1776–1890*. New York: Oxford University Press, 1974.

Bender, Averam Burton. *A Study of the Mescalero Apache, 1846–1883*. New York: Garland Publishing Co., 1974.

Bennett, James A. Forts and Forays: *A Dragoon in New Mexico, 1850–1856*. Albuquerque: University of New Mexico Press, 1948.

Betzinez, Jason. *I Fought with Geronimo*. Edited by Wilbur Sturtevant Nye. Harrisburg, Pa: Stackpole Co., 1959.

Bieder, Robert E. *Science Encounters the Indian,1820–1880: The Early Years of American Ethnology*. Norman: University of Oklahoma Press, 1989.

Bolton, Herbert E. *Coronado: Knight of Pueblo and Plains*. New York: McGraw Hill, and Albuquerque: The University of New Mexico Press, 1949.

Bourke, John G. *On the Border with Crook*. New York: Charles Scribner's Sons, 1891.

Brown, Joseph Epes. *The Spiritual Legacy of the American Indian*. Lebanon, Pa: Sowers Printing Co., 1964.

Burdett, Charles. *Life of Kit Carson*. New York: The Perkins Book Co., n.d.

Capps, Benjamin. *The Old West: The Indians*. New York: Time Life Books, 1973.

Cleland, Robert Glass. *This Reckless Breed of Men: The Trappers and Fur Traders of the Southwest*. New York: Alfred A. Knopf, 1952.

Cochrane, C. N. *Christianity and Classical Culture: A Study of Thought and Action from Augustine to Augustus*. New York: Oxford University Press, 1972.

Cremony, John C. *Life Among the Apaches*. Lincoln: University of Nebraska Press, 1990.

Crook, George. *Apache Problem. Resume of Operations Against Apache Indians, 1882–1886*. London: Johnson-Taunton Military Press, 1971.

Culin, Stewart. *Games of the North American Indians*. Washington, D.C.: Government Printing Office, 1907.

Cummins, D. Duane. *William Robinson Leigh: Western Artist*. Norman: University of Oklahoma Press, 1980.

Dale, Edward Everett. *The Indians of the Southwest*. Norman: University of Oklahoma Press, 1988.

Darlington, C. D. *Genetics and Man*. Harmandsworth, England: Allen and Unwin Penguin Books, 1966.

Dary, David. *True Tales of the Old-Time Plains*. New York: Crown Publishers, 1979.

Debo, Angie. *Geronimo: The Man, His Time, His Place*. Norman: University of Oklahoma Press, 1982.

Diaz del Castillo, Bernal. Translated by A. P. Maudsley. *The Discovery and Conquest of Mexico*. New York: Farrar, Straus and Cudahy, 1956.

Dickey, Roland F. *New Mexico Village Arts*. Albuquerque: University of New Mexico Press, 1970.

Dictionary, Mescalero Apache. Mescalero, N. M.: Mescalero Apache Tribe. Mescalero, N. M., 1982.

Dobyns, Henry F. *The Mescalero Apache People*. Phoenix, Ariz.: Indian Tribal Series, 1977.

Eban, Abba. *Heritage: Civilization and the Jews*. New York: Summit Books, 1984.

Emerson, Dorothy. *Among the Mescalero Apaches: The Story of Father Albert Braun, OFM*. Tucson: University of Arizona Press, 1980.

Fergusson, Erna W. *Murder and Mystery in New Mexico*. Albuquerque, N. M.: Merle Armitage Editions, 1948.

_____. *Our Southwest*. New York: Alfred A. Knopf, 1946.

Fergusson, Harvey. *Rio Grande*. New York: Tudor Publishing Co., 1945.

French, Captain William. *Recollections of a Western Ranchman*. Silver City, N.M.: High Lonesome Books, 1990.

Greene, A. C. *The Last Captive*. Austin, Tex.: Encino Press, 1972.

Gregg, Josiah. *Commerce of the Prairies*. Edited by Max L. Moorhead. Norman: University of Oklahoma Press, 1954.

Griffen, William B. *Apaches at War and Peace*. Albuquerque: University of New Mexico Press, 1988.

_____. *Utmost Good Faith*. Albuquerque: University of New Mexico Press, 1988.

Haley, J. Evetts. *Charles Goodnight: Cowman and Plainsman*. Norman: University of Oklahoma Press, 1979.

Haley, James A. *Apaches: A History and Culture Portrait*. Garden City, N. Y. Doubleday and Co., 1981.

Hammond, George P. and Agapito Rey. *Don Juan de Oñate: Colonizer of New Mexico, 1594–1628*. Vols. 5, 6. Albuquerque: University of New Mexico Press, 1953.

Hening, H. B., ed. *George Curry, 1861–1947: An Autobiography*. Albuquerque: University of New Mexico Press, 1958.

Hoijer, Harry. *Chiricahua and Mescalero Apache Texts*. With Ethnological Notes by Morris Edward Opler. Chicago: University of Chicago Press, 1938.

Horgan, Paul. *The Heroic Triad: Backgrounds of Our Three Southwestern Cultures*. Austin, Tex.: Monthly Press, 1987.

_____. *Josiah Gregg and His Vision of the Early West*. New York: Farrar, Straus, Giroux, 1979.

_____. *A Distant Trumpet*. New York: Farrar, Straus and Cudahy, 1960.

_____. *The Great River*. 2 vols. New York: Rinehart and Company, 1954.

Hunter, J. Marvin, ed. *The Trail Drivers of Texas*. 2 vols. New York: Argosy-Antiquarian, 1963.

Hylton, William H., ed. *The Rodale Herb Book* (Emmaus, Pa.: Rodale Press, 1974).

Keleher, William A. *The Fabulous Frontier*. Santa Fe, N. M.: Rydal Press, 1946.

_____. *Turmoil in New Mexico, 1846–1868*. Santa Fe, N. M.: Rydal Press, 1952.

_____. *Violence in Lincoln County,1869–1881*. Albuquerque: University of New Mexico Press, 1957.

Klasner, Lily. *My Girlhood Among Outlaws*. Edited by Eve Ball. Tucson: University of Arizona Press, 1972.

Klinak, Richard E. *Land of Room Enough and Time Enough*. Albuquerque: University of New Mexico Press, 1953.

Lekson, Stephen H. *Nana's Raid: Apache Warfare in Southern New Mexico, 1881*. El Paso: Texas Western Press, 1989.

Lewis, C. S. *Surprised by Joy: The Shape of My Early Life*. New York: Harcourt Brace Jovanovich, 1955.

Lockwood, Frank C. *The Apache Indians*. New York: Macmillan Co., 1938. Reprint: Lincoln: University of Nebraska Press, 1990.

Lummis, Charles F. *The Land of Poco Tiempo*. Albuquerque: University of New Mexico Press, 1952.

_____. *Flowers of Our Lost Romance*. Boston: Houghton Mifflin Company, 1929.

Markham, Edwin. *The Man with the Hoe*. New York: Harcourt, Brace and Co., 1942.

Marriott, Alice. *The Valley Below*. Norman: University of Oklahoma Press, 1949.

Martin, Luis. *Daughters of the Conquistadors*. Albuquerque: University of New Mexico Press, 1983.

Menninger, Carl, et al. *The Vital Balance*. Gloucester, Mass.: Peter Smith, 1985.

Merk, Frederick. *History of the Westward Movement*. New York: Alfred A. Knopf, 1978.

Miller, Alfred Jacob. *The West of Alfred Jacob Miller*. Norman: University of Oklahoma Press, 1951.

Mills, W. W. *Forty Years at El Paso*. El Paso, Tex.: Carl Hertzog, 1962.

von Mises, Ludwig. *Human Action*. Chicago: Regnery Press, 1963.

Morgan, Lewis Henry. *The Indian Journals, 1859–1862*. Edited by Leslie A. White. Ann Arbor: University of Michigan Press, 1959.

Murphy, Lawrence R. *Frontier Crusader: William F. M. Arny*. Tucson: University of Arizona Press, 1972.

Myers, Sandra L. *Westering Women and the Frontier Experience, 1800–1915*. Albuquerque: University of New Mexico Press, 1982.

Neihardt, John C. *Black Elk Speaks*. New York: Simon and Schuster, 1972.

Nock, Albert Jay. "A Study in Manners," In *On Doing the Right Thing and Other Essays*. New York: Harper & Brothers Publishers, 1928.

Ogle, Ralph H. *Federal Control of the Western Apache*. Albuquerque: University of New Mexico Press, 1940.

Olmstead, Frederick Law. *A Journey Through Texas*. Austin: University of Texas Press, 1982.

O'Neil, Paul. *The Old West: The Rivermen*. New York: Time Life Books, 1975.

Oppenheimer, Franz. *The State*. Translated by John M. Gitterman. New York: Vanguard Press, 1922.

Ortega y Gasset, José. *History as a System and Other Essays toward a Philosophy of History*. Translated by Helen Weyl. New York: Norton and Company, 1961.

_____. *Man and Crisis*. Translated by Mildred Adams. New York: W. W. Norton and Company, 1958.

_____. *Man and People*. Translated by Willard R. Trask. New York: W. W. Norton and Company, 1957.

Parkman, Francis. *LaSalle and the Discovery of the Great West*. New York: Signet Classic, 1963.

Pesman, M. Walter. *Meet Flora Mexicana*. Globe, Ariz.: Dale S. King, Publisher, 1962.

Pike, Donald G. *Anasazi: Ancient People of the Rock*. Palo Alto, Calif.: American West Publishing Company, 1975.

Remington, Frederick. *Crooked Trails: A Facsimile of the 1898 Edition*. New York: Bonanza Books.

Riegel, Robert Edgar. *The Story of the Western Railroads, From 1852 Through the Reign of the Giants*. Lincoln: University of Nebraska Press, 1926.

Ruxton, George Frederick. *Life in the Far West*. Edited by Leroy R. Hafen. Norman: University of Oklahoma Press, 1955.

Schilz, Thomas F. Lipan. *Apaches in Texas*. El Paso: Texas Western Press, 1987.

Schroeder, Albert H. *A Study of the Apache Indians*. New York: Garland Publishing Co., 1974.

Schweitzer, Albert. *Nobel Peace Prize Address: The Problem of Peace*. New York: Albert Schweitzer Hospital Fund, 1954.

Sides, Dorothy Smith. *Decorative Art of the Southwestern Indians*. New York: Dover Publications, 1961.

Smith, James Morton, ed. *Seventeenth Century America: Essays in Colonial History*. New York: W. W. Norton and Co., 1972.

Smithwick, Noah. *The Evolution of a State or Recollections of Old Texas Days*. Austin: University of Texas Press, 1984.

Sonnichsen, C. L. *The Mescalero Apaches*. Norman: The University of Oklahoma Press, 1982.

_____. *Tularosa: The Last of the Frontier West*. New York: Devin-Adair Co., 1961.

_____. ed. *Geronimo and the End of the Apache Wars*. Lincoln: University of Nebraska Press, 1986.

Stanley, F. *Fort Union.* The World Press, 1953.

Stegner, Wallace. *Beyond the Hundredth Meridian: John Wesley Powell and the Second Opening of the West.* Boston: Houghton Mifflin Company, 1954.

Thomas, Alfred B. *The Mescalero Apache, 1853–1874.* New York: Garland Publishing Co., 1974;

Thompson, Jerry D. *Desert Tiger: Captain Paddy Graydon and the Civil War in the Far Southwest.* El Paso: Texas Western Press, 1992.

Thrapp, Dan L. *Encyclopedia of Frontier Biography.* 3 vols. Glendale, Calif.: Arthur H. Clark Company, 1988.

_____. *The Conquest of Apacheria.* Norman: University of Oklahoma Press, 1985.

_____. *Victorio and the Mimbres Apaches.* Norman: University of Oklahoma Press, 1980.

Twitchell, Ralph Emerson. *The Leading Facts of New Mexican History.* 3 vols. Cedar Rapids, Ia: Torch Press, 1917.

Underhill, Ruth M. *The Navajos.* Norman: University of Oklahoma Press, 1956.

Unruh, John D. *The Plains Across: The Overland Emigrants and the Trans-Mississippi West, 1840–1860.* Chicago: University of Illinois Press, 1979.

Untermeyer, Louis. *Modern American Poetry.* New York: Harcourt, Brace and Co., 1942.

Utley, Robert M. *High Noon in Lincoln: Violence on the Western Frontier.* Albuquerque: University of New Mexico Press, 1990.

_____.*The Indian Frontier of the American West, 1846–1890.* Albuquerque: University of New Mexico Press, 1984.

_____. *Frontiersmen in Blue: The United States Army and The Indian, 1848–1865.* Lincoln: University of Nebraska Press, 1981.

Van Every, Dale. *Forth to the Wilderness.* Vol. 1 of History of Early America. New York: Mentor Books, 1961

Webb, Walter Prescott. *The Texas Rangers: A Century of Frontier Defense.* Austin: University of Texas Press, 1985.

Weber, Max. *The Protestant Ethic and the Spirit of Capitalism.* Translated by Talcott Parsons. New York: Charles Scribner's Sons, 1958.

Weems, John Edward. *To Conquer a Peace: The War Between the U.S. and Mexico.* College Station: Texas A & M University Press, 1974.

Wellman, Paul I. Glory, *God and Gold: A Narrative History.* Garden City, N. Y.: Doubleday and Company, 1954.

_____. *Indian Wars of the West.* Garden City, N. Y.: Doubleday and Company, 1947.

Wooten, Mattie Lloyd, ed. *Women Tell the Story of the Southwest.* San Antonio, Tex.: The Naylor Company, 1940.

Worcester, Donald E. *The Apaches.* Norman: University of Oklahoma Press, 1979.

ARTICLES

Abel, Annie Heloise, ed. "Indian Affairs Under the Administration of William Carr Lane from the Journal of John Ward." *New Mexico Historical Review* 17 (April 1941).

Ball, Eve. "The Apache Scouts: A Chiricahua Appraisal." *Arizona and the West,* 7 (Winter 1965).

Bender, A. V. "Frontier Defense in the Territory of New Mexico, 1846–1853." *New Mexico Historical Review,* 9 (July 1934).

_____. "Frontier Defense in the Territory of New Mexico, 1853–1861." *New Mexico Historical Review* 9 (October 1934).

_____. "Government Explorations in the Territory of New Mexico, 1846–1859." *New Mexico Historical Review* 9 (January 1934).

Bieber, Ralph P., ed. "Letters of William Carr Lane, 1852–1854." *New Mexico Historical Review* 3 (April 1928).

Blazer, A. N. " The Fight at Blazer's Mill in New Mexico." *Frontier Times* (August 1939).

_____. "Blazer's Mill." *New Mexico Magazine* (January 1938).

_____. "Beginnings of an Indian War." *New Mexico Magazine* (February 1938).

_____. "Loaded for Bear." *New Mexico Magazine* (November 1938).

Bourke, John G. "The Folk Foods of the Rio Grande and Northern Mexico." *Journal of American Folklore* 8 (1895).

_____. "Notes on Apache Mythology." *Journal of American Folklore* 3 (April-June 1890).

Burton, Estelle Bennett. "Volunteer Soldiers of New 1863." *Old Santa Fe* 1 (April 1914).

Charles, Tom. "The Old Scouts of the Mescaleros." *New Mexico Magazine* (August 1931).

Crimmins, Colonel M. L. "The Mescalero Apaches." *Frontier Times* 8 (September 1931).

Flannery, Regina. "The Position of Women Among the Mescalero Apache." *Primitive Man* 5 (April-July 1932).

Goodwin, Grenville. "A Comparison of Navajo and White Mountain Apache Ceremonial Forms and Categories." *Southwestern Journal of Anthropology* 1 (1945).

_____. "The Characteristics and Function of Clan in a Southern Athapascan Culture." *American Anthropologist* 39 (1937).

_____. "Clans of the Western Apache." *New Mexico Historical Review* 8 (July 1933).

Hammond, George P., and Agapito Rey. "The Crown's Participation in the Founding of New Mexico." *New Mexico Historical Review* 32 (October 1957).

Hoijer, Harry. "Classificatory Verb Stems in the Apachean Languages." *International Journal of American Linguistics* 11 (January 1945).

Kaut, Charles R. "Western Apache Clan System. Its Origin and Development." *University of New Mexico Publications on Anthropology* 9 (1957).

Kaywaykla, James (as told to Eve Ball). "Witchcraft." *Frontier Times* (February-March 1965).

Matson, Daniel S., and Albert H. Schroeder, eds., "Cordero's Description of the Apache—1796." *New Mexico Historical Review* 32 (October 1957).

Miles, Susan. "Mrs. [Bridget Coghlan] E. B. Taylor of Bismarck Farm." *The Edwards Plateau Historian* 8 (1983–1989).

Myers, Lee. "Military Establishments in Southwestern New Mexico: Stepping Stones to Settlement." *New Mexico Historical Review* 43 (January 1968).

_____. "The Enigma of Mangas Colorada's Death." *New Mexico Historical Review* 41 (April 1966).

McNeil, Irving. "Indian Justice." *New Mexico Historical Review* 19 (October 1944).

Nicholas, Dan. "Mescalero Girl's Puberty Ceremony." *El Palacio* 46 (September 1939).

Opler, Morris E. "Reaction to Death Among the Mescalero Apache." *Southwestern Journal of Anthropology* 2 (Winter 1946).

_____. "The Creative Role of Shamanism in Mescalero Apache Mythology." *Journal of American Folklore* 59 (July-September 1946).

_____. "The Sacred Clowns of the Mescalero Apache Girls Puberty Ceremony." *El Palacio* 44 (March 9–16–23, 1938).

_____. "The Concept of Supernatural Power Among the Chiricahua and Mescalero Indians." *American Anthropologist* 37 (June 1937).

Opler, Morris Edward, and Catherine E. Opler. "Mescalero Apache History in the Southwest." *New Mexico Historical Review* 25 (January 1950).

Opler, Morris E., and Edward F. Castetter. "The Ethnobotany of the Chiricahua and Mescalero Apaches." *Ethnobiological Studies in the American Southwest* 7 (1936).

Pack, Joseph F. "The Apaches in Mexican-American Relations, 1846–1861. A Footnote to the Gadsden Treaty." *Arizona and the West* 3 (Summer 1961).

Reeve, Frank D. "The Federal Indian Policy in New Mexico, 1858–1880." *New Mexico Historical Review* 12 (July 1937); 13 (January, April, July 1938).

Rippy, Fred. "The Indians of the Southwest in the Diplomacy of the U.S. and Mexico." *Hispanic American Historical Review* 2 (August 1919).

Rope, John. "Experiences of an Indian Scout." Recorded by Grenville Goodwin. *Arizona Historical Review* 3 (January-April 1936).

White, Charles B. "A Comparison of Theories on Southern Athapascan Kinship Systems." *American Anthropologist* 59 (June 1957).

Worcester, Donald E. "The Beginning of the Apache Menace in the Southwest." *New Mexico Historical Review* 16 (January 1941).

GLOSSARY

amole—soap-weed
besh dilhentee—metal jingles
bytah—fox
carrate—coil
carretas—wagons
ch'eeke—young women
Chete Neh—devil, malignant
    influence, evil
chuchupate—white angelica
ede—upper garment
etsee(s)—water-tight basketry jug
Eyata—God, something above the
    sky, good
gunesnane tu—ten-hundred
guuche—hog-filthy
haheh—dance of the adolescent girls
hazhah—hunt
hoddentin—cattail flags
isdza/iszhah—women
iskenyeh—child/children
juu—ornaments
kahne jah—the length of a forearm
    from wrist to elbow
kotulh—tepee of special design
    where the ceremony of haheh
    was carried out

kukeh—firepit
lha asti—much talk
lhizhin—black
Mal Pais—lava beds
metates—grinding stones
palmilla—a species of yucca
sazh—hide trunk
shapaz—hoop pole
shizhi—white one
Ta incha—big father
tan ju—enemy
tendejon—combination of general
    store and grocery
tiswin—corn liquor
tsitse—stick and stone
tubisno—abstaining guards
tubisno deh neh—not drinking
    anything strong
tule—large bulrush common to
    swampy areas of the Southwest
tulhiba—fermented drink made
    from corn
wickiup—a traditional shelter
yadeche—priestess-chaperone